# Recovering the U.S. Hispanic Literary Heritage

# Volume VII

# Recovering the U.S. Hispanic Literary Heritage

## Board of Editorial Advisors

# Recovering the U.S. Hispanic Literary Heritage, Volume VII

Edited by Gerald E. Poyo
and Tomás Ybarra-Frausto

Recovering the U.S. Hispanic Literary Heritage

Arte Público Press
Houston, Texas

This volume is made possible through grants from the City of Houston through the Houston Arts Alliance and by the Exemplar Program, a program of Americans for the Arts in collaboration with the LarsonAllen Public Services Group, funded by the Ford Foundation.

*Recovering the past, creating the future*

Arte Público Press
University of Houston
452 Cullen Performance Hall
Houston, Texas 77204-2004

Jacket design by Pilar Espino

The Library of Congress has catalogued Volume I of
*Recovering the U.S. Hispanic Literary Heritage* as follows:

Recovering the U.S. Hispanic literary heritage / edited by Ramón Gutiérrez and Genaro Padilla
p. cm.
ISBN: 978-1-55885-063-7 $34.95
ISBN: 978-1-55885-058-3 (trade pbk.) $17.95
1. American literature—Hispanic American authors—History and criticism. 2. Hispanic American literature (Spanish)—History and criticism. 3. Hispanic Americans—Intellectual life. 4. Hispanic Americans in literature. I. Gutiérrez, Ramón A., 1951- II. Padilla, Genaro M., 1949-
PS153.H56R43 1993

92-45114
CIP

ISBN: 978-1-55885-139-9 (Volume II)
ISBN: 978-1-55885-251-8 (Volume III)
ISBN: 978-1-55885-361-4 (Volume IV)
ISBN: 978-1-55885-371-3 (Volume V)
ISBN: 978-1-55885-478-9 (Volume VI)
ISBN: 978-1-55885-526-7 (Volume VII)

The paper used in this publication meets the requirements of the American National Standard for Information Sciences—Permanence of Paper for Printed Library Materials, ANSI Z39.48-1984.


Printed in the United States of America

9 0 1 2 3 4 5 6 7 8 10 9 8 7 6 5 4 3 2 1

# Contents

# Part III
## Amparo Ruiz de Burton: Literature and History



# Part IV
## Language Representation and Translation

# Introduction

## Gerald E. Poyo and Tomás Ybarra-Frausto

Recovering the U.S. Latino Literary Heritage project is ambitious and tackles big goals and ideas; it has done so since its inception in 1990. Its trajectory is documented in the six previous volumes of this series. This seventh contribution derives from the ninth biannual conference, "Encuentros y Reencuentros: Making Common Ground," held in St. Louis, Missouri, in collaboration with the Western Historical Association in October 2006. Here also the Recovery program organizers set expansive goals for participants, including reaching out explicitly to historians of the west and encouraging scholars to consider methodological approaches to integrating the diverse U.S. Hispanic story. "It is fitting that this geographic center of the United States, serve as the place for our historic encounter: that of western history and Recovery scholars," noted Nicolás Kanellos, director of the program. Common themes, he said, are plainly evident in "the intersecting paths of our intellectual and cultural concerns, the conflict and contestation so apparent in western and Latino histories of the United States, as well as the confluence, cooperation and syncretism." [from Introduction of the Recovery Conference Program]

Besides continuing the practice established in the seventh and eighth conferences of partnering with scholarly groups interested in similar pursuits (the American Studies Association in 2002 and the University of New Mexico Spanish and Portuguese Department in 2004), this conference constituted the Recovery project's first collaboration with an association of historians. "Making common ground" with historians has been a Recovery project goal since early on and this joint meeting represented an effort to promote institutional scholarly collaboration. The meeting made eminent sense since Recovery's work is inherently historical and western history of the United States is intricately linked with the history of Hispanic peoples since the sixteenth century.

Recovery project scholars routinely place the literary and historical in dialogue, which involves examining recovered literary documents within their historical contexts and interpreting them through diverse cultural, textual and linguistic analytical approaches. This endeavor begins with the practical process of identifying and making available for scholars the written record of Hispanic populations during four and a half centuries. Recovery scholars have interpreted unknown, or little known, literary texts fully within their historical context, in this way linking the rich Hispanic literary tradition to the historical trajectory of the United States. The historical contextualization by Recovery project scholars of the writings of Cabeza de Vaca, Amparo Ruiz de Burton, Daniel Venegas or Jovita González, for example, have helped interpret historical moments, just as continuing research into the historical moments themselves clarify and explain the texts. As the available body of Hispanic documentary texts grows, scholars also engage in a continuing reinterpretation of the historiographic record. Despite the still "insufficient theorization of the historical presuppositions underwriting the endeavor" observed by Kenya Dworkin y Méndez and Agnes Lugo-Ortiz in the fifth volume of this series, this process of literary and historical "dialogue" has deepened scholarly understanding of the political, socioeconomic and cultural effects and legacies of the United States conquest of the regions from Texas to California on the lives of the people.

With this methodology in mind, Recovery scholars at the ninth conference succeeded in creating openings and opportunities for cross-disciplinary and intra-ethnic discussions. For their part, they highlighted the rich Hispanic literary contributions and encouraged Western historians to incorporate recovered texts in their research and courses. On the other hand, a seamless engagement grounded in shared intellectual and logistical concerns between the Recovery project's essentially literary constituency and historians proved challenging. Divergent assumptions, methods, discourses and rhetoric often prevent effective interaction across disciplinary boundaries, always challenging for those interested in promoting multidisciplinary scholarly approaches. Nevertheless, the experience identified a fruitful collaborative path and initiated conversations that resulted in the inclusion of Recovery-sponsored panels at the 2008 Western History Association meeting in Salt Lake, City Utah.

In addition to the collaborative scholarly goals involving literature and history, conference organizers also used the common ground theme to encourage literary critics and historians of the Hispanic experience to integrate research "in Latina and Latino Studies disciplines, from Chicano to Cuban to Dominican to Puerto Rican studies to Sephardic Studies and beyond" as a complement to the previous conference's focus on region. Calling for the use of "trans-disciplinary, trans-national and trans-cultural" methodologies, Recovery project organizers encouraged scholars to analyze and interpret texts and themes beyond specific ethnicities, creating aperture for convergence of similar issues across diverse national groups. [from Recovery Conference, Call for Papers, 2006]

This integration also proved challenging. While one conference plenary session addressed the intra-ethnic character of the Recovery project's work, the overall integrative enterprise remains in its infancy. The unbalanced scholarly production favoring Mexican-American and southwest studies observed in most Recovery conferences and volumes persists. This tendency reflects demographic and other realities, including a strong commitment by Recovery scholars to what Dworkin y Méndez and Lugo-Ortiz describe as "questions of territoriality and regionalism deemed proper to the Southwestern experience." Together, this collection and volume six, for example, include only two articles that focus on "other" Hispanics which highlights the need to further encourage Recovery scholars to advance writing about the broad Latino experience. Certainly, sufficient research material exists. During the last fifteen years the Recovery project has identified and made available valuable literary and historical sources pertaining to all the historical communities that await interested scholars.

If the conference faced challenges, it also accomplished the primary and essential function of all Recovery conferences: to bring together scholars dedicated to presenting new knowledge about the Hispanic experience in the United States. Recovery contributions to the joint conference included seventeen panels with formal presentations, two plenary sessions, several roundtable discussions, literary readings and receptions that provided scholars the opportunity formally and informally to engage a wide-range of themes on mostly Mexican-American topics. Not surprisingly then the eleven essays included here organized into four sections reflect this continuing interest. In some ways these essays represent a continuation of the regional theme that informed volume six; indeed, it seems fitting that collaboration with the Western History Association resulted in a volume that deals essentially with the Hispanic West.

Part I brings together three essays on "History, Culture and Ideology," uncovering aspects of historiography, cultural identity and exile thought. The collection begins with an exploration of the way in which the once much maligned sixteenth century chronicle over a century gained acceptance as a legitimate source of historical "truth." José Antonio Gurpegui and Carmen Gómez Galisteo's, "Describing the 'New World': *De dicto* vs. *de re,* Historians vs. Eyewitnesses," traces the development of Spanish historiography of the sixteenth and seventeenth centuries through the eyes of historians and chroniclers. In the sixteenth century, historians viewed themselves as uniquely positioned and trained to offer accurate historical accounts. Though historians relied on first person accounts in combination with other sources to offer their version of events, they considered chroniclers biased eyewitnesses with inherently limited perspectives. By the time of the publication of Bernal Díaz del Castillo's *Historia verdadera de la conquista de a Nueva España,* the chronicler established greater legitimacy and gained "the right of historicizing himself in the events in which he had so actively participated."

The relationship between culture, representation and power is the subject of Alicia Verónica Sánchez Martínez's, "Recuperando la memoria cultural: Cleofas Jaramillo y las recetas originales de Nuevo México." Sánchez's examination of a cookbook of "recetas originales" raises many interesting issues related to the complicated legacy of class, race and ethnicity in Hispanic New Mexico. Sánchez points out that in representing her "authentic" New Mexican dishes as "Spanish recipes," Cleofas Jaramillo ignores the Mexican and indigenous influences from which her dishes emerge. "Se destacan," notes Sánchez, "los mecanismos que las instituciones tienen para producir y reproducir el poder y la ideología."

Alejandra Balestra's, "Women Writers in the Nineteenth-Century Hispanic Southwest: Letters, Discourses and Linguistics," examines the historical role of women in the U.S. Southwest. This examination of Spanish-language correspondence by Hispanic women who belonged to the privileged classes demonstrates their involvement in quotidian matters and concern with protecting their families and possessions, seeking justice and commenting on society in general.

Part II, "Women's Voices: Gender, Politics and Culture," includes three essays that explore women's political, socio-cultural and economic critiques and engagement with the world around them. In "Recovering the Self: The Unnamed Characters of Luisa Capetillo's *How Poor Women Prostitute Themselves,*" Nancy Bird-Soto explores the worldview of Puerto Rican activist Luisa Capetillo, a subject of previous attention in volume five of this series. Bird-Soto analyzes Capetillo's play *Cómo se prostituyen los pobres* (1916), which revolves around an unnamed prostitute who is a metaphor for the life of poor women everywhere who become prostitutes "whenever they enter an unequal relationship that subordinates them, financially, politically and personally."

Pilar Melero follows with her essay, "*El héroe agachado* or the Hero that Wasn't: Virile Language and Women's Quest for Political Participation," which examines gender representations in the writings of *activistas* Juana Belén Gutiérrez and Andrea Villarreal González during the Mexican Revolution. Melero reveals how the writings of the women activists sought to shame men into involvement in revolution and to "rearticulate femininity away from the confines of passivity" toward greater involvement in politics.

Commentary by women on politics, economics and society is also the subject of how Mexican expatriates constructed a "México de Afuera" in the 1920s is the topic of Gabriela Baeza Ventura, "Treacherous Women in the *crónicas* of

Quezigno Gazavic: A Strategy in Creating Commmunity." Particularly concerned with the expression of gender ideology as part of an overall strategy of promoting traditional Mexican values in the United States, Baeza analyzes a *crónica* that appeared in San Antonio's *El Heraldo Mexicano* in the 1920s. The *crónica* "demanded that Mexican women remain Catholic, that they treasure their traditions and culture and they not lose their language."

The three essays in Part III, "Amparo Ruiz de Burton: Literature and History," reflect the continuing interest in the writings of Ruiz de Burton. As noted in the fifth volume of the Recovering the U.S. Hispanic Literary Heritage series, *The Squatter and the Don* "is the only recovered work that consistently reappears as an object of obsessive critical attention." After an abeyance in volume six, Ruiz de Burton appears again.

"Mechanical imagery" is the focus of Kevin Anzzolin's "Building a Bridge to the Twentieth Century: Ruiz de Burton's Novel Techne in *The Squatter and the Don.*" By concentrating on three nineteenth century technological innovations—telephones, trains and cameras—Azzolin analyzes how the subtle use of mechanical imagery becomes a primary organizing trope in the novel. In his reading, "it is the divestiture of technological know-how that ultimately derails the *californio* plans for national assimilation and reconciliation."

Timothy P. Gaster, "Irony and Laughter in Ruiz de Burton's Public Sphere," examines how an incipient public sphere is represented in the novel through the literary devices of irony and humor. Framed by Michael Baktin's notion of the carnivalesque, Gaster elucidates how laughter is the medium through which the *californios* loss of socio-political status is critiqued and challenged.

Alberto Varon, "The Interior Frontier Man: *The Squatter and the Don,* the Conquest of Manhood and the Making of Mexican-American Literature," contrasts forms of masculinity in the Southwest frontier. The Anglo-frontiersman devoid of feeling represented by the Squatter is contrasted to Don Mariano Alamar who exemplifies the sentimental self-aware male characterized by a dialectic of patriarchy and defeat. These two myths of American manhood become integrated with questions of identity and subject formation in the subsequent evolution of Mexican-American literature.

Part IV treats the subject of "Language Representation and Translation" in two essays. In "Representations of Language in Three Early Novels by U.S. Latinos," María Irene Moyna considers the divergent language strategies used to represent bilingualism in the work of María Amparo Ruiz de Burton, Daniel Venegas and Jovita González. Ruiz de Burton's protagonists employ "elite Spanish-English bilingualism" while Venegas' main characters are working-class Spanish monolingual speakers who use non-standard forms "including rural dialect and urban caló." González uses English to represent Spanish to a mostly monolingual English-speaking audience. Each author's choice of strategy reflected their particular social environment and literary goals.

In the final essay of the volume, Ethriam Cash Brammer de Gonzales argues that a faithful translation of any work of literature must remain consistent with the original text in form, genre and historical period. In "'Keeping it Real': The Translation of *El sol de Texas,*" Brammer de Gonzales offers a painstaking literary analysis that reveals Conrado Espinosa's text to be a realist novel with some elements of naturalism, a finding that must inform a translator's decisions when rendering the work into another language.

Like previous volumes, the essays in this seventh compendium respond to questions of nomenclature, genre, subject and identity formation, gender and the omnipresent themes of cultural resistance and affirmation. Scholars attend to the heterogeneous class positions and aspirations of writers and how they relate to their literary production. There is continual attention to gender and how historically women have nurtured interstitial social spaces to voice their concerns. Also how dominant myths of manhood are revised and re-articulated by Latino writers and thinkers. The papers push forward the primary goal of the Recovery project as a whole—to make new knowledge about the texts and socio-historical contexts of Hispanic literary production within the United States from the colonial period through 1960.

Latinos are now the largest ethnic group in the United States and the Recovery enterprise is a critical part of a larger multicultural and multilingual Latino Cultural project encompassing Latina/o images and imaginations in all the arts. Today's Latina/o culture is nurtured within local, national and international spaces and is vibrant in the formation of new mobile identities, incipient collations and solidarities and possible social formations of connection, communications and conciliation within national groups and across borders. Shared historical processes such as colonization, immigration, mestizaje and resistance are seen as possible links for cultural convergence in the Americas.

At the turn of the twenty-first century, Latina/o scholars and activists continue a quest to imagine and sustain public spheres of inter-cultural dialogue and the maintenance of an intellectual commons that affirms both difference and common ground. The envisioning of what cultural theorist Arjun Appadurai calls "communities of sentiment across borders." Recovering the U.S. Hispanic Literary Heritage Project remains a foundational enterprise for seeding, nurturing, gathering and disseminating the intellectual and symbolic production of U.S. Latino writers as integral components of an inter-dependent global community.

# Part I

## History, Culture and Ideology

# Describing the "New World": *De dicto* vs. *de re*, Historians vs. Eyewitnesses

**JOSÉ ANTONIO GURPEGUI**
Universidad de Alcalá

**CARMEN GÓMEZ GALISTEO**
Universidad de Alcalá

> Pero uno es escribir como poeta y otro como historiador: el poeta puede contar o contar las cosas, no como fueron, sino como debían ser; y el historiador las ha de escribir, no como debían ser, sino como fueron, sin añadir ni quitar a la verdad cosa alguna.
>
> Miguel de Cervantes: *El Quijote*

In the sixteenth and seventeenth centuries there was a trend, particularly acute in Spanish historiography, that more value was attributed to that retold by a historian rather than what was told by an eyewitness of the very event reported. That is, in the Renaissance mind, more value was given to men of letters with a formal background (that is, historians) than to less knowledgeable eyewitnesses. Only those statements coming from an authority (*de dicto*) were straightforwardly accepted; those coming from a firsthand testimony (*de re*) and unmediated were considered suspicious and untrustworthy on the grounds of a bias which those who had not directly participated in the event described lacked.

The most common accusation against eyewitnesses was that "they may lie by authority, because none can controule them," as William Wood, eyewitness and author of *New Englands Prospect* (1634), put it (quoted in Franklin, 1979: 39). Direct testimony was considered biased by one's personal motivations and goals, obviating the fact that even official chroniclers had certain personal motivations and goals in mind, since all "chronicles were written for pragmatic as well as academic purposes, and even those that served theoretical ends had at stake practical goals of influencing policy or opinion" (Adorno, 1992: 211).

Following this view, *de re* was rejected in favor of a supposedly more objective (though indirect and maybe incomplete) point of view. It was the historian's trained eye that was the only one that could (and was sanctioned to) discern what might be exaggeration or amazement in order to render for readers the naked truth in an objective manner. The eyewitnesses that undertook the task of writing their chronicles were well aware of this distinction, though. In the very prologue to his *Historia verdadera*, Bernal Díaz del Castillo made a distinction between eyewitnesses (*testigos de vista*) in opposition to historians (or chroniclers, "coronistas" in sixteenth-century spelling):

> Digo que sobre esta mi relación pueden los **coronistas** sublimar y dar loa al valeroso y esforzado capitán Cortés, y a los fuertes conquistadores, pues tan grande empresa salió de nuestras manos, y lo que sobre ello escribieron diremos los que en aquellos tiempos nos hallamos como **testigos de vista** ser verdad, como ahora decimos las contrariedades de él; que, ¿cómo tienen tanto atrevimiento y osadía de escribir tan vicioso y sin verdad, pues que sabemos que la verdad es cosa bendita y sagrada, y que todo lo que contra ello dijeron va maldito? (Díaz del Castillo, 1976: 30-31) [bold ours]

Historians were also aware that their not being eyewitnesses had some disadvantages—they might make some mistakes given that they had not actually seen what they reported. To account for their flaws, historians gave several excuses, claiming the primacy of *de dicto* over *de re*, and considering that, all in all, the flaws of the historian would, nonetheless, be less serious than those of the eyewitness. Truth was to be found in the manner—though not completely accurate—in which events were told, "a kind of 'natural truth' of the deeds and a 'moral truth' of their narration" (Adorno, 1992: 217). That way, they claimed for themselves an authority that was unavailable to eyewitnesses.

Their greater authority was used by historians to their advantage in their altering the original sources (i.e., eyewitnesses' accounts) as extensively as they wanted. Fernández de Oviedo in his *Historia general y natural de las Indias* rewrote Cabeza de Vaca and his companions' *Joint Report* so much that his interpolations cannot be separated from the text itself.[1] Moreover, often these interpolations, additions and comments were not only made in the printed version of the original document, but in the very document itself. Thomas Prince, one of those who had the original manuscript of *Of Plymouth Plantation* in his possession for awhile, added his own comments in the margins, making it very difficult (if not impossible) to distinguish his from Bradford's.[2] These alterations were so common and widespread that these "armchair travellers"—historians who had not been to America—even corrected and denied the veracity of eyewitnesses' accounts. For example, Samuel Purchas, who never went to America himself, corrected eyewitness James Rosier's account in reference to Indian women's nakedness (Kupperman, 1997: 201).

That way, only the professional historian was entitled to write histories, a confining vision of historiography that has persisted up to our days (Pocock, 1962: 210). What an eyewitness might write was a mere report, for a historian to criticize, use freely and rewrite as he found convenient in order to turn this nonhistorical material into historical substance. Consequently, for the eyewitness, the problem of describing the New World was two-fold—"the recognition of new objects and experiences and the communication of the newly acquired knowledge to his European audience" (Murray, 1994: 33) for which there were no words available and the "battle against the current 'facts' and dogmas of the learned" (Boorstin, 1983: xv). At the same time that they lacked both the concepts for describing these new, unheard-of realities, eyewitnesses also struggled with words. Communicating the knowledge of the New World to their European addressees involved the skilful use of linguistic resources eyewitnesses did not feel comfortable with. Many writers of the period, prior to their turning to writing, had to come to the conclusion that "un grado de excelencia narrativa no era requisito imprescindible para relatar sus vivencias" (Beltrán Llavador, 1994: 22).

At a time where formal knowledge was difficult to obtain and reserved just for the upper classes, eyewitnesses (being basically soldiers and the like, in the case of explorations and colonizations) were not likely to possess it. This lack made them unable to render their visions in the expected mode and more often than not they could not express themselves in a flowery prose, a flaw their critics exploited to the maxim. As pointed out by Friederici, "in no country is there so great a number of soldier-chroniclers as in Spain. Characteristic of these is their scorn for bookish erudition, even though they try to exhibit their own ingenuously and repeatedly" (Iglesia, 1940: 525). For example, John Smith showed his scorn for bookish erudition in *A Map of Virginia*, when he accused calumniators of having received a tender education without any military instruction and both Fernández de Oviedo and Bernal Díaz del Castillo agreed in that historians of the time regarded style as more important than truth. So aware were eyewitnesses that their works would be attacked on the grounds of stylistic conventions, that Díaz del Castillo

> equipara la elevación de estilo y la distancia del cronista profesional con la deformación de la realidad histórica, para sugerir que, puesto que él, Bernal, no utiliza un estilo *sublimis* y lo tuvo todo "delante de los ojos" (*evidentia*), no se aparta de la verdad. (Serés, 2004: 117)

Francisco López de Gómara's own history, *Historia general de las Indias,* is representative of the limitations imposed on eyewitnesses. López de Gómara, a professional historian, was given the assignment of composing the authorized historical chronicle of Hernán Cortés's conquest of Mexico. That is, given his erudite knowledge, he was to collect and historicize the experiences of an eyewitness, Cortés. Certainly Cortés did not regard himself as the "soldier-scholar of the Renaissance" Pagden saw in him (quoted in Murray, 1994: 63) and assumed that, in contrast, López de Gómara's account would be more authoritative. Had Cortés been certain that a history written by himself (rather than by López de Gómara) would have had the same credibility and reception as if written by a professional historian, Cortés could and most probably would have gone without the help of López de Gómara, his personal chaplain. Thus, López de Gómara turned into a history Cortés's firsthand account in order to provide historical legitimacy and avert criticism.

Not even Cortés, the paradigm for a conquistador, could be like Gonzalo Fernández de Oviedo, an eyewitness as well as "hombre de pluma en todos los sentidos, escritor a la vez que escribano, aficionado íntegramente a este instrumento en torno al cual hizo girar su vida" (Esteve Barba, 1992: 66), whose writings earned him the post of "cronista de Indias" for twenty-five years. The ideal historian-eyewitness, somebody like Fernández de Oviedo or, even better, Francisco Cervantes de Salazar, author of *La crónica de la Nueva España* (1557), a scholar writing from New Spain, was almost impossible to find.

To make things worse for eyewitnesses attempting to make a name for themselves in the field of history as they already had in the battlefield, the concept of history both as science and literature was not clearly defined in the same terms as it is nowadays. In the sixteenth and seventeenth centuries, following "the Erasmian notion of knowledge as a unified *Wissenschaft*," the methods, ideas, and practices of a discipline were usually applied to the rest of disciplines (Fussner in Woolf, 1987: 11). Thus, history and literature came to be so closely associated that history, to qualify as such, had to meet certain literary standards, which, roughly, were the same required from a poet or novelist. The blurring of any possible distinction that might exist between history and literature was a certainty in sixteenth-century Spain and England. So extreme was this confusion that all but any writing—fictional or not—could be included under the label "history."

Eyewitnesses were aware that their writings would, at best, be suspected, on the grounds of their coming not from professional historians but from soldiers and explorers turned into historians. At worst, their works would be taken as fictional works, with no resemblance to the truth whatsoever. This fear was expressed by most of them; among them, Bernal Díaz del Castillo, John Smith, Pedro Castañeda, and by Cabeza de Vaca, who forewarns in his proem that "aunque en ella se lean algunas cosas muy nuevas y para algunos muy difíciles de creer, puede sin duda creerlas" (2000: 4). This concern dated back from Columbus's discovery journeys. The admiral himself had expressed his fear of not being trusted and begged the Catholic monarchs not to think he was exaggerating. Rather, he affirms that, if anything, he is just falling short of the truth, telling only a one hundredth of the reality he has seen.

Given that historical authority was grounded on flowery prose, a vast formal knowledge of the classics, and other standards that historians could claim, which were unavailable to eyewitnesses, conquistadors, and explorers had to find a new type of authority that would legitimate their works. In so doing,

> the answer was an appeal not to other texts (for there were none), nor to internal coherence, the logic of argument, the structure of analogy, and so on, but to the authorial voice. It is the "I" who has seen what no other being has seen who alone is capable of giving creditability to the text. If the reader chooses to believe what he or she reads, it is because he or she is willing to privilege that writer's claims to authority over all others and not, in this case, because it might seem to the reader to be inherently plausible or internally consistent. (Pagden, 1991: 150–151)

As well as vindicating an authority for themselves, they at the same time undermined historians' *auctoritates*. Fernández de Oviedo, who had spent three decades in America, "casts doubts on the truth of the versions of other authors who wrote histories of the Indies in Latin and the vernacular. They never set foot in the region, but they attempt to make up for the truth as an eyewitness observer" (Murray, 1994: 104). In the same fashion of Pliny the Elder, Fernández de Oviedo counteracted his own limitations (his inadequate style and his young age) with the justification that he had been an eyewitness and attacked Peter Martyr, who wrote his *Decadas de Orbe Novo*[3] from Spain. Notwithstanding his attacks against Martyr, Fernández de Oviedo, though, was more generous than other eyewitnesses were in criticizing historians, for he conceded that Martyr "deseaba escribir lo cierto si fielmente fuera informado;[4] mas como habló en lo que no vido . . . , sus *Décadas* padecen muchos defectos" (quoted in Esteve Barba, 1992: 78).[5]

For men like Díaz del Castillo and Fernández de Oviedo, what the historian might tell was completely useless, unless they had been eyewitnesses. Díaz del Castillo asserted that historians

> les parece que placen mucho a los oyentes que leen sus historias y no lo vieron ni entendieron cuando lo escribían; los verdaderos conquistadores y curiosos lectores que saben lo que pasó claramente les dirán que si todo lo que escriben de otras historias va como lo de la Nueva España, irá todo errado. (1976: 30)

In a similar way, Fernández de Oviedo constantly reminds his readers "that elegance of style and erudition are of no use unless one has lived what he wishes to relate" (Iglesia, 1940: 525–526). It is only the truth (which can only be obtained if the writer is an eyewitness) which is of any importance in a historical work, not the style in which it is composed: "las historias no son de presciar ni tener en muncho, sin con la verdad no son acompañadas," claimed Fernández de Oviedo (quoted in Esteve Barba, 1992: 74).

For all the above reasons, Las Casas, Bernal Díaz del Castillo, and Fernández de Oviedo, in order to legitimize their works, all insisted on the eye being more reliable than books, which led to the logical consequence that their own books were more authoritative and truthful than anybody else's (Pagden, 1991: 154; Cerwin, 1962; Iglesia, 1940: 525–526). This is the same belief inspires Smith's *A Map of Virginia* (1612), in which he attacked his opponents by indicating how accounts that differed from his should be evaluated—

> Those who visit with the annual supply ship, but do not settle, he says, find it in their interest to give false reports, since no actual colonist is present back in England to challenge them. Such calumniators, he writes, "Being for the most part of such tender education and small experience in martiall accidents, because they found not English cities, nor such faire houses, nor at their own wishes any of their accustomed dainties, with feather beds and downe pillows, Tavernes and alehouses in every breathing place, neither such plenty of gold and silver and dissolute liberty as they expected had little or no care of any thing, but to pamper their bellies, to fly away with our Pinnaces, or procure their meanes to returne to England." (quoted in Ziff, 1996: 513)

Having discredited professional historians, in turn, eyewitnesses had to redefine the conception of "historian" to create a new definition which fitted their own situation. John Smith came to accept "the historian's role as equal to that of soldier-statesman and of history as the site of the meanings that unmediated experience alone cannot yield" (Ziff, 1996: 517). When in *A Map of Virginia* he compared others' writings to his very own, he was proposing that his own writings were from then onwards held as the standard for all subsequent works on Virginia, but also demanding that eyewitnesses' accounts (especially those who had stayed in America for quite a long time), in general, were to be taken as the standard to compare more doubtful accounts.

But in demanding credibility and authority for themselves, not only did eyewitnesses have to counteract historians, but they also had to face the "many scandalous and false reports upon the Country, even from the sulphurious breath of every base ballad-monger," as William Wood bitterly complained (quoted in Franklin, 1979: 39). That is, they had to work against historians' accounts and against those whose ignorance about America did not prevent them from spreading their own ideas about what America was like.

However, eyewitnesses, in the writing of their histories, sometimes resorted to exactly the same mechanism they criticized so much in historians—using other eyewitnesses' testimony (be it written or oral), not their own. Las Casas collected thousands of documents for the writing of his *Historia*, as did Fernández de Oviedo. Even Bernal Díaz del Castillo, who wanted to give his own point of view only, could not witness all the events he claims—some of them happening simultaneously. John Smith, too, in his *The General History of Virginia, New England, and the Summer Isles* (1624), not only compiled his previous writings but also added information that was almost in everybody's mouth in London at the time.

To excuse themselves, they stated that what they had not witnessed themselves, had been witnessed by reliable eyewitnesses: "Y lo que no hubiere visto, direlo por relación de personas fidedignas, no dando en cosa alguna crédito a un solo testigo, sino a muchos en aquellas cosas que mi persona no hubiere experimentado," Fernández de Oviedo argued (quoted in Serés, 2004: 108). They also pointed out the inability of anyone to be an eyewitness of all events. Still, they failed to acknowledge that these two circumstances applied to historians as well.

The kind of authority Bernal Díaz del Castillo and Cabeza de Vaca could claim was "the kind of historical authority that supplied sworn testimony in an official investigation and rested on the claim of having been an eyewitness" (Adorno, 1992: 218). Eyewitnesses, lacking formal knowledge in most cases, were forced to resort to other, more authoritative sources, in search for authority and legitimacy. They attained this—or at least, tried to—by means of inserting quotations from authorities in their works, with mixed results. In some cases, the quotations are appropriate to the topic at hand, but more often than not, quotations become excessive, as it happened to Las Casas.

In order to defend themselves from criticism, another strategy that eyewitnesses resorted to was making use of ancient models to compare themselves to. The most useful and profitable ones were the Roman military and political leader Julius Caesar (100 B.C.–44 B.C.) and the Roman historian Pliny the Elder (23–79 A.D.), also used as models for antiquarians in Tudor England—particularly the latter (Woolf, 1987: 13). Thucydides, Polybius, Josephus, and Tacitus were also mentioned to illustrate the case of active participants in events they also recorded, since "this sort of man had the personal experience and social stature necessary to the re-teller of remote events and indispensable to the historian of recent times" (Woolf, 1987: 25).[6]

That eyewitnesses in writing their reports chose to compare themselves to historical figures of the past was no accident, since "the men of the Renaissance looked to classical antiquity for models not only of literary elegance but also of conduct to imitate and outrival" (Armstrong, 1953: 88). Van Cromphout advances a further reason:

> the [Renaissance] humanists turned to the classics because they were inspired by "the firm belief that in order to write and to speak well it was necessary to study and to imitate the ancients." They approached classical literature "almost exclusively as style," and they valued style "chiefly as a model for imitation." (1977: 327)

Recurrent among eyewitnesses was the argument that their strategies were not too different from Julius Caesar's, whom they considered as their main model. Bernal Díaz del Castillo reminded his readers that Julius Caesar[7] not only recorded his military successes, but at the same time, in so doing, he presented himself as a hero, without having had to face criticism—just the contrary. Actually, Bernal Díaz del Castillo felt he was even more entitled than Caesar to record his glory, since he had participated in more battles than Caesar himself (Esteve Barba, 1992: 164).

John Smith also looked up to Caesar as a model and wondered: "Where shall we looke to finde a Julius Caesar, whose achievements shine as cleare in his owne *Commentaries*, as they did in the field?" (quoted in Ziff, 1996: 516). The choice of Julius Caesar was especially significant: "Smith's choice of Caesar as a model may be vainglorious, but it also marks his recognition of the fact that historical meaning is reconstructed in the report rather than constructed in the event" (Ziff, 1996: 517).

Instead of relying on Julius Caesar, Fernández de Oviedo turned to Pliny for a model, of which there were several precedents in the Middle Ages, like Gerald of Wales (Woolf, 1987: 13). The same view Fernández de Oviedo held about history was shared by Pliny, who stated that "the historian must cite who he heard something from, what sources he read, and what he saw as an eyewitness." (Murray, 1994: 101) As a result, Fernández de Oviedo tried to impose a loose Plinian model on his *Historia* (Pagden, 1991: 150).[8] Not only did Fernández de Oviedo find in Pliny a model, but the figure of the Roman historian helped him vindicate his own role even more effectively, since he could be considered in some aspects even greater than Pliny, for Fernández de Oviedo had undergone sea perils in his voyages to America.

The writings and chronicles of Bernal Díaz del Castillo, Las Casas, Cabeza de Vaca and many others were suspected and questioned due to a tradition in Spanish historiography of undervaluing eyewitnesses' accounts in favour of professional historians. In Spain the main concern and the main criteria for a history to qualify as such and for the author to be considered a historian and not an upstart trying to advance his own self-promotion, was that it came from an authority and not from an eyewitness.

In England, though, the situation was somewhat different. Due to its insular condition, the Renaissance and the new airs it brought took more time to be perceived. History was not different in this respect and, consequently, "the Renaissance tendency to write history more critically was but slightly felt until the third decade of the sixteenth century" (Trimble, 1950: 30). Eyewitnesses' testimonies were likely to be "qualified" by the more authoritative voices of non-eyewitnesses (i.e., armchair travellers) or disqualified, but in England their main concern was not *de re* vs. *de dicto*.

If the accounts by Spanish *conquistadores* were neglected and scorned on the grounds of a Spanish tradition of discrediting eyewitnesses and their accounts, English explorers being taken as more seriously than their Spanish counterparts lies on a tradition in English historiography of previous chroniclers being followed verbatim without raising any question about their accuracy. This lack of questioning of authorities allowed for mythical elements to pass unnoticed—and not criticized—in histories, "without any sense of discrimination Biblical narratives and fictitious events were included" as well as "unsubstantiated traditional events and mythological events" (Trimble, 1950: 31).

Contrary to Fernández de Oviedo's accusations of historians having collected their knowledge from many books and his having obtained his own from personal experience, in England, to start with, the very conception of truth and its rendering were completely different—"a chronicler should not be considered as affirming the truth of what he wrote, but only what he had seen in other books" (Trimble, 1950: 32). Consequently, claims like Fernández de Oviedo's or John Smith's that historians were unable to report events on the grounds of their not having witnessed them were less forceful in England. As long as it was in a book, it was true; seeing was not a question of being an eyewitness of events but of being an "eyewitness of books."

That way, in England, although Smith's writings were suspected, it cannot be said that this tendency to distrust eyewitnesses in Spanish historiography was thoroughly shared by English historiography. As an example,

> latter-day historians, anthropologists, ethnologists, and the like have been so willing to trust early English eyewitness accounts that, for instance, they construct virtually their entire picture of the Powhatan society out of them, right down to telling us its settlement patterns, political forms, burial, and marriage practices, tribute systems, sumptuary rules, puberty rites, and the like, on the basis of little more than the perceptions of thoroughly Anglo-

> centric and prejudiced men, not one of them trained for the track. (Sale, 1990: 389)

Not only did English historians apply this credibility to their own chroniclers and recorders, but also to Spanish chroniclers. For instance, the first English edition (1583) of Las Casas's *Brevísima relación*, titled *The Spanish Colonie, or briefe chronicle of the acts and gestes of the Spaniards in the West Indies, called the Newe World,* attributed to Las Casas the condition of historian whose words should be considered true. Notwithstanding that one of the reasons why they considered Las Casas a historian right away was that it was most convenient for the English to give credit to stories denouncing the brutality and wrongdoings of the Spaniards in America, it is significant that they gave full credit to Las Casas's words. Also, the Dominican friar was not the only Spanish eyewitness given credit as a historian by English historiography. Not less important were the translations of Peter Martyr by Richard Eden, López de Gómara, and Fernández de Oviedo, which aroused interest in England for the colonization venture.

Eventually it would be the reforms brought up by the Renaissance that would help eyewitnesses in their claims to a role in history-writing. Eyewitnesses benefited from a change in the concept of history:

> the Renaissance, which saw the flowering of humanist historiography, also witnessed a revolt against the humanist concept of history as a branch of rhetoric, i.e., "as a form of literature susceptible to rhetorical and stylistic refinement," and against the humanist concept of historical truth as verisimilitude. (Van Cromphout, 1977: 328)

Eyewitnesses' writings thus helped confirm and reinforce this tendency due to two things: they were written by eyewitnesses, whose testimony up to then had been considered valueless without the mediation of historians and their writings dealt with the New World.

By 1632, the publication of Bernal Díaz del Castillo's *Historia verdadera de la conquista de la Nueva España* revealed that the old dichotomy between testimony (*de re*) and authority (*de dicto*) was breaking down. "A century of writing on the Indies had shifted the boundaries of the discursive encounters and made possible the incorporation of authors undreamed of a hundred years earlier" (Adorno, 1992: 228) and eyewitnesses' testimonies were progressively paid more credit. Therefore, the eyewitness ("the historical actor," in Adorno's words) was finally granted the right of historicizing himself the events in which he had so actively participated.

## Notes

[1] The possibility of contrasting it to the original manuscript is hindered since the latter is lost.

[2] Some of Prince's comments are misidentified as Bradford's in some editions of *Of Plymouth Plantation.*

[3] However, its author not having set foot in America did not prevent that this history is considered to be the first general history of the Indies (Esteve Barba, 1992: 55).

[4] Martyr obtained all his information in the Spanish court, talking with people who had been to America (Hanke, 1986: lxix).

[5] López de Gómara would make use of the same excuse when publicly accused of not having published anything but lies (Hanke, 1986: l).

[6] Puritan historians also relied on classical models. The most popular among them were Plutarch, Livy, Tacitus, Polybius, Herodotus, Xenophon, Diodurus Siculus, Dionysis of Halicarnassus, Suetonius, and Herodian (Murdock, 1976: 68-69).

[7] Curiously enough, Bernal Díaz del Castillo compares Cortés to Caesar as well—and also to Hannibal and Alexander the Great.

[8] For Esteve Barba, as pervasive as the excess on erudite quotations was among priests was the tendency of humanists to deform reality according to their classical readings (1992: 9).

## Works Cited


Adorno, Rolena. "The Discursive Encounter of Spain and America: The Authority of Eyewitness Testimony in the Writing of History." *William and Mary Quarterly*. 49.2 (1992): 210–228.

Armstrong, A. MacC. "The Conquistadores and the Classics." *Greece & Rome*. 22.65 (1953): 88–89.

Beltrán Llavador, Fernando. "Introducción." In William Bradford. *De la plantación de Plymouth*. León: Secretariado de Publicaciones de la Universidad de León, 1994. 9–50.

Boorstin, Daniel J. *The Discoverers: A History of Man's Search to Know His World and Himself*. New York: Random House, 1983.

Cerwin, Herbert. *Bernal Díaz: Historian of the Conquest*. Norman, Oklahoma: U of Oklahoma P, 1963.

Díaz Del Castillo, Bernal. *Historia verdadera de la conquista de la Nueva España*. 1632. 11th edition. Joaquín Ramírez Cabañas (ed.) México, D.F.: Porrúa, 1976.

Esteve Barba, Francisco. *Historiografía indiana*. 2nd revised edition. Madrid: Gredos, 1992.

Franklin, Wayne. *Discoverers, Explorers, and Early Settlers*. Chicago: U of Chicago P, 1979.

Hanke, Lewis. "Bartolomé de las Casas, historiador." In Millares Calvo, Agustín (ed.) *Historia de las Indias, por fray Bartolomé de las Casas*. 2nd edition (1965). Vol. 1. México, D.F.: Fondo de Cultura Económica, 1986. ix–lxxxvi.

Iglesia, Ramón. "Two Articles on the Same Topic: Bernal Díaz del Castillo and Popularism in Spanish Historiography and Bernal Díaz del Castillo's Criticisms of the History of the Conquest of Mexico, by Francisco López de Gomara." *Hispanic American Historical Review*. 20.4 (1940): 517–550.

Kupperman, Karen Ordahl. "Presentment of Civility: English Reading of American Self-Presentation in the Early Years of Colonization." *William and Mary Quarterly*. 54.1 (1997): 193–228.

Murdock, Kenneth B. *Literature and Theology in Colonial New England*. 1949. Westport, CT: Greenwood P, 1976.

Murray, James C. *Spanish Chronicles of the Indies: Sixteenth Century*. New York: Twayne Publishers, 1994.

Núñez Cabeza De Vaca, Álvar. *Naufragios*. 1542. [N. p.]: El Aleph, 2000.

Pagden, Anthony. "*Ius et Factum*: Text and Experience in the Writings of Bartolomé de Las Casas." *Representations*. 33. Special Issue: The New World (1991): 147–162.

Pocock, J. G. A. "The Origins of Study of the Past: A Comparative Approach." *Comparative Studies in Society and History*. 4.2 (1962): 209–246.

Sale, Kirkpatrick. *The Conquest of Paradise: Christopher Columbus and the Columbian Legacy*. New York: Alfred A. Knopf, 1990.

Serés, Guillermo. "La crónica de un testigo de vista: Bernal Díaz del Castillo." In Arellano, Ignacio, and Fermín del PINO (eds.) *Lecturas y ediciones de crónicas de Indias: Una propuesta interdisciplinaria*. [N.p.]: U de Navarra / Iberoamericana / Veuvert, 2004. 95–135.

Trimble, William Raleigh. "Early Tudor Historiography, 1485–1548." *Journal of the History of Ideas*. 11.1 (1950): 30–41.

Van Cromphout, Gustaaf. "Cotton Mather: The Puritan Historian as Renaissance Humanist." *American Literature*. 49.3 (1977): 327–337.

Woolf, D. R. "Erudition and the Idea of History in Renaissance England." *Renaissance Quarterly*. 40.1 (1987): 11–48.

Ziff, Larzer. "Conquest and Recovery in Early Writings from America." *American Literature*. 68.3 (1996): 509–525.

# Recuperando la memoria cultural: Cleofas Jaramillo y las recetas originales de Nuevo México

ALICIA VERÓNICA SÁNCHEZ MARTÍNEZ
Tecnológico de Monterrey

En este artículo sobre las recetas originales de Nuevo México, hemos querido reconstruir, con los datos que aporta un pequeño folleto cuya autora es Cleofas Jaramillo, la visión de una mujer que manifiesta en su escrito, la voz de protesta contra el olvido de una de las prácticas más ancestrales en toda cultura: la preparación de alimentos. Para Cleofas Jaramillo las recetas, sus recetas, cobran importancia por el valor cultural que representan, ya que son el reflejo de las prácticas cotidianas ancestrales de su comunidad, Nuevo México, en sus propias palabras: "In this collection of Spanish recipes, only those used in New Mexico for centuries are given, excepting one or two Old Mexico récipes." Para Jaramillo, este tipo de prácticas culturales están en peligro de perderse, de ahí que al dejar por escrito lo que tradicionalmente es transmitido de manera oral, refleja el anhelo de una mujer que considera que las recetas originales ancestrales están en peligro de caer en el olvido.

Existen numerosos estudios relacionados con las comidas, por ejemplo, en Inglaterra, Douglas y Isherwood *(El mundo de los bienes: hacia una antropología del consumo)* ha estudiado las comidas como un microcosmos donde se reflejan, a manera de ritual, las estructuras sociales que dan sentido al mundo a través de los alimentos; los bienes, para estos autores, son al mismo tiempo el "componente material e inmaterial de un sistema de información cuya preocupación principal es verificar su propio desempeño" (88). En su libro, Douglas e Isherwood consideran los alimentos como mercancías que señalan la jerarquía de valores que practica un grupo social a través de las elecciones que hacen los individuos al escoger ciertas mercancías. De manera que las recetas de Jaramillo permiten conocer el universo valorado y apreciado que manifiesta ésta a través de su recetario. Así, a través de las recetas de cocina se observa cómo las instituciones culturales han sido parte fundamental en la circulación y permanencia de las prácticas de preparación y consumo de los alimentos en cualquier sociedad.

Por otra parte, el hogar es para la mujer el espacio de trabajo y de realización, es ahí donde a través de la preparación de los alimentos se manifiestan las prácticas sociales que revisten importantes significados de apropiación cultural de las ideologías circulantes en un cierto tiempo y espacio. Como responsable de su hogar, pero sobre todo como representante de la cultura nuevo mejicana, Jaramillo demuestra en sus escritos la importancia que reviste la herencia culinaria española que ella detenta. La materialidad de los alimentos, ofrece entonces importantes significados sociales que podemos analizar en las recetas ya que estas forman la parte visible de las culturas, donde se manifiesta el universo de valores de una sociedad.

La alimentación es considerada una actividad ritual ya que es ahí donde se refleja lo que dispone y consume el individuo. En este sentido, el consumir ciertos alimentos, nos habla de las costumbres, la familia, la región y la cultura. En 1939, Cleofas Jaramillo escribe un recetario cuyo objetivo es presentar lo que considera son las recetas genuinas de Nuevo México. En este recetario la voz de la autora se manifiesta desde su lugar social (Pêcheux *Hacia el análisis automático del discurso*, 89) desde el cual pretende defender la "herencia genuina de la tradición culinaria" de esa región.

La historia de Nuevo México evolucionó de una manera particular ya que, de acuerdo con Erlinda González-Berry y David R. Maciel (*The Contested Homeland a Chicano History of New Mexico*), el desarrollo de esta región se caracterizó por originarse a partir de la lucha entre España y los nativos americanos. Cuando los españoles llegaron a la región, ubicada en el centro y norte de Nuevo México, ésta ya se encontraba habitada por grupos sedentarios denominados Pueblos. El territorio de Nuevo México (la provincia interna) se transformó en la zona más poblada de la frontera norte del Imperio español (12).

Los nuevo mexicanos se desarrollaron aislados de las leyes de España, ese factor permitió el impulso a un cierto tipo de patrón social, cultural y político que transformó su historia. La relativa independencia con que vivían los nuevo mexicanos produjo modos de vida y de tradiciones con fuertes lazos a la tierra.

En este contexto, las recetas de Jaramillo tienen un gran interés histórico ya que se relacionan con las luchas de poder y la influencia entre culturas culinarias diferentes: la española y la americana. Es a través de las recetas como se observa esta lucha por preservar las "tradicionales comidas de Nuevo México" y evitar así que bajo la influencia más poderosa de la cultura norteamericana, se pierdan o se transformen las recetas originales. Es interesante observar que Cleofas Jaramillo se considera a sí misma una poseedora de las verdaderas recetas de Nuevo México, por lo que su texto se transforma en una defensa de las costumbres culinarias ancestrales de esa región.

Una lectura minuciosa del recetario de Jaramillo nos plantea la visión de una mujer que pretende dejar para la posteridad las recetas de sus ancestros, evitando así que se pierda la memoria de su cultura: la española. A pesar de que en su texto se percibe claramente lo que podemos llamar una cocina latinoamericana, que es la síntesis de cocinas amerindias y española producto de la conquista, sin embargo, la autora no hace suyo este concepto ya que en sus recetas, evita por ejemplo nombrar a México como parte de sus raíces hereditarias.

Durante la conquista se introdujeron entre otras muchas prácticas, el usar manteca de puerco para freír los alimentos, una práctica desconocida por los nativos de América. Este ejemplo, en el contexto más amplio del análisis de las cocinas culturales, sugiere que durante los periodos de conflicto el país triunfador impone sus propios hábitos alimenticios a la nación derrotada, aun y cuando aparente una cohabitación de cocinas en la forma de un mestizaje amistoso.

Es importante considerar también la forma en la cual se transmiten las prácticas culinarias, tomando el concepto de habitus de Bourdieu en tanto que son sistemas de disposiciones durables y transferibles, estructuras estructuradas predispuestas a funcionar como estructuras estructurantes que integran todas las experiencias pasadas y que funciona en cada momento como matríz estructurante de las percepciones, las apreciaciones y las acciones de los agentes cara a una coyuntura o acontecimiento y que él contribuye a producir (Bourdieu en *Esquisse d'une théorie de la pratique, precede de tríos études d?ethnologie kabyle*, Droz, Ginebra, 1972, p. 17).

Por lo tanto, para preservar la ancestral tradición culinaria de Nuevo México, Cleofas Jaramillo presenta setenta y cinco "deliciosos platillos españoles" que forman parte de " . . . Spanish recipes, only those used in New Mexico for centuries are given, excepting one or two Old Mexico recipes". En este corto preámbulo, Jaramillo manifiesta la larga tradición que se halla en estas recetas que datan de una historia de cientos de años de antigüedad pero que la autora no percibe como comidas mexicanas sino españolas. Es interesante considerar las formaciones imaginarias que hace la autora acerca de sus posibles lectores: primero podría pensarse que el recetario va dirigido a la familia, pero la tradición de preparación de alimentos es generalmente oral, por lo que esta posibilidad, aunque importante, no es la principal. Por lo tanto, podemos deducir que el lector a quien va dirigida la obra es a las mujeres de la región que comparten sus mismas raíces españolas. El objetivo es no permitir que las recetas "centenarias" queden en el olvido.

Ya desde el título del libro *The Genuine New Mexico Tasty Recipes*, Jaramillo expresa que lo que el lector o lectora va a encontrar son recetas originales y genuinas que son parte de la tradición de Nuevo México. Este pequeño libro que no pasa de treinta y tres páginas deja ver, ya desde la primera página, la intención de llamar atención sobre los alimentos sabrosos, "Tasty Recipes" que van a encontrar contenidos en el libro. Un factor interesante es que, además del título, el texto lleva un subtítulo en español (Potajes sabrosos). El uso de los dos idiomas, inglés y español, refleja el aspecto ideológico que subyace al texto de recetas, aunque para la fecha en que se publica el texto el inglés es el idioma oficial en Nuevo México, el uso de español refleja sus raíces españolas que se evidencia al momento de la escritura, como veremos en lo títulos de sus "recetas originales" como llama Jaramillo a sus preparaciones culinarias.

Bajo su nombre en la parte inferior de la página titular, Jaramillo formula un agregado que expresa la antigüedad así como la cantidad de las recetas incluidas en su libro: *Old and Quaint Formulas for Preparation of Seventy-five Delicious Spanish Dishes.* Es interesante notar que a pesar de que Cleofas Jaramillo describe las recetas como de origen español y no mexicano, las comidas como el "pipián", las "enchiladas" "chile Caribe", "corn tortillas", etc. representan el mestizaje entre dos cocinas: la autóctona prehispánica y la española.

Así mismo, en sus recetas, la autora expresa una de las expresiones de género más antiguas: la preparación y realización de las comidas, una práctica ligada al rol de la subordinación de la mujer en la historia de las diferentes culturas.

A través del discurso de las recetas es posible reconstituir los sabores tradicionales de esa región. Las comidas son el reflejo del lento proceso de adaptación que una sociedad lleva a cabo y el aprovechamiento que hace de los ingredientes autóctonos para satisfacer una de sus necesidades básicas del ser humano: la alimentación.

Esta adaptación está relacionada con el clima, la geografía, la historia y la religión, elementos que forman parte de la cultura y que producen y reproducen en forma recíproca una de las constantes de cualquier sociedad: sus gustos. Sin embargo, estos hábitos enmascaran otro tipo de prácticas más sutiles: las comidas y su preparación ocultan las luchas de poder y la ideología que subyacen a dichas prácticas.

En la escritura, por otra parte, difícilmente se transcribe lo que se pretende ya que existen coacciones en el lenguaje que determinan nuestra manera de hablar (Reboul, *Lenguaje e Ideología*). De acuerdo a esto en este recetario se puede ver cómo se manifiesta la ideología de la autora en cuanto a sus orígenes. Jaramillo se considera con raíces españolas, no es por lo tanto ni mexicana ni americana, de este modo expresa su identidad al comentar que dichas recetas son "Seventy-five Delicious Spanish Dishes" aunque al interior del texto incluya "excepting one or two Old Mexico recipes" (1). Vemos cómo el discurso de Jaramillo presenta una ideología que Reboul define como *difusa,* la que se manifiesta por reflejar creencias extendidas que tienen por función justificar el poder establecido (Reboul, *Lenguaje e Ideología*). Es interesante observar cómo la autora refleja en el texto su propia identidad, por un lado evitando nombrando lo que considera de poco valor: como el considerarse con ancestros mexicanos; y por el otro lado afirmando que las recetas, sus recetas, son de origen español y forman parte de las representaciones de una colectividad cuyos ancestros vinieron desde el viejo continente a conquistar y poblar la región.

Las recetas están escritas en dos lenguajes: español e inglés lo que refleja la importancia que le da Jaramillo al lenguaje materno, siendo que vive en Nuevo México, un estado que pertenece a Norteamérica desde la guerra de 1847. A pesar de lo anterior y como un ejemplo de su identidad "difusa", en la segunda página del recetario encontramos un apartado titulado "Dishes prepared with chile and dry corn" donde la autora proporciona la receta para preparar el maíz para "nistamal, corn for the posole tamales, and tortillas . . . ." En dicho apartado la autora nos relata que la preparación data de los tiempos de su abuela y siguiendo la estructura de la escritura de recetas va dando los pasos de esta preparación que "it takes a great deal of time and labor". Los utensilios que utiliza para estas preparaciones giran alrededor del ancestral "metate" donde se muele el maíz ya preparado con dos días de anticipación.

Para Foucault (1987), en toda sociedad la producción discursiva está controlada mediante diversos procedimientos que son sostenidos por las diferentes instituciones sociales. Uno de los procedimientos por los cuales se manifiesta la relación del discurso con el poder, según Foucault, es la imposición de un discurso oficial por parte de las instituciones. Esta imposición se produce mediante una serie de prácticas como la relacionadas con los roles de género, la de la pedagogía, el sistema de libros, o las bibliotecas, una autoridad sobre lo que ha de considerarse "verdadero" o "falso" (*El orden del discurso).* De esta manera, la preparación de los alimentos conlleva cierto tipo de práctica con instrumentos "apropiados" para su elaboración como el metate, una herramienta ancestral y cuya práctica requiere no sólo habilidad sino fuerza física. Este instrumento de origen prehispánico está hecho de piedra volcánica en forma rectangular, cuenta con tres patas chicas, una al frente, y dos en la parte posterior. Además tiene un mango que sirve para triturar el maíz. Las indígenas utilizaban este instrumento en cuclillas, cabe preguntarse si Cleofas

Jaramillo utilizaba el instrumento, ya que comenta que su abuela le dio la receta de la preparación del maíz de la tortilla en el metate. El moler el maíz con el metate se vuelve aquí una elección que marca la identidad cultural y una oposición al discurso cultural español pretendido por Jaramillo a través del libro. La utilización de este utensilio arcaico se contrapone a la negación discursiva de la herencia mexicana por parte de la autora.

Otro procedimiento de control discursivo, según Foucault, se refiere a la autoría, en el sentido de que quien habla o escribe, no es el autor o "creador" de lo expresado, sino sólo su repetidor. En el discurso se entrecruzan diversos saberes históricos, sociales y culturales que se ocultan detrás de una aparente subjetividad creativa, de tal forma que "el tiempo del discurso no es el tiempo de la enunciación" (Foucault, 1987, p. 354). Los enunciados representan una exterioridad que es colectiva, el habla y la escritura son, en realidad, la manifestación de representaciones del "otro" en el discurso; no es uno quien habla sino "otras voces" del pasado a quienes nosotros repetimos sus discursos (p. 204). En las recetas de Jaramillo, quien habla es el pasado que se transmite de generación en generación mediante las prácticas que se van heredando también de generación en generación. Así, por ejemplo, una de sus recetas, el *Pipian*, representa el pasado prehispánico con sus ingredientes originales: las semillas de calabaza tostadas, el maíz blanco, y sus dos tipos de chile. Este platillo representa también el mestizaje de Jaramillo pues lo prehispánico se presenta mezclado con elementos españoles como el pollo es agregado a la salsa o pipian en su receta.

Otro aspecto interesante en las recetas de Cleofas Jaramillo, es la manera en que destaca las diferencias de sabor del maíz blanco y del azul; según la autora en el México antiguo "only the white corn is used, but the blue corn has a better flavor". Esta anotación refleja lo que para Foucault (1987) es el tabú del objeto, como hemos visto, la autora se representa como española y en este contexto prohibido es hablar de su "mexicanidad", a riesgo de provocar rechazo. Dentro de la cultura norteamericana Jaramillo forma parte de una minoría doblemente marginada: mujer y además mexicana ya que aunque intente ocultarlo sus ancestros nacieron en México aun cuando Jaramillo se enmascare como española. De esta forma la autora evita "el tabú del objeto", aquello que no se puede decir, lo prohibido, lo que se debe evitar nombrar debido a esa doble opresión: ser mujer y tener raíces mexicanas. Jaramillo, por lo tanto, remarca su origen español aunque en su discurso, al hablar de la preparación de ciertos alimentos como por ejemplo del maíz, se reflejan los hábitos de la cultura mexicana. El maíz y el chile, por lo tanto, son una marca de mexicanidad ya que son ingredientes fundamentales en la cocina mexicana y no forman parte de la dieta española.

QUESADIAS

> Roll out thin, small pieces of biscuit dough into thin, round tortillas; spread with slices of fresh cheese; fold in half to cover cheese and bake on griddle, turning to brown both sides.

Entre los platillos que describe Jaramillo, no pueden faltar las tortillas de maíz en sus distintas presentaciones como en las enchiladas de salsa de chile rojo.

Otras comidas tradicionales presentadas en el texto son la carne adobada, la carne con chile, los tamales, el pie de chile, los chicharones (sic), el posole (sic), los frijoles y entre las bebidas destaca el pinole, bebida a la cual nos referiremos posteriormente.

Estos alimentos son parte de la cocina autóctona nuevo mexicana y se pueden considerar de origen mestizo pues en ellos se encuentran elementos de ambas culturas como el puerco que fue traído por los españoles a la Nueva España. Es interesante observar cómo a través de las comidas se manifiesta la identidad de una cultura en este caso de una cultura mestiza producto de la transformación de las recetas originales españolas e indígenas creando un nuevo platillo con un sabor propio y regional nuevomexicano. Este mestizaje se puede observar en la receta denominada *Green Chile with Cheese*:

> Stew in milk to moisten, as many peeled, chopped green chiles as you wish to serve. Add yellow cheese cut up in small pieces and salt to taste. Simmer a few minutes to melt cheese; serve. (8)

En esta receta se puede observar que a la preparación de los chiles verdes se le añade queso amarillo en cuadros, el ingrediente "queso amarillo" es uno de los elementos que forman parte de la cocina norteamericana ya que en la receta original mexicana, el ingrediente utilizado tradicionalmente es el "queso blanco".

Otro de los elementos españoles que Jaramillo incorpora a su cocina es el aceite de oliva. La autora describe la preparación de la salsa de tomate con cebolla cortada a la que se añade chile verde, tomates en rajas y un diente de ajo molido a lo cual le añade aceite de oliva. Este último ingrediente marca no sólo la incorporación de un elemento no tradicional sino que también marca una esfera social específica ya que el aceite de oliva es un elemento económicamente caro.

Entre las recetas también se encuentran tres tipos de preparación de arroz, entre ellos el *Aroz con tomate* es otro platillo que presenta aspectos de interés como es que el título esté escrito en español, aunque la receta con sus ingredientes esté en inglés (9). Llama la atención además que el título esté escrito con una "r" en vez de dos, lo que parecería una representación fonética de la pronunciación oral de una persona cuya lengua materna no es el español, lo que probablemente es el caso de Cleofas Jaramillo. Las otras dos recetas de arroz están escritas en inglés: Spanish Rice (New Mexico Style) y Spanish Rice (Old Mexico Style) (10).

En la primera receta al arroz se le agrega cordero en piezas, sal, cebolla, pimienta blanca y un poco de menta mientras que en la receta al estilo del México antiguo, aunque se repiten elementos como la sal, cebolla, pimienta, en vez de cordero, lleva un ingrediente que es de origen prehispánico, el tomate en jugo. Este es el elemento culinario que determina que el arroz se considere de procedencia mexicana.

Las recetas en español están mezcladas con recetas en inglés, *Avocados with green chile*, lo que repite el bilingüismo que hemos mencionado anteriormente. Esta combinación de recetas en inglés y en español no tiene una aparente lógica, al parecer es un se reflejo de la costumbre oral de nombrar dichas recetas de la manera en que la autora aprendió a hacer dichos platillos.

Otra receta que lleva el sello de Nuevo México es la *Capirotada,* un postre que se prepara en época de Cuaresma:

> CAPIROTADA (Bread Pudding)
>
> Cover bottom of a pudding pan with a thick layer of toasted stale bread broken into small pieces or sliced. Over this spread a layer of yellow American cheese cut into inch pieces. Add a layer of seeded raisins, then bread crumbs and cheese to fill pan 2/3 full. Pour over this a hot syrup made of hot water, 3 tablespoons red syrup or molasses, cinnamon and brown sugar to make it quite sweet. Pour over the bread to moisten well, place in oven for about ten minutes until cheese threads; cool and serve with brandy sauce or cream. (11)

Esta receta lleva como ingrediente una vez más "yellow american cheese", queso amarillo, mientras que en la receta mexicana el queso que se utiliza es blanco. Estos tipos de queso: amarillo y blanco, funcionarían como marcas de identidad cultural. Se observa cómo cada cultura va adaptando los alimentos a los gustos socio-culturales lo que agrega, a su vez, un valor al elegir ciertos alimentos sobre otros.

Entre las bebidas que menciona Cleofas Jaramillo varias de ellas son de origen prehispánico como el pinole que la autora describe de la siguiente manera: "This tastes something like milk. Toast to golden brown a cup of maiz concho, dry sweet corn. Grind into fine powder. Dissolve in fresh milk, sweeten with maple sugar, and mix" (14). Esta bebida, en la receta de Jaramillo, representa el mestizaje entre elementos prehispánicos, como el maíz, y elementos españoles, como la leche y el azúcar de maple que es un elemento de la cultura norteamericana. Otra bebida prehispánica altamente valorada es el chocolate y Jaramillo lo prepara al estilo español: con leche, huevos batidos al contrario de la manera nativa, en la que el chocolate se bate con el molinillo de madera, instrumento de origen prehispánico que permite que se produzca la espuma en el chocolate (15).

Los atoles son altamente valorados desde la época prehispánica y Jaramillo menciona varios tipos de ellos: colados, azul, de leche, y el champurrado. Los españoles y criollos adaptaron esta bebida al cambiar el agua, ingrediente original, por la leche, la que le da un sabor característico a esas bebidas.

Los postres forman otro apartado importante en las recetas de Jaramillo y son fundamentales en la herencia de la cocina española y mexicana. Aquí la autora presenta varias recetas:

> BUNELOS DE VIENTO (Puff Fritters)
>
> Make a thick batter of wheat flour and water about like cornbread batter, add salt, aniz seed, and sugar to sweeten slightly. Boil slowly, stirring continually for about % hour until it thickens to consistency of soft biscuit dough. Remove from fire, cool and add 4 eggs to each pint of batter. Mix well and drop into deep hot lard by spoonfuls; hit with a stick constantly to keep turning until they puff up and brown on all sides.

Los "bunuelos de viento", representan la memoria histórica de las recetas tradicionales en la cocina mexicana, de la misma manera esta receta en Nuevo México representa las raíces culturales de esa región.

Por otra parte, al final del recetario, Cleofas Jaramillo nos presenta una serie de menús con varias opciones para el desayuno, la comida y la cena, así como varios tipos de meriendas (teas) completas:

BREAKFASTS

1. Pork Posole, Pork or Lamb Feet, Toast, Café.
2. Tamales, Torta de huevo con camarón, Bonelos, Café.
3. Menudo, Scrambled eggs with green chile, Tortillas, Café.

DINNERS

1. Albondigas, Green chiles rellenos, Spanish Rice, Capirotada pudding with cream, Café.
2. Frijoles, Red chile con carne, Quelite greens, Tortillas, Bonelos de viento, Café.
3. Enchiladas, Frijoles, Aros con tomate, Panocha, Café.
4. Pollo relleno, Green squash and green corn, Fideos, Natias.
5. Canffainita, Helotes or chicos, Salsa de tomates, Helado de pina, Café.
6. Pollo marzeno, Chile verde rescoldado (green chile peeled roasted and fried with garlic), Green corn, Requeson, Cajeta.

SUPPERS

1. Fried carne seca, Green squash with green peas, Bonelos enmielados, Atole con leche.
2. Pipian or Morcias, Chile Pie, Asaderos or chongos with cane syrup or jam.
3. Torrejas, Rueditas, Atole de leche, Cuajada and jam.

TEAS

1. Chocolate, Sopaipas, Puchas or Marquesote cake.
2. Mistela, Puchas, Biscochitos.
3. Champurrado, Empanaditas, Bollette.
4. Atole de leche or Ormiguillo, Pastelitos, Sospiros.

Es importante señalar que estos menús muestran los hábitos de alimentación de una época y que además siguen formando parte de las prácticas que se han trasmitido de generación a generación. La memoria permite mantener en circulación los alimentos a pesar del dinámico evolucionar de las diferentes preparaciones e influencias. Con el tiempo van surgiendo nuevas formas de "dieta" que se adaptan a los cambios socio-históricos de las culturas que evolucionan con las nuevas tecnologías y retos de la sociedad moderna.

La historia de Nuevo México no estaría completa sin la recuperación de las recetas de comidas tradicionales, ya que en ellas se manifiesta una fuerte carga histórica y cultural. La importancia de "The Genuine New Mexico . . . " de Cleofas Jaramillo radica en que, de acuerdo con la autora, refleja la necesidad de dejar por escrito la memoria de la práctica culinaria, herencia de los ancestros españoles que forjaron Nuevo México.

Este acercamiento histórico a las recetas de Cleofas Jaramillo, nos permite afirmar que las prácticas culinarias ligadas a la historia de Nuevo México están relacionadas con las características geográficas y las costumbres de esa región. Además, en su obra, Jaramillo refleja una de las prácticas más antiguas de toda cultura, la cocina, y que ha estado ligada al anónimo papel que ha jugado la mujer como participante activa en la cultura y sin embargo, ha sido una práctica "invisible" con una fuerte tradición oral que necesita ser revalorada como parte importante de la identidad sociocultural de los sujetos.

De los ingredientes que más se repiten en el recetario de Cleofas Jaramillo, destaca el chile, un condimento de origen prehispánico que sin embargo, se mezcló con las comidas españolas y de los descendientes de Nuevo México. Estas fusiones son el reflejo de la identidad mestiza donde a los elementos nativos mexicanos como el maíz, chile, calabacitas, frijoles, se suman los ingredientes españoles como el arroz, el aceite de oliva, la manteca de puerco y el queso, entre otros muchos con los que se fundieron y lograron un mestizaje culinario que se refleja en las recetas de Cleofas Jaramillo.

El concepto del tabú del objeto de Foucault que nosotros articulamos al discurso culinario de las recetas de Jaramillo nos permiten analizar estos textos en cuanto a su relación tanto con la religiosidad. Textos culinarios considerados "religiosos" —como es la época de la cuaresma—, así como en las prácticas culinarias y su relación con el género: quien cocina es la mujer aunque tiene el *derecho* de escribir sobre dichas prácticas en el recetario de Jaramillo, por ejemplo, se incluye como coautor de las recetas su hermano, Reyes N. Jaramillo.

Las recetas de Cleofas Jaramillo reflejan de manera clara los modos de producción, circulación y consumo de alimentos de una región y una época particular que son el reflejo de prácticas sociales que los individuos internalizan a través de la experiencia, y de reglas de conducta que se aplican en la vida cotidiana.

## Works Cited


Douglas, Mary, y Baron Isherwood. *El mundo de los bienes: hacia una antropología del consumo*. México: Grijalvo, 1990.

Foucault, Michel. *El orden del discurso*. Barcelona: Tusquets Editores, 1987.

González-Berry Erlinda y David R. Maciel. *The Contested Homeland a Chicano History of New Mexico*. Albuquerque: U of New Mexico P, 2000.

Pêcheux, Michel. *Hacia el análisis automático del discurso*. Trad. Manuel Alvar Ezquerra. Madrid: Gredos, 1978.

Reboul, Oliver. *Lenguaje e Ideología*. Fondo de Cultura Económica: México, 1986.

# Women Writers in the Nineteenth-Century Hispanic Southwest: Letters, Discourses and Linguistics

**ALEJANDA BALESTRA**
Independent Scholar

Throughout the nineteenth century, the region that is presently constituted by the states of California and New Mexico displayed a cultural diversity characteristic of a society that was thrice colonized during the very same century. Both regions were affected first by Spanish colonization, followed by Mexican colonization, and lastly, by Anglo-American colonization, after the Treaty of Guadalupe Hidalgo (1848). Concomitant with these changes in government, other changes in social and economic structures also occurred, which inevitably influenced the daily lives of women and the roles they had in society—roles that in the history of writing were often obscured by male oppression. In *Writing the History of Women,* Georges Duby and Michelle Perrot explain the ways in which women were marginalized throughout history:

> At one time, a history of women would have seemed an inconceivable or futile undertaking. The roles for which women were destined were silent ones: motherhood and homemaking, tasks relegated to the obscurity of a domesticity that did not count and was not considered worth recounting. Did women so much as have a history? In the minds of the ancients, they were associated with cold: they were inert constituents of an immobile world, while men, burning with heat, were active. Remote from the stage of history, upon which the men who controlled their destinies clashed, women were poorly placed to serve as witnesses. At times, they might play minor roles, but they rarely took the leading parts, and when they did their weaknesses were all too apparent. Generally they were subjects, ready to hail

> conquerors and to weep when heroes went down in defeat. No tragedy was complete without a chorus of women's tears. (ix)

According to Duby and Perrot, women were banished from the history of writing. The only time they became visible was to show what they could *not* do, or what men thought they could do, or what men thought they were. In recent years, a recovery of texts from archives has begun to reconstruct a new history of women, a history told *by* them and not *for* them. This essay aims to support this new trend by showing that women did not have a passive role in history but rather *made* it, just as men did. Furthermore, I hope to illustrate that in a pre-capitalist, colonial society such as the one that existed in the western part of the present-day United States, women who at first spoke only the language of the colonizer and only later the language of the colonized, with the arrival of Anglo-Americans between 1846 and 1848, were protagonists in the construction of the region's history, often times precisely through the use of language. In the beginning, they adhered to the language of the first empire—Spanish. Later, they protested in English, the language of the other empire, the Anglo-Saxon one. No one better represents this contentious attitude toward the language of Empire(s) than María Amparo Ruiz de Burton, a native Spanish speaker who knew English from a very young age. Notwithstanding, she wrote her letters in Spanish as a way to position herself in *californio* (Spanish-Mexican California) society. Even when she moved to the northeastern part of the United States, and used English more frequently, Ruiz de Burton always did so in an ironical manner, to criticize the social constructs of the Anglo-American colonizer, as we shall see below. On the other hand, New Mexican women used Spanish, as seen in their letters, but also used English, which served as a form of silent resistance in their writing.

A detailed analysis of the written discourse of the women who lived in what was to become the Southwest of the United States reveals some characteristics of the social context that necessarily influenced the manner and topics about which women would wrote, since they represented what Van Dijk (1997) called 'the dominated group.' In the case of *nuevomexicano* and *californio* societies, women were part of one dominated group within another. They were first part of the Spanish colonizers' group that took women along for the purpose of reaching the Empire's objectives. Later, they became part of the group of inhabitants whose regions was subjected to the Anglo-American colonizing project.

Critic Van Dijk (1997) provides us with an understanding of the context in which this type of discourse analysis can take place, defining it as: "[a] structure that involves all the properties or attributes of the social situation that are relevant in the production and understanding of such discourse" (106). In this way, contextual traits influenced (written and oral) discourse, and members of the dominated groups either chose to reproduce the discourse of those in power in that social and historical context, or resist it. According to Van Dijk, we find these signs at all levels of discourse, in the contexts in which participants' social characteristics have a fundamental role, e.g., when gender is seen as a type of social grouping. Through their writing, women writers manifested the social limits of that context, yet in certain cases, they resisted the circumstances. We shall see that the moment some women who wrote in Spanish in the nineteenth century abandoned their expected functions (self-sacrificing wives, self-denying mothers or grandmothers), they went beyond the social limits of the time and turned to fulfilling social functions outside the home—making decisions and influencing their husbands' decisions. While they were obeying the power of the group to which they belonged, they were also challenging it, changing, in creative ways, the social norms and rules for them.

For the purpose of this essay, I use approximately twenty-five letters written by women from California and New Mexico between 1800 and 1915. María Antonia Pico, María Amparo Ruiz de Burton, María Ignacia Soberanes, Tomasa Pico de Alvarado, Benicia Vallejo, María de la Concepción Arguello, María Ignacia García, Josefa and Laureana Cuevas, Josefa Carrillo de Fitch, Benicia Vallejo, Concepción Ruiz, María del Refugio Amador, Refugio Ruiz de Amador, Amada E. de Frías, and Julieta Amador are among the letter-writers I consider. One way or another the women who wrote these letters belonged to a privileged social class, since not everyone in nineteenth-century *californio* or *nuevomexicano* society had access to learning the written language. In general, educational possibilities for women were far fewer than for men; however, this situation was not similar for all women, as we shall see.

## Recovering Women's Voices

The first step involved in writing women's history is to recover their voices: what they said and not what was said on their behalf. All along, the history of women has been constructed from men's perceptions. The belief was that women did not write about topics or subjects that deserved inclusion in official history. A recovery of women's voices from the midst of the patriarchal and colonial past of nineteenth-century California and New Mexico is no easy endeavor. There have been devoted archivists dedicated to meticulously keeping the millions of texts written by men but only a few writings by women. Even so, some of these women's texts have been recovered and allow us to "listen" to women's voices, to their own perceptions about reality.

There are two reasons that some writings by Hispanic women from California and New Mexico have been spared the destructive processes of time, abandonment and neglect: either the women who penned them belonged to a privileged social class or the writings dealt with women who corresponded with powerful men in society—governors, priests, military men, and ranchers. These texts were not preserved because of their content, per se, but rather because those women engaged in dialogue with an important male figure, a fact that can be confirmed by the collection of letters that appears in the De la Guerra, Misiones and Amador family archives.

In general, writing women's history, and a history of women from societies such as those in California and New Mexico, implies a project of meticulous recovery, long hours of research in the interminable archives dedicated to men. However, this history *can* be reconstructed and those voices *can* be recovered. By just reading what those women wrote, we re-examine their role in the structuring of their societies, thus rendering a more complete vision of the pre-capitalist colonial society that later became part of the United States. Furthermore, we better understand the role women played in the imposition of first the Spanish colonizer's language and then how the Anglo-American empire's language, itself, was imposed on them.

## Writing and Participation

During the first stages of Spanish colonization, in what later became United States territory, the presence of women in the societies of the *californio* or New Mexican missions was considered to convey tranquility and peace to indigenous tribes, thus allowing missionaries to dedicate time to evangelization. Fray Junípero Serra considered that the presence of women and families in California missions made possible the spiritual progress of the conquest. His role, as can be deduced from Serra's affirmations, quoted by Castañeda (1993), were to teach natives the foundations of a Catholic family life, "including the subservience of women to men, the sanctity and permanence of holy matrimony, the respect for authority, and the saving grace of Baptism" (Castañeda 1993: 80). Women maintained the language and customs of the colonizers' patriarchal society that dominated the period. Castañeda points out that California's colonization was supported by a body of laws that acknowledged women's centrality in Spanish society in America and incorporated the sex/gender element as a main component in the expansion and colonization politics of frontiers (77). Although this gave the impression that women served a patriarchal society that imposed its rules, these women on many occasions resisted the norms imposed on them by the contextual structure. In general, historians have reported the ways in which men lived a different culture and life on the frontiers; yet very few of them have evaluated the role of women in the formation of this new colonial space (Castañeda 1993: 88) and the way women, with the use of Spanish, resisted the language of the Anglo-American empire. These women were responsible for enabling the use of Spanish to persist beyond the period in which this language was considered dominant. The same phenomenon continues to take place in the present: women in many regions in the United States continue to use Spanish and pass it on to their children and grandchildren.

During the Hispanic period of these regions (1800–1848, for our study), the role that women were permitted influenced social, cultural and linguistic forms. They were brought from remote places, first, to accompany the men in the conquest of these isolated zones located in the center of New Spain's viceroyalty, and, later, in the center of the Mexican government territories. In her testimony, Eulalia Pérez (1994: 39) pointed out that in the missions some natives were taught how to pray and others how to read and write. Historians have frequently focused on women's deficiencies, their lack of participation outside the home and lack of formal education; however, as Castañeda indicates, "they [historians] have missed the value the people placed on learning and knowledge. Women were not indifferent to literacy and education, and went to great lengths under the most difficult circumstances to learn to read and write and to pass that knowledge on to others" (1993: 86). Women taught reading and writing to their own and other children; they learned the native languages to facilitate communication with native women, and memorized poems, hymns and dialogues of pastoral stories, or *pastorelas* (Castañeda 1993: 86). In many instances, they became literacy tutors in communities to which formal education had not extended and to places where it would soon be extended in systematic fashion with the Anglo-American presence. Formal education continued to be a site of conflict. The Anglo-American colonization would bring about formal education and with it an increase in the presence of Hispanic children in schools (Griswold del Castillo 1979: 85). Yet, as time went by, education in English was imposed and this would once more signify the losing of Spanish-speaking women's voices since they would not attend school. Many Hispanic parents did not consider trustworthy an education in the colonizer's language that was not associated with Catholicism (1979: 87).

In addition to the preservation of Spanish as a means of communication and resistance to the language of the (new) empire, one can see that some of the women writers whose letters I use in this article fought for their own property rights, for the right to manifest their political ideas, and for their security in this early missionary period. For instance, in the letters of Luisa Varela, Demetria Martínez, Valeriana Lorenzana, Juana Inocencia Reyes and María Luisa Reyes written to Antonio de la Guerra y Noriega, the governor of California, in 1822, they requested that they and their families be granted security so they could avoid economic ruin due to the irregular actions of their husbands:

> Mi venerado señor nos bemos precisadas por razon de las mui numerosas familias, de que temerosas a los mayores estragos que se nos muestra en nuestras familias a causa de las cotidianas impertinencias ocasionadas de los groseros echos de nuestros esposos, nos destraigan de nuestras casas i bienes de nuestras mantenciones . . . (February 1, 1822).[1]

It is possible to begin to see the active and not passive role of women, the latter having been the history that has been written by men through time. In addition, these manifestations can also seem unusual in patriarchal societies, guided by Catholic religious principles, such as the societies of California and New Mexico in the nineteenth century. These women united and fought for their rights, claimed the debts that other members of society owed them, organized the family, and demanded that their children be responsible for their families. In short, these women participated in social issues that affected not only the men but them, too, as members of that society.

Resistance to representatives of power is evident in numerous letters. In 1818, María Rufina Hernández wrote to the governor of California to request assistance in the matter of collecting money that was owed to her. Her husband was deceased and she needed to be paid back either with money or goods:

> Mui señor mío pongo a las plantas de V con el devido respeto que deve I su misión quedava hasiendo [ininteligible] del tiempo que me debe Sor. Martín Noriega la cantidad de sien ps en ganado que desde el tiempo de mi difunto finado Sebastián Alvitre causó esta dependencia hasta la presente no a avido resulta de pago alguna por donde aclamo a la piedad de V. se digne aserle que me pague, pues me hallo [ininteligible] y caresiendo de dicha dependencia i tamvien deviendo por otra parte ahora yo no le pido dinero sino que me pague en frutos como sevo y generos pues todo es pagar [ininteligible] . . . María Rufina Hernández, somos 14 noviembre de 1821.

Rufina Alvitre de Hernández is requesting what belongs to her, but she must do this by pleading with a man, the governor: it is not enough for her to make this demand of her debtor because, from her position as a woman, she cannot successfully secure respect and have restitution made to her.

In the period between 1832 and 1848, which in this study is connected to a third period (1849–1900), Mexican laws established social limits for women to follow: if they stepped outside those imposed boundaries, they would lose their rights or respect (Haas 1995: 82). During this period, women could be owners and manage their own properties. We find two types of property owners: those that received properties from the government for their collaboration in educational and colonization policies, and those who were part of a privileged elite, although, as we shall later see, even as part of said elite these women always found themselves in subordinate positions, which on some occasions caused them to reject their condition as (privileged) women in order to regain control of their possessions. Apolinaria Lorenzano belonged to the former group, while María Amparo Ruiz de Burton, who was owner and manager of her ranches, and owned a mine, among other possessions, belonged to the latter. Even though they were both property owners, there were social differences between them.

Lorenzano is representative of the relatively poor landowners who owned lands that had been transferred to them for services rendered in missions and *presidios* (prisons). In general, these property owners continued to perform manual labor all their lives. On the other hand, María Amparo Ruiz de Burton exemplifies those *californios* who belonged to an elite group. Ruiz de Burton was a member of a colonial military family. After the Anglo-American colonization [of California], she married an Anglo-American military officer in 1849. Although there is a contrast in the source of Lorenzana's and Ruiz de Burton's wealth, they shared the right to own their possessions (Haas 1995: 80). Both also had in common the Spanish language and they used it in their correspondence or testimonies.

The right of women to own property came from Spanish and Mexican laws that allowed women to manage their lands and wealth, and separately manage possessions they acquired before contracting marriage. However, in contrast to men, who were not required to practice decorous conduct to preserve their possessions, women could lose their property if they did not closely subscribe to the social rules or just if they did not turn to a man for protection. These rights and their concerns about the possession of their lands can be traced in the writings of these two women. In 1857, María Amparo Ruiz de Burton wrote to Matías Moreno:

> Me parece que le oí decir hace algún tiempo que hay un decreto nuevo regulando la manera de dar posesiones, y también los costos o derechos que se deben cobrar a los propietarios; si Ud. tiene ese decreto le agradeceré me lo preste, o si Ud. sabe algo con respecto a este particular, que me lo diga pues me interesa y tal vez tendré que hacer uso de esa información pronto. (María A. Ruiz de Burton to Matías Moreno, 1857, 147)

María Antonia Pico also writes to her son concerning legal issues:

> Mi apreciable hijo: Hay algunas noticias de los comisionados de quienes hiciste encargue que desde el mes pasado han llegado á la ciudad de San Francisco que han principiado ha trabajar en su comision.

> De este lugar han salido algunas personas con el objeto de arreglar sus documentos, á quienes estamos aguardando su vuelta para darte noticias mas seguras para que prevengas tu viaje á este punto há arreglar nuestros titulos y demas asuntos. (María Antonia Pico to Manuel Castro, February 15, 1852)

Women could also remain in charge of their children and grandchildren's care if their husbands died. The right to inheritance was among the other rights women had, which in this particular case was equal to that of their male siblings.

María Amparo Ruiz de Burton kept constant correspondence with Mariano Guadalupe Vallejo, a prominent nineteenth-century figure in California. In this epistolary exchange, our female writer discusses extremely varied topics: the position of *californios* in the social pyramid [and] differences among *californios*, which through personal details allows a glimpse at the condition of women in nineteenth-century *californio* society. As Sánchez y Pita (2002) have indicated, Ruiz de Burton positions herself as superior among *californios* and also as someone who "always found herself both 'insider' and 'outsider' in whatever circles she moved . . . ." (74), in reference to her status as a Californian, American or Mexican (woman). She was also an "insider/outsider" in terms of the language she used. To sustain a dialogue with her "compatriots," she used Spanish; to criticize the Anglo-American colonizer and also allow him to understand what she had to say, she used English. One can appreciate as much in her novels *Who Would Have Thought It*? and *The Squatter and the Don*, which are not the focus of this study but are worth mentioning, since they represent the first novels written in English and from a *californio*'s point of view. English is also sprinkled in her Spanish-language correspondence: she uses it to ridicule the empire's attitude. In a letter addressed to Mariano Guadalupe Vallejo on November 30, 1851, María Amparo Ruiz de Burton addresses the subject of her superiority within the circle of *californios*, her position within society and her condition as a woman:

> Si no me animara el pensamiento que estoy hablando con un buen compatriota seguramente acabaría por decir nada, pero el título de paisana vale demasiado para no hacer uso de él; conozco que no debo hablar a Ud. con rodeos, ( . . . ) dejaremos pues para con los extranjeros, el uso de todas esas bagaletas, y para entre nosotros los paisanos la franqueza. ( . . . )
>
> Ahora conozco cuán bueno y útil que haya entendimiento entre dos compatriotas, ¡qué lástima que no haya muchos como nosotros dos! ( . . . ) Sí, parece que quedamos de acuerdo en que somos un par de prodigios ( . . . ) estoy persuadida de que nosotros nacimos para hacer algo más que simplemente vivir, esto es, que nacimos para otra cosa más, que el resto de nuestros

> pobres paisanos . . . (María A. Ruiz de Burton to Mariano G. Vallejo, 1851, 75)

It is evident that she positions herself in a place of power and adopts the discourse of those who exert that power in order to keep herself within the imposed parameters. The theme of gender reappears in a letter written to Mariano Guadalupe Vallejo, from New Castle, Delaware. Ruiz de Burton had advised Vallejo to negotiate personally in the U.S. Congress the usurpation of lands that was taking place in California, but Vallejo did not heed her advice. In reference to this, Ruiz de Burton states: "Todavía creo que si Ud. hubiera seguido mi consejo y venido a Washignton en '60 o '61, otro habría sido el resultado de este negocio. Pero Ud. es hombre y no me creyó con la suficiente seguridad para (seguir) mi buen consejo" (March 18, 1863, 261). In another letter addressed to Matías Moreno, she points out: "La perseverancia aún en una mujer a veces vence obstáculos" (September 2, 1863, 263). Ruiz de Burton even questions decisions made by her husband, Henry Burton, as is evident in the following section of a letter, when she asks Mariano Guadalupe Vallejo to recover documents that belong to her that her husband left in the hands of George C. Johnson, the agent the Burtons had hired to establish a mine company in southern California:

> Dígale Ud. de mi parte al Sr. Johnson que me ha sido muy perjudicial el carecer por tan largo tiempo de esos documentos y que espero me haga el favor de no detenerlos por más tiempo. Dígale también que sin que yo lo supiera, sin mi consentimiento, que Enrique dejó así mis papeles, y que cuando lo supe, lo desaprobé ( . . . ) y tengo derecho a reclamarlos.
>
> Un abogado en Washington me dijo que mujeres casadas no pueden legalmente dar "poderes" ni aún a sus maridos. Así es, el poder que yo le di a Enrique fue de muy dudosa legalidad, y no creo que él haya tenido el derecho de dejar mis títulos sin mi consentimiento. (September 12, 1868, p. 277)

One can clearly see the contrasting situation of women in California in María Amparo Ruiz de Burton's correspondence. She knew that being a woman in that society was not an advantage but rather a disadvantage and she preferred to emphasize the fact that it was more advantageous to be a man before she ever thought about trying to change that situation. Yet, in an indirect manner, she was bringing about changes by addressing topics and subjects that were not the expected pursue of women. From previous examples, one can also see that there were limitations on women's rights—they could own property yet were not allowed to confer power (of attorney) to anyone else.

This same author also discusses daily topics, such as the boring life in Monterey, California: "Ningunas noticias interesantes hay que comunicarle; todo está lo mismo, como siempre, nada saca a Monterey de su continuo feliz letargo; todo reposa en perfecta quietud," she tells Mariano Guadalupe Vallejo in a letter written on April 24, 1852. In the same letter, she criticizes the Anglo-Saxon capitalist position, a position that years later she herself adopts when she receives a *recertificacíon* [license] of behalf of Benito Juárez's government to exploit the lands she owns in Ensenada:

> No, nosotros los montereyanos no somos como esa gente ambiciosa de por allá arriba que no tiene más deseo que atesorar dinero o procurárselo, no importa cómo, para gratificar sus pasiones, eso es horrible. Nosotros no, nuestro objeto (si tuviéramos alguno) no sería tan indigno; Sí, estoy segura que si tuviéramos más energía y menos flojera ganaríamos dinero y lo emplearíamos mejor; compraríamos bonitos vestidos- ¿No es verdad que esto es muy inocente? sólo gratifica una muy simple vanidad, y es más, es de gente decente tener buenos trapos . . . (79)

As regards the aforementioned use of English in her correspondence, she does it in an ironic manner to deconstruct Anglo-American activities. In an 1867 letter addressed to Mariano Guadalupe Vallejo, in which she seems to be replying to another one by Vallejo in which he defends Anglo-American actions and defends the American Republic, Ruiz de Burton resorts with irony to English:

> Veo que se enoja Ud. y me dice que su admiración por los Yankies 'no es crónica pero que ellos son los hombres de América.' Por supuesto que sí lo son, si aún los más ilustrados mexicanos les doblan las rodillas. Por supuesto que sí lo son, cuando los mismos mexicanos se apresuran a remover todo obstáculo y barrer todo impedimento para que su marcha triunfal siga sin interrupción. Lo único que lo habría interrumpido habría sido una monarquía en México. Ellos lo previnieron y de allí nació el amor repentino por la "Sister Republic" . . . (271)

She also is critic about enlightened Mexican people who accept and congratulate the U.S. advances over Mexican territory. In another 1868 letter, Ruiz de Burton once more resorts to English in ironic fashion: "¿Qué le parece a Ud. del pleito de gatos del Congreso y el Presidente? Lindísimo—I suppose- puesto que todo es chulísimo si sólo es un gobierno *republicano*, no? ¡Qué vergüenza—si la tuvieran—declamar tanto del respeto de las leyes y después pisotearlas" (273). In a letter from 1869, she states: "Si yo pudiera creer en el "Manifest Destiny" dejaría de creer en la justicia ( . . . ) No amigo mío, el Manifest Destiny no es otra cosa que "Manifest Yankie trick" . . . " (281). Throughout several extensive letters in which she used English, she used it to ridicule and continue to state her opposition to republics that are forced to yield to other countries and to object to Vallejo's position with regard to that subject.

María Amparo Ruiz de Burton is an example of a nineteenth-century privileged woman who had an elite education, who owned lands, who married an American officer. This lifelong situation created an almost schizophrenic position for her in which she constantly questioned, openly or implicitly, the Anglo-Saxon government. She sometimes positioned herself as a Californian or Mexican woman, or would adopt a capitalist stance that on yet other occasions she would criticize, making her appear more like an Anglo-American than her Californian compatriots. It was through the many small gaps that society left them where women found a space for expression through writing.

The kinds of concerns that one finds in women's letters are not only those that have often only been attributed to men, e.g., legal or economic matters, land ownership, and questioning the Anglo-American government's actions. Women were also concerned with the everyday topics that were part of the social networks that were coming into being in U.S. Hispanic society. Many letters were written to announce illnesses, inquire about the health of family members, provide news, and recount their routines. Even those women who write about economic, cultural, and political topics do not leave aside daily subject matters. The following examples illustrate the kinds of topics that women addressed in their correspondence:

> Mi muy amado hermano José:
> Si no supiera que tanto es lo que tengo que hacer, y todo lo dejo ahorita para ponerle á Ud. estas mal hechas letras. Pues que me tiene con cuidado su silencio, y deseo saber cual es el motivo de que no me haiga contestado mi carta que hase mas de un mes que le escribi. (Josefa Carrillo de Fitch to her brother José Carrillo, May 27, 1860)

> Mi querídisima hermanita Refugio.
> Cuanto hemos padecido mi mamá y yo y sin tener el consuelo de berte, á mi me paresía que no bolbio á berte nunca, que me moría sin ber á mi unica hermana á mi querida Cuca, pero por fin estoy ya restablecida; y la pobre de mi mamá es la que apenas comiensa a sentir alivio: paralitica todavía del braso y la pierna isquierda permanese son poder andar. (Belén Ruiz de Escobar to Refugio Ruiz de Amador, May 24, 1871)

A particularly noteworthy letter is one written by Benicia Vallejo to one of her sons, some time after the beginning of 1869, in which she complains to her sons and to all her children about the lack of interest they show in family matters once they have left their home:

> Querido Platon
> Tome pluma para saludarte a ti y a Lili tu esposa para los dos es esta carta. Platon dile a Lili que no le he escrito porque escribo mui mal: solo la necesidad que tengo de saber algo de mis hijos: Yo no sé porqué desde que salen de aquí ya no se acuerdan mas de su mamá. Andonico no tiene mamá . . . . Napoleón no tiene mamá: Frani no tiene Mamá, Adela no tiene Mamá: Ninguno se acuerda de mi, ni una cartita siquiera para saludarme y todos saben bien escribir . . . (Benicia de Vallejo to Platón Vallejo, January 7, 1869)

Sometimes women who did not have the social presence of someone like María Amparo Ruiz de Burton inserted an opinion about some aspect of the society in which they lived in the middle of a letter in which daily topics abounded. In a letter written by Belén de Escobar, she talks about daily subjects: diseases, family members who are ill, forgotten objects in a house that was visited. However, in two lines she comments on the great need that is being endured in Las Cruces, New Mexico, at the end of the nineteenth century: "Por aquí no hay mas nueba que las comedias que estan dando a benefisio de los pobres, y la necesidad de comida que hay, por lo demas todo muy muy triste" (Belén de Escobar to Refugio E. de Amador, Las Cruces, NM, May 10, 1880). In another letter, another woman from Las Cruces, in the middle of a series of greetings and errands, mentions that she is a landowner:

> Aquí tengo el cucharoncito de Corina que trajeron de la "Popular", dile que se lo mando por correo, yo no le mandé por que temo que se quiebre. Dime cuanto mas se le pagó a Leiva ya este mes vencido tiene que pagar Primitivo doce pesos. Alex puede que vaya para esa dentro de dos o tres días va con un agente que se interesa por mi terreno si algo se les ofrece me escriben luego y puedo mandar con el los encargos.
> Recuerdos de los dos para todos a los nenes besos y para ti otros de tu fiel. María. (María to Julieta, Las Cruces, NM, November 18, 1895)

In a letter written by Amada E. de Frías to Julieta Amador de García, one catches a glimpse of the performance of the period's postal system's performance and of women's humor:

> Y lo que sucedió, fué que la remesa no fue por Express, sino por correo, creyendo que la Oficina se los llevarian á Ustedes lo mismo que cualquiera carta. De manera es, que sin duda los botes se han quedado allá en el Correo, en espera de que los manden recoger. ( . . . ) Y ahora no hay mas que pedirles me excusen por aquel equivoco: y te suplico te informes si estan todavia allí los botecitos o si ya se los comieron en el Correo al ver que nadie los reclamaba. (Amada E. de Frías to Julieta Amador de García, Las Cruces, NM, November 7, 1895)

Sometimes these references in the midst of other daily issues allow us to reconstruct the history of these women and of the place from the perspective of women who write in Spanish. As I said earlier, this is a history that has been veiled, hidden, due to the fact it was written by men. In addition, here in the part of the world that later became the United States, history ended up being written in English with an Anglo-American perspective. Nevertheless, through their letters, women show us another point of view.

As Van Dijk has indicated, in some instances women's discourse from their position in a colonial and imperialist society transmitted patriarchal and colonial values. But other times one can see signs of resistance, even from within the limitations that these women had to face. From the very little space that was left for them, they tried to resist social impositions.

## Conclusion

In conclusion, during the period between 1800 and 1900, one can see that women fulfilled roles that were imposed upon them from without: they had to intervene as guardians of the transmission and imposition of culture imposed by the colonizers and in the language of said colonizers. However, women always constructed their own spaces in the interstices that were permitted them in patriarchal societies. In those gaps, we find that women had other concerns that went beyond the limits of their homes. We have seen that they were concerned with the preservation of their possessions, justice, the caretaking of their families, and commenting on the society in which they lived. Furthermore, they carried out these activities in a language that later became the conquered language: Spanish. Through their written discourse, women conveyed aspects of the post-1848 histories of California and New Mexico that were not addressed either by men in the period of Spanish domination or by Anglo Americans, in general.

This study is part of a larger historical and sociolinguistic research project on Spanish in nineteenth-century California and New Mexico and has among its major proponents Glenn Martínez (2000), who studies nineteenth-century judicial law in Texas; Irene Moyna, et al. (2005), who study the contact between the Spanish and English languages in nineteenth-century California; Magdalena Coll (1999), who analyzes linguistic aspects of Doña Teresa de Aguilera y Roche's letter to the Court of the Inquisition in 1664; and Acevedo (2000) and Balestra (2002, 2006), who study the Spanish verbal system used in California. All these researchers began to study some linguistic aspect of Spanish in a society in which this language came to displace the languages of natives and was later itself displaced by the language of the new Anglo-American conquerors. Reviewing the archives in order to collect what was written in Spanish allows us to observe the absence of women's writings, or their limited presence, and to gain access to those few written materials that are actually available. In this manner, an interpretation of the social history of these regions from women's point of view, from the perspective of the conquered, is possible. This is just the beginning of a vast amount of research that still needs to be done with respect to women's writings. I hope that this study will encourage other researchers to engage the topic too.

## Note

[1] I have kept the original spelling of the correspondence (in the Spanish versions).

## Works Cited

Acevedo, Rebeca. "Perspectiva histórica del paradigma verbal en el español de California." *Research on Spanish in the United States. Linguistic Issues and Challenges.* Ed. By Ana Roca. Somerville: Cascada P, 2000. 110–20.

Balestra, Alejandra. *Del futuro morfológico al perifrástico: un cambio morfosintáctico en el español de California*, 1800–1930. Diss. U of Houston, 2000.

Castañeda, Antonia. "Presidarias y pobladoras: Spanish-Mexican women in frontier Monterey, Alta California, 1770–1821." *Chicana critical issues.* Ed. Norma Alaracón. Berkeley: Third Woman P, 1993. 73–94.

Coll, M. M. *Un estudio lingüístico-histórico del español en Nuevo México en la época de la colonia: análisis de la carta de Dona Teresa de Aguilera y Roche al Tribunal de la Inquisición en 1664*. Diss. U of California, Berkeley, 1999.

Duby, Georges, and Michelle Perrot. "Writing the History of Women," in *A History of Women: From Ancient Goddesses to Christians Saints*. Cambridge and London: The Belknap P of Harvard UP, 2000. ix–xxi.

Griswold del Castillo, Richard. *The Los Angeles Barrio, 1850–1890: A Social History.* Berkeley, Los Angeles and London: U of California P, 1979.

Haas, Lisbeth. *Conquests and Historical Identities in California*. Berkeley, Los Angeles, London: U of California P, 1995.

Martínez, G. 2000. *Topics in the Historical Sociolinguistics of Tejano Spanish 1791–1910: Morphosyntatic and Lexical Aspects.* Diss. U of Massachusetts, Amherst, 2000.

Moyna, Irene, Wendy Decker, and M. Eugenia Martín. "Spanish/English Contact in Historical Perspective: 19th Century Documents of the Californias." *Selected Proceedings of the 7th Hispanic Linguistic Symposium.* Ed. David Edington. Somerville, MA: Cascadilla Proceedings P, 2005. 169–79.

Sánchez, Rosaura, and Beatrice Pita, eds. *Conflicts of Interest: Letters by María Amparo Ruiz de Burton*. Houston: Arte Público P, 2001.

Van Dijk, Teum. *Racismo y análisis critico de los medios*. Barcelona and Buenos Aires: Paidós, 1997.

## Letters Cited

María Rufina Alvitre de Hernández to José Antonio de la Guerra. Pueblo de los Ángeles, 1821. Huntington Museum and Library, HUNT De la Guerra Family Collection.

María Amador to Julieta Amador. Las Cruces, NM, Archives and Special Collections Department, NSMU Library, Amador Family Papers, 1836–1949, MS 0004, Box 40, Folder 3.

María de la Concepción Arguello to Jose de la Guerra y Noriega, 1829. Huntington Museum and Library, HUNT De la Guerra Family Collection.

María Josefa Buelna to Manuel Castro. 1853, June 17. Manuel de Jesús Castro Collection, Bancroft Collection, BANC MSS C-B 483, Folder 184.

Josefa Carrillo de Fitch to her brother José Carrillo. Rancho del Polin. 1863, May 27, Bancroft Collection, Fitch Family Papers BANC MSS C-B 357 v.1.

Josefa Castro de Roldán to Juan and Francisco Sepulveda. Tepec, 1849, June 13. Manuel de Jesús Castro Collection, Bancroft Library, BANC MSS C-B 483.

Josefa Castro de Roldán to Manuel Castro. Tepec, 1849, July 14. Manuel de Jesús Castro Collection, Bancroft Collection, BANC MSS C-B 483.

Amada E. de Frías to Julieta Amador de García. Las Cruces, 1915, November 7. Archives and Special Collections Department, NSMU Library, MS 0004, MS 0004 Box 40, Folder 3.

María Ignacia García to José Antonio de la Guerra. 1821, August 24. De la Guerra Family Collection, Huntington Museum and Library, HUNT 315.

Juliana López de Orema to Josefa Carrillo de Fitch. San Diego, 1852, May 15. Fitch Family Papers, Bancroft Collection, BANC MSS C-B 357 v.1.

María Josefa (López) de Vejar to Crisóstomo Vejar, Los Angeles, 1854, June 21. Vallejo Family Papers, Emparán Purchase. No. 45. 73/122 C, California Miscellany Additions, Folder 45.

Francisca Moreno to Matías Moreno. 1847. Huntington Library, Helen Long Collection, HUNT Box 1.

María Antonia Pico to José de la Guerra y Noriega. Monterey, 1819, August 18. Huntington Museum and Library, de la Guerra Family Collection, HUNT 179.

María Antonia Pico to Manuel Castro, 1853, March 15. Manuel de Jesús Castro Collection, Bancroft Collection, BANC MSS C-D 483, Folder 173.

Tomasa Pico de Alvarado to Manuel Castro. San Diego, 1854, May 4. Manuel de Jesús Castro, Bancroft Collection, BANC MASS C-B 483 Box 2, Folder 226.

María Amparo Ruiz de Burton to Mariano Guadalupe Vallejo. Monterey, 1851, November 30. (*Conflicts of Interest: The Letters of María Amparo Ruiz de Burton.* Ed. Rosaura Sánchez and Beatrice Pita. Houston: Arte Público P, 74–76.)

María Amparo Ruiz de Burton to Mariano Guadalupe Vallejo. Monterey, 1852, April 24. (*Conflicts of Interest: The Letters of María Amparo de Burton*. Ed. Rosaura Sánchez and Beatrice Pita. Houston: Arte Público P, 78–80.)

María Amparo Ruiz de Burton to Matías Moreno, Jamul, 1857, December 22. (*Conflicts of Interest: The Letters of María Amparo de Burton*. Ed. Rosaura Sánchez and Beatrice Pita. Houston: Arte Público P, 147.)

María Amparo Ruiz de Burton to Mariano Guadalupe Vallejo. New Castle, Delaware, 1863, March18. (*Conflicts of Interest: The Letters of María Amparo de Burton*. Ed. Rosaura Sánchez and Beatrice Pita. Houston: Arte Público P, 261–62.)

María Amparo Ruiz de Burton to Matías Moreno. Pittsburg, Pennsylvania, 1863, September 2. (*Conflicts of Interest: The Letters of María Amparo de Burton*. Ed. Rosaura Sánchez and Beatrice Pita. Houston: Arte Público P, 277–79.)

Antonia M. de Sánchez. San Francisco, 1854, April 26. Manuel de Jesús Castro Collection, Bancroft Collection, BANC MSS C-B 483, Box 2.

Benicia de Vallejo to Platón Vallejo. 1869, January 1, Sonoma, Huntington Library and Museum.

Luisa Varela, Demetria Ramírez, Baleriana Lorenzana, Juana Ignacia Reyes and María Luisa Reyes. Pueblo de los Angeles, 1822, February 1. De la Guerra Family Collection, Huntington Museum and Library, HUNT 1000.

# Part II

## Women's Voices: Gender, Politics and Culture

# Recovering the Self: The Unnamed Characters of Luisa Capetillo's *How Poor Women Prostitute Themselves*

**NANCY BIRD-SOTO**
University of Wisconsin-Milwaukee

To approach Luisa Capetillo (1879–1922) is to encounter a writer and activist who lived admirably according to her egalitarian convictions in both words and actions. The characters of her short plays enact and expose the social environment in which they lived as men and as women. These characters often exemplify how much an individual conforms his or her self to the social norm of gendered behavior or how much they are able detach from it. It is usually the women protagonists in her plays who enact the power of their convictions just like Capetillo herself did throughout her lifetime.[1] These women protagonists are, as Lara Walker keenly describes, "agents of social change" (98). In the play *Cómo se prostituyen las pobres* (*How Poor Women Prostitute Themselves*), the Boricua[2] writer exposes the paradigm of exploitation that kept women subordinated to patriarchal domination at the end of the nineteenth century and beginning of the twentieth.[3] My goal here is to demonstrate how the answer to the question offered in the title of the play lies in the woman protagonist's ability to recover herself by challenging the norm of women's subordination.

The Arecibo-born writer was well aware of the climate of oppression that encircled the Puerto Rican society of her time. It was a paternalistic society bound by hierarchies in which men and the affluent would position women and the working classes in a status of dependence as if they were inferior.[4] Moreover, Capetillo noticed how exploitation was not just an insular problem, since it was affecting workers, women, and marginalized groups around the globe. Capetillo's travels to different factories in different towns in Puerto Rico, and also to

New York, Tampa, and Cuba, plus her role as reader of literature and news at tobacco factories, gave her a broad and firsthand view of the scope of the oppressive social and economic structure she consistently denounced. As an anarchist of her time and as a woman, Capetillo devoted her life and her writings to confronting social dynamics that created injustice, especially for workers and for women. Her numerous essays, letters and short plays convey her commitment to improving the lives of those who had limited to nonexistent choices at their disposition to fully detach themselves from their status of subordination. In *Cómo se prostituyen las pobres*, Capetillo decries gender-based exploitation in the context of a specific venue of unequal exchanges: the house of a prostitute. I will, thus, illustrate the manner in which this play questions prevailing notions of the role(s) of women in society, that is, how it addresses the topic of gender disparity entrenched in the social foundation of a patriarchal and paternalistic nation.

In appreciating the relevance of the social critique offered by Capetillo, the cultural constraints for a woman in early twentieth-century Puerto Rico must be acknowledged. These constraints are based upon an oppressive mode of social conditioning that permeates the education and therefore the interactions between men and women. Capetillo's *Cómo se prostituyen las pobres*, from *Influencia de las ideas modernas* (1916), was a "project that had been gestating since her days in Tampa (Matos Rodríguez, xxiii). The present analysis is enhanced by different yet equally important components of its contextualization. The first aspect is the social and cultural climate in the Puerto Rico known to Capetillo. Part of the repertoire of an active observer and commentator, Capetillo's other writings[5] address the injustice that characterized social dynamics between the sexes and between social classes.

Closely linked to this first aspect, I include a sample of instances in which the author questions the social norms of the time through her essays and letters. This way, we will see how Capetillo was not a mere observer of the scaffolding of the Puerto Rican nation. By exposing her critique in an array of writings, including short plays, Capetillo actively represents how gender and class disparity are problematically rooted in the elaboration of such nationhood. Thus, establishing the social context and her consistent denouncement of any form of exploitation will serve as a backdrop for the situation represented in the play. As the characters speak, they can embody, adhere or challenge the very norm that limits them. By creating characters that (re)present the social situation as lived by many, Capetillo allows for individuals to reclaim their selves beyond social prescriptions of behavior.

## Paradigms and Challenges

In this analysis, I use different terms that function as particular articulations of the general paradigm of class and gender oppression. One of these terms is the adjective "patriarchal." It is used in the sense of the privileging of the male, which in social terms means the privileging of the *pater* (father) or the patriarch. In this sense, a patriarchal society is one where the male principle rules, a dynamic that extends over men and women and their gender(ed) relations. In the problematic patriarchal enmeshment of the terms "man" and "woman" with the articulation of gender and gender roles, it is important to consider Judith Butler's postulation of how it appears that "sex is absorbed by gender" (5). When applying this observation to the analysis at hand, the fact that in normative behavior terms gender or gender roles may trump sex (as in individual man or individual woman), it becomes evident how traditional patriarchal patterns would thrive as a result of the aforementioned enmeshment.[6] If being an individual woman (sex) is disregarded in favor of behaving like a woman (gender), then that particular woman is being judged as socially fit as to how she complies with her sexual and social subordinated role.[7]

The subordination of women to the authority of men is an obvious manifestation of the oppressive paradigm embedded in a patriarchal society. Subordination implies a structure of domination, another term used in this analysis to depict the unequal dynamics Capetillo denounces in *Cómo se prostituyen las pobres*. "Domination" is another term that as well characterizes the oppressive paradigm that limits the possibilities for justice for subordinated social sectors, mainly women and workers. Following Marcia Rivera Quintero's study about women joining the capitalist workforce toward the end of the nineteenth century in Puerto Rico and into the twentieth, it is evident how patriarchal biases, subordination, domination and exploitation are all expressions of a generalized oppressive climate. As she explains,

> Women from dispossessed classes were recruited to take on jobs that served to reinforce the hegemony of one class over another, and that maintained women in a subordinated position, subject to a constant economic, social, and sexual exploitation.[8] (Rivera Quintero 48–49)

This environment of exploitation that Rivera Quintero illustrates is what Capetillo, via the protagonist of *Cómo se prostituyen las pobres,* calls attention to in order to demonstrate the lack of fair options women were facing. Such limitations were obstacles in the process of emancipating themselves from the forms of oppression they had learned to cope with and endure.

Luisa Capetillo's primary biographer, Norma Valle Ferrer, has aptly described the writer as a "pioneer Puerto Rican feminist," which is the title of her 2006 book on the Arecibo-born author. As an activist, Capetillo was challenging herself in all areas of her life while contesting her prescribed social role as a woman. In her writings, especially her essays and letters, that challenge is in many ways her inspiration. A play such as *Cómo se prostituyen las pobres* demonstrates the challenge of how to achieve full emancipation from subjugating ways. This task is enacted as the characters are allowed to express their perceptions of who they are. The oppressive climate already mentioned is the constant target of Capetillo's critique, a critique aimed at transforming a social paradigm anchored in unfair and unbalanced relations, especially between men and women.[9]

The consistent denouncement of inequality in Capetillo's work is an asset in underscoring the power of her convictions and also in assessing her social critique when, in the scope of a play, different characters have the opportunity to debate and dialogue in order to highlight it. An example of the unequal social expectations for men and women, and the implied conceptual double standards can be found in Capetillo's remarks in her essay *Lo que hacen los hombres*:

> . . . la mujer no encuentra igual sinceridad en el hombre, que el hombre encuentra en la mujer. La mujer cuando un joven la enamora, si á ella le agrada, es sincera y afectuosa, y atenta y fiel, el hombre cuando esa mujer lo enamora, es pedante, injusto, grosero, importuno, y por fin la desprecia. Todo esto es debido á las costumbres establecidas, pero después que se acostumbren ambos, á ser libres, ya variarían de procedimiento. (Ramos 208)

By decrying that lack of honesty in men and the rude behavior that characterizes their romancing rites, Capetillo is not merely describing unbalanced mating techniques between men and women. She is offering an impugnation of the patriarchal mentality that molds the inequality between the sexes. Moreover, she accurately contextualizes the gender-based behavior as a product of the social and cultural circumstances, asserting that with the appropriate change in how people are educated, both women and men will be able to overcome the indoctrination of rigid gender roles.

Adding to the social contextualization of *Cómo se prostituyen las pobres*, Capetillo also calls attention the lack of balance between social classes and how the poor find themselves subordinated to those higher in the social hierarchy. This is why she openly criticizes throughout her writings the role of dominant institutions such as the State (the governmental institution) and the Church (the religious institution) in maintaining an unequal society. In regards to the State and its politics, Capetillo affirms herself as a socialist of her time by saying: "aspiro a que todos los adelantos, descubrimientos e invenciones establecidos, pertenezcan a todos, que se establezca su socialización sin privilegios. Algunos lo entienden con el Estado para que éste regule la marcha, yo lo entiendo sin gobierno" (Ramos 87). In her vision of an advanced society where everyone has the same access to resources, the State appears to be obsolete. The thinker from Puerto Rico disapproves of State regulation, and institutional regulations in general, because she notices the manner in which they exploit those they regard as inferior or unworthy.

The way in which the working class and women are relegated to live in ignorance about who they are as potential agents of change is what prompts Capetillo to also demand accountability from the religious institution. In a letter to her daughter, Manuela Ledesma Capetillo, she recommends that her daughter be a real presence for those who are in need instead of just praying for them. In Luisa Capetillo's own words:

> En vez de ir a oír misa, visita los pobres y socórrelos, que podrás hacerlo: en vez de confesarte y comulgar, visita los presos, llévales consuelos, algo que los instruya. No olvides que los [que] abundan en las cárceles y presidios son los pobres y los ignorantes, las víctimas de siempre, de todas las explotaciones.[10] (Ramos 96)

It is the contrast between what is established in theory as the goal of politics and in this case the Christian (Catholic) religion, and the reality and practice of social hierarchies characterized by inequality which incites Capetillo's discontent with the State and the Church. Capetillo was able to separate the compassionate (and Christian) tenets she valued and saw fit for an emancipated humanity from the injustices she observed in the religious institution. This is why she calls for tending to those in jail who are just as worthy of compassion as anybody else. In her view, they may have broken a law that very well could have been unfair to those with fewer or zero resources.

As Capetillo saw the correlation between exploitation and the presence of poor people in jail, her desire for economic and social justice became much more urgent. In the cited fragment of the letter, she was advocating for egalitarianism. However, given the patriarchal bias of the society in question, Capetillo also faced obstacles in reaching her daughter when the latter was at the Colegio de la Inmaculada Concepción in Manatí. As Félix Matos Rodríguez points out after quoting Valle Ferrer in regards to the issue of the nuns at the school censoring the correspondence between Capetillo and Manuela,[11] "the nuns considered Capetillo's influence over her daughter undesirable and dangerous" (xxvi).

This general contextualization of the social climate of Capetillo's time and her discontentment with it allow us to approach the analysis of the play proper by truly asking the very question in the title: *Cómo se prostituyen las pobres*, and also *why*? If for the sake of the nation—and in the specific case of this play it is Puerto Rico, but may be applied elsewhere—people are condoning unfair social practices, then the "how" and the "why" indeed go hand in hand. These social practices include workers' exploitation and gender disparity. It is no wonder that in her famous feminist manifesto *Mi opinión sobre las libertades, derechos y deberes de la mujer* (1911) Capetillo criticizes those who oppose equality for the sake of the nation, regarding them as "frauds" (Sánchez González 31). All of this happening at a time when Puerto Rico had gone through the consequences of 1898, passing from Spanish to U.S. rule. A detailed review of those social and political consequences exceeds the scope of this analysis. However, what is important to consider is that aside from those consequences, the patriarchal paradigm was already established in Puerto Rico by 1898, and the mentality of domination and subordination followed the transformations in the economy and the workforce. In this sense, the gender disparity was still at the forefront of the struggles an activist like Capetillo strove to overcome.

The cited excerpts I have included of Capetillo's other writings illustrate the prevailing social paradigm and how it prevented women from fully achieving emancipation from limitations imposed on them in terms of gender. At a time when women were still not allowed to vote, and thus were not been equally regarded in the political realm, it is clear that they were dependent on a system that saw them as inferior. If they were dependent, they were subordinated. Some had the option of being part of the religious institution. Nonetheless, given the example of the nuns at the Colegio de la Inmaculada Concepción and how they handled Capetillo's correspondence with her daughter, it is evident that they were enacting their own role of subordination to patriarchal rule in the unfairness of censorship. Considering this problematic situation for women in society, the response to the queries of *why* and *how* poor women prostitute themselves, is answered and enacted by the protagonist of the play.

## Words Enacted

*Cómo se prostituyen las pobres* is a two-page play in which none of the characters has a proper name. It begins with a woman entering the scene "followed by a well-dressed man who gives her money" (Kanellos 433). This man subsequently leaves the scene although it is not noted in the text. Even before the characters begin their dialogue, with just this piece of information the overall social context depicted in the play is established. The protagonist is a prostitute. The man who just paid her has financial solvency and belongs to the affluent class. Why she is a prostitute is actually the basis of the dialogue that soon follows.

The dialogue quickly begins with "el joven" ("young man") asking "una mujer" ("a woman") if she is happy with her life. In her response, and as it appears in the original version in Spanish, she becomes "la mujer" ("the woman") directly answering "no," and adding that she actually has no other options (Ramos 214; Kanellos 433). As they interact, "el joven" exhorts her to consider working at a factory. Albeit his good intentions, the simplification he shows in regards to the woman's situation demonstrates his poor understanding of how patriarchal and exploitative dynamics operate in his own social realm. Through the woman's response, he learns about the humiliation that workers continually face in the factories due to low wages and sub-standard working conditions. That is, by entering the space of this woman to approach her about her trade, his understanding of how society works is challenged.

He also shows his concern for the illnesses and troubles ailing a woman like her. He tries to convince her that "Mother Nature doesn't make those choices. For her, the virgin is the same as the prostitute. She is the equalizer the lever par excellence" (433). This is his rather naive response to a very insightful query by "la mujer" in which she asks which woman deserves more respect even after death: a virgin or a prostitute. She does not want to be lectured on the topic of "respect," because she has come to understand how "we women will always be sacrificed in the infinite holocaust to a hypocritical social lie." Moreover, she condemns the role of the religious institution, the "Christian morality" in her own words, in maintaining the status quo. This is one of the instances in which we see the protagonist enacting Capetillo's social critique and presenting herself as an individual aware of the social and economic difficulties women face. Indeed, she demonstrates a better grasp of how her society functions than does the young man.

Another significant aspect of the observations "la mujer" brings to the fore is that the ideas postulated by "el joven," who is a young man of public presence and social conscience, are countered with the reality of this particular woman. While his assertions about how Mother Nature is nonjudgmental may be true or comforting, the woman presents him with other socio-economic layers that he may have been unaware of or may have just plainly overlooked. Part of him appears interested with the betterment of the condition of women; an interest that nonetheless comes off rather simplistic when he says that "[a]ll women have the right to be happy, to be respected" (433). Moreover, his approach becomes more paternalistic when, challenging the woman's decrying of "useless words" such as "respect," he calls her "selfishness incarnate in an ignorant lady" (433). If we read him as a potential Puerto Rican "patriot," we can detect an implicit commentary on how the island's elite was out of touch with the harsh realities of the lives of women and workers. Ironically, he is the one who is being "educated" as to how and why she is a prostitute and the socio-structural difficulties that keep women subordinated.

After their frank exchange, the young man leaves, not without apologizing to the woman for his questions. By doing this, he is conveying the fact that his dialogue with her has presented him with difficulties and experiences that had been so far rather foreign to him. He says he may return some day, leaving open the possibility of continuing the dialogue. On her part, she continues her own reflections about women, their role(s) and their place in society. For the character of the woman, working at a factory, getting married, and working as a prostitute are all the same because they are all based on an economy of gender disparity and exploitation. Voicing her own mental dialogue:

> if everything is for sale, why worry so much because we charge a fee? If she who joins herself with man—through civil marriage or through some religion—also sells herself, doesn't the husband have to cover all the costs? Very few of them go to the factories, but isn't that a kind of sale? (434)

What "la mujer" is articulating is how women lack real access to routes to emancipate themselves. Her examples amply describe their predicament. The factory worker endures degrading treatment. The wife yields to the acquisitive power of her husband. This yielding to the role of the man as the provider is rooted in the political and religious culture where men have the active role in being the "breadwinners" of the household. It is significant that the woman does not include life in a convent as one of her options. A reason could be that as a prostitute she would not fit the ideal for a nun. It could also be that, as Capetillo experienced herself with the censorship and even destruction of her letters to her daughter, being part of the religious institution was still another context prone to unfair practices. This is one of the reasons Capetillo is so critical of both the role of the State and of the Church in issues of gender disparity.

Capetillo's unapologetic critique of institutions coincides with Carmen Centeno Añeses remarks about the Arecibo-born writer's sharp style when conveying her ideas. As the aforementioned critic describes, "[c]on su lengua víbora, metáfora ésta que representa la ruptura del silencio, invade los sacros recintos de la palabra masculina" (199). It is in the same spirit of the "serpent tongue" (lengua víbora)—a tongue that will not yield to the subordination of women to the ideal of their passivity and acquiescence—that *la mujer* (the woman) in *Cómo se prostituyen las pobres* enacts Capetillo's biting denouncement of women's exploitation. "La mujer" understands how the inherent plurality of the experiences of individual women is silenced and forced into a paradigm of subordination.

Just as the woman reflects upon how women, via the factory, marriage, or prostitution, end up giving in to economic exploitation, the character of "el hombre" (the man) enters the scene. As her client, he treats her violently, both physically and verbally, calling her and all women like her "thieves—not even paying you makes you listen. Let's go or I'll whip you" (434). Her conclusion to all this violence and contempt is that suicide would be the antidote to her situation, a "solution" that is very revealing of the oppressive environment that encircled her as a woman. Beyond the literal sense, suicide may stand for the forceful removal of the self due to crushing and stagnant conditions. The unavailability of real options for a woman as an individual is what paves the way for that metaphorical suicide. In any case, what "la mujer" refers to is to the absence of opportunities for being an individual woman emancipated from gender disparity.

The fact that none of the characters in this play has a name stresses the idea that anyone in society can either maintain the status quo or become an agent of subversion who can expose and challenge oppressive norms. There are two speaking male characters, "el joven" and "el hombre" plus the one that is barely in the scene when leaving the stage at the beginning of the play. Meanwhile, there is only one woman. She is the protagonist and a very sharp social commentator, just like Capetillo. Anonymity in this play becomes possibility of liberation and equality, if so the individual chooses.

The absence of names erases differences. In this case, they are referred to only by their gender. The two speaking male characters are different in how they treat the woman. The young man is courteous, yet he cannot hide his unawareness of the socio-structural disparities that ail all women, be it as workers, wives, or prostitutes. On his part, the other male character arrives drunk to his encounter with the woman. His level of unawareness is at such a point that he expresses the utmost contempt for her, not just because of her trade, but because she is a woman. Thus, the contrast between the two men is that the older one has embraced the social prescription for gender roles to the extreme, which undoubtedly puts into question his individuality as a man. The younger one appears to have learned something from his dialogue with the woman, and may be able to reflect upon it and perhaps revise his simplistic and paternalistic approach to women. It is through the dialogue that "el joven" is challenged to delve deeper into the dynamics that create and maintain exploitation. In contrast to the two of them, the woman appears as the only female character, and a very knowledgeable and individualized one at that, all obstacles notwithstanding.

Still, there is another unnamed character that is represented in the plural and that forms an integral part of the title of the play. "Las pobres" (poor women) is that collective character. It represents a variety of individuals, once again defined by their gender and the historical circumstances that have relegated them to a state of inferiority. Thus, the title gives a certain amount of contextualization as well as a preview on how the character of "las pobres" is a depiction of the mentality that subordinates women to a mere classification that circumvents their agency as individuals. Capetillo subverts that mentality by presenting how women did not have real options at their disposition for their advancement in society. If we follow the character of "la mujer" in her demand on how women—workers, wives and prostitutes—are all to a degree subordinated to the patriarchal paradigm, then no matter the social class and the resources they may have available, they are all *pobres* as long as they yield the power of their individuality, that is power of their selves, to that which limits them as human beings.

How is it then that poor women prostitute themselves? The protagonist's assessment of the generalized subordination for women directly answers that question. According to her, women prostitute themselves whenever they enter an unequal relationship that subordinates them, financially, politically, and personally. In her recognition that she has no other choice besides being a prostitute, she is underscoring not just her particular situation, but also the overall problem of the role(s) of women in her society. As an arena where nationhood and its values are played out, this society certainly demonstrates not only the subjugation of women, but also how the structuring of such nationhood actually depends on keeping women, workers, and the marginalized in a constant state of subordination. That is, it shows the inherent inequality of its dynamics. This is the complete opposite of the vision of the egalitarian Puerto Rico and transnational society that Capetillo so ardently advocated for in her writings and throughout her labor union activism.

To conclude, in agreement with Capetillo's commitment to the cause of women's emancipation, it is "la mujer" in this play who finds herself by understanding her predicament as a woman and by questioning the social factors that enable such predicament. Aware of the social norm that fuels gender disparity, the character of the woman knows how and why (poor) women prostitute themselves. By knowing and expressing this, she is destabilizing the paradigm of the paternalistic and patriarchal nation. Assertively, Capetillo allows the reader/spectator to hear it directly from a woman, thus validating the protagonist's active contribution to the quest for social justice and egalitarianism.

## Notes

[1] In the play "Influencia de las ideas modernas," Angelina, the protagonist, may be read as an alter-ego of the author/playwright.

[2] In her book *Boricua Literature*, Lisa Sánchez González regards Capetillo "as one of the earliest and most pivotal Boricua literary figures" (21–22). This usage of the term "Boricua" refers to Puerto Ricans who had a permanent or

temporal exile in the United States or had a migratory relationship between the two nations. The assessment by Sánchez González underscores how Capetillo is an important and versatile figure in Puerto Rican, American, and U.S. Latino/Hispanic, and Boricua literature.

[3] Referring to the impact of the 1898 change of sovereignty in Puerto Rico and the effects of U.S. dominion and educational plans for the island, Marcia Rivera Quintero describes how "the family was one of the institutions that used the educational process to reaffirm the development of a generation of docile, pro-American, citizens. The traditional patriarchal family of the XIX Century kept its social hegemony and the new textbooks depicted the ideal family in this way: the woman subordinated to the man, with no other work besides domestic chores, like the women in landowning families (hacendados)" (58–59, translation mine). All translations are mine except where noted.

[4] *Literatura y paternalismo en Puerto Rico,* Juan Gelpí addresses the paternalistic aspect of Puerto Rican traditional culture, especially in terms of the island's literary canon. In regards to both Capetillo's context and her legacy in Puerto Rican letters, the fact that such a versatile literary figure is virtually absent from the island's literary canon is indeed telling of this traditional paternalistic approach that Gelpí discusses.

[5] Aside from the most studied *Mi opinión sobre las libertades, derechos y deberes de la* mujer (1911) and *Influencia de las ideas modernas* (1916), in her lesser-known works: *Ensayos libertarios* (1907) and *La humanidad del futuro* (1910) Capetillo maintains her egalitarian goals in the quest for social justice.

[6] In the article "Rompiendo el molde . . . " I discuss the problematic use of "sex," "gender," and "masculine/feminine," especially used interchangeably. If applied as such it denotes a learning process in which gender roles continue to be internalized (165–166).

[7] In *Historia de una mujer proscrita*, Norma Valle Ferrer describes how Capetillo was judged and proscribed due to the notion that women were expected to be subordinated to male authority (100).

[8] "Las mujeres de las clases desposeídas se reclutaban para desempeñar trabajos que servían para reforzar la economía social de una clase sobre otra, y que mantenían a las mujeres en una posición subordinada, sujetas a una constante explotación económica, social y sexual" (49, original text in Spanish).

[9] Félix Matos Rodríguez also highlights this goal while following Yamila Azize Varga's discussion about emancipation and how it "would only come with an overhaul for the social, economic, and cultural structures advocated by the labor movement (88, 166)" (Matos Rodríguez, xxix) (referring to Azize Vargas's *La mujer en la lucha*).

[10] From the Julio Ramos edition, *Amor y anarquía*. All quotes in Spanish from the play *Cómo se prostituyen las pobres* are from this edition. All quotes from the play in English are from the translation in the anthology *Herencia*, edited by Nicolás Kanellos.

[11] From Valle Ferrer's *Historia de una mujer proscrita*, 57.

## Works Cited


Azize Vargas, Yamila. *La mujer en la lucha*. Río Piedras: Editorial Cultural, 1985.

Bird-Soto, Nancy. "Rompiendo el molde o arráncandose el corset: La propuesta educativa de Luisa Capetillo." *Identidades*. 5 (2007): 161–175.

Butler, Judith. *Bodies that Matter: On the Discursive Limits of "Sex."* New York: Routledge, 1993.

Centeno Añeses, Carmen. *Modernidad y resistencia: Literatura obrera en Puerto Rico (1898–1910)*. San Juan: Callejón, 2005.

Gelpí, Juan G. *Literatura y paternalismo en Puerto Rico*. Río Piedras: UPR, 1994.

Kanellos, Nicolás. Ed. *Herencia. The Anthology of Hispanic Literature in the United Status*. New York: Oxford, 2002.

Matos Rodríguez, Félix V. *A Nation of Women: An Early Feminst Speaks Out. Mi opinión sobre las libertades, derechos y deberes de la mujer* (Luisa Capetillo). Houston: Arte Público P, 2004.

Ramos, Julio. *Amor y anarquía: Los escritos de Luisa Capetillo*. Río Piedras: Huracán, 1992.

Rivera Quintero, Marcia. "Incorporación de las mujeres al mercado de trabajo en el desarrollo del capitalismo." *La mujer en la sociedad puertorriqueña*. Ed. Edna Acosta-Belén. Río Piedras: Huracán, 1980. 41–65.

Sánchez González, Lisa. *Boricua Literatura. A Literary History of the Puerto Rican Diaspora*. New York & London: NYUP, 2001.

Valle Ferrer, Norma. *Luisa Capetillo: Historia de una mujer proscrita*. Cultural, 1990.

______. *Luisa Capetillo, Pioneer Puerto Rican Feminist*. New York: Peter Lang, 2006.

Walker, Lara A. *Luisa Capetillo: Beyond Border Feminism and Class Struggle*. 13 pp. 2002. <http://coh.arizona.edu/spanish/symposium/AnnualProceedings/2002actas/cntents>.

# *El héroe agachado* or the Hero that Wasn't: Virile Language and Women's Quest for Political Participation

PILAR MELERO
University of Wisconsin-Whitewater

> Ahora que muchos hombres flaquean y por cobardía se retiran de la lucha . . . aparece la mujer, animosa y valiente, dispuesta a luchar por nuestros principios, que la debilidad de muchos hombres ha permitido que se les pisotee y se les escupa . . .
>
> *Regeneración*, May 15, 1901

> [A]nte la República acusamos al cobarde que atropella y a los cobardes que se inclinan para que el atropello pase, aún cuando al hacerlo sea por sobre ellos mismos . . .
>
> *Vésper*, May 15, 1903

Men who hesitate. Cowards. Emasculated men. Men who bend over and allow abuse. Men who fail to stand up to their abusers. These and other images of and about gender that appear to reproduce traditional cultural patterns of masculinity, such as those highlighted in the passages cited, overcome the reader of the Magonista press.[1] Curiously, the images of failed masculinity appear almost uniformly opposed by images of women forced to step up to defend their rights and those of their children, symbolically left in orphanages by the inactivity of their fathers. In this paper, I examine gender images in an article in *Regeneración*, by the Flores Magón brothers, and in articles by *activistas* Juana Belén Gutiérrez de Mendoza and Andrea Villarreal González. I propose that the Magonista press used traditional models of masculinity and femininity—particularly the image of *el hombre agachado*, a term anthropologist Roger Bartra uses to refer to the antihero made popular in early twentieth-century philosophical representations of Mexican masculinity—to coax men into action against the Díaz government. In addition, I argue that the female activists' use of the *héroe agachado figure*, or the crouching hero, has a double intention. It seeks to cajole men to engage in the Mexican Revolution as well as to rearticulate femininity away from the confines of passivity, thus creating a niche for female participation in the politics of the early 1900s.

## Action and Masculinity

In *La jaula de la melancolía, identidad y metamorfosis del mexicano*, Bartra identifies a number of stereotypes and myths codified by the Mexican intellectual elite during the first half of the twentieth century. He argues that these stereotypes portray the Mexican male as a lonely, melancholy subject overcome by a profound sense of inferiority. One of these myths, created in the 1930s by a group of intellectuals known as Los Contemporáneos (Samuel Ramos, Emilio Uranga, and Jorge Carrión, among others), has been propagated further by figures of enormous cultural relevance, such as Diego Rivera, and, more recently, Octavio Paz in *El laberinto de la soledad* (1959). Bartra proposes that the myth of the hero who fails to be one is the figure that "Rivera consagró en el hombre acurrucado en su sarape y bajo un enorme sombrero" (96).

Bartra warns that archetypes such as those highlighted about the character of "lo mexicano" rather than being reflection of popular Mexican consciousness, are "una proyección cultural de la imagen que se ha formado la intelectualidad—o al menos una parte de ellos—del pueblo (92). He dubs one of these archetypes, the archetype of the Mexican male dominated by his own feelings of inferiority, *el héroe agachado* and argues that Mexican culture of the first half of the twentieth century "ha creado un formidable mito: los mexicanos llevan dentro, como un homúnculo, al indio, al bárbaro, al salvaje, al niño" (93). Bartra also warns that this *homúnculo* (from the Latin "homunculus" or "small man"), is an *homúnculo roto*, or what Carrión would define in the following image: "Tronchada la infancia, antes de cumplirse su derrotero, aparece el mexicano como un niño proletario y sin juegos, juguetes ni sonrisas, inmerso en la vida adulta de trabajos y objetivos inadecuados a su ritmo de crecimiento."[2]

Bartra faults the Contemporáneos and the generation that followed them (among them Paz) for the creation of the myth of the stooping hero. The Contemporáneos wrote most of their texts between 1920 and 1932, well after the *Magonista* articles I am discussing (written between 1900 and 1920) were published. The archetype of the *héroe agachado,* however, is still pertinent in our examination of the Magonista notions of masculinity since the Contemporáneos base their philosophical reflections on Mexican masculinity on their perception of Mexican culture in the decades that precede their writing; that is, the decades they have lived.[3] Therefore, even though no name has been given to the myth of the fallen hero before 1920, at least not by the members of the intellectual elite, the myth of *el héroe agachado* is already present in Mexican culture. Indeed, the Flores Magón brothers, and the *activistas*, attempt to coax men into joining their call for a Mexican Revolution by appealing to their sense of pride and to what they hope will be their fear of not being identified as *héroes agachados*.

According to writer Manuel Matus Manzo, Oaxacan women successfully evoked the image of the *héroe agachado* to coax men into action during the French intervention in Mexico in the 1860s. Since Oaxaca is the home state of the Magón brothers, it is likely that they are themselves following a precedent established during the French intervention when they appeal to the image of *héroe agachado* as a call to arms, as they do in a *Regeneración* article, published on May 15, 1901, where they welcome *Vésper* (Gutiérrez de Mendoza's newspaper) to the progressive movement. The article reads:

> Ahora que muchos *hombres flaquean y por cobardía se retiran de la lucha*, por considerarse *sin fuerzas* para el combate encaminado a la reivindicación de nuestras libertades; ahora que muchos *hombres sin vigor* retroceden espantados ante el fantasma de la tiranía, y *llenos de terror* abandonan la bandera liberal para evitarse las fatigas de una lucha noble y levantada, aparece la mujer, animosa y valiente, dispuesta a luchar por nuestros principios, que *la debilidad de muchos hombres* ha permitido que se les pisotee y se les escupa. (Lau and Ramos 176, my emphasis)

An article published in *Vésper* two years later, on May 15, 1903, signed by Juana Belén Gutiérrez de Mendoza and Eliza Acuña y Rossetti, echoes strikingly similar sentiments. In the article, the *activistas* accuse men of being cowards for not standing up for their rights and for "bending over" so that the government can "violate" their rights as citizens. In the article, the Díaz regime appears in the role of the violator, and the common Mexican man appears as a willing participant in the violation. The article reads: "ante la República acusamos al *tirano que atropella* y a *los cobardes que se inclinan* para que el atropello pase aún cuando al hacerlo sea por sobre ellos mismos" (Lau and Ramos 177, my emphasis). The image of *el héroe agachado* is clearly visible in the image of the *cobardes que se inclinan.* In fact, it is this image—of the hero that is not one—the image that Gutiérrez de Mendoza evokes when she tries to provoke Mexican men into action against the Díaz regime:

> Cuando los ciudadanos que han depositado su confianza en los periodistas honrados *permiten el atropello, lo toleran y lo dejan pasar*, *¿No se comete un acto indigno, de incalificable bajeza y cobardía*? ¿No se complican en el crimen y se confunden con el criminal mismo? Por eso ante la República acusamos al tirano que atropella y a *los cobardes que se inclinan* para que el atropello pase aún cuando al hacerlo sea por sobre ellos mismos. (Lau and Ramos 177-81)

Bartra's assertion that archetypes permeate society in general—rather then merely reflect it—are illustrated by the images populating the discourse of *activistas* such as Gutiérrez de Mendoza. In a manner similar to that of the Flores Magón texts, the model after which Gutiérrez de Mendoza produces her own opposition paper, Gutiérrez de Mendoza's articles reproduce the myth of the potential hero who fails to take action and therefore becomes a coward. Gutiérrez de Mendoza uses the myth of the *héroe agachado* to appeal to men's sense of pride so that they take up arms against the Díaz regime. She does so through her treatment of two concepts traditionally tolerated and even encouraged in femininity, but shunned if associated with masculinity: cowardice and passivity. Gutiérrez de Mendoza accuses "a *los cobardes que se inclinan* para que el atropello pase." Through this accusation, she scorns the potential heroes for their passive (cowardly) posture in the face of the Revolution.

It could be argued that when Gutiérrez uses the masculine to speak of the cowards she is simply using conventional rules of gender in language, which, in Spanish, call for the use of the masculine version of grammatical structures (*ellos, inclinados*) when speaking in general terms. But that is not so. When Gutiérrez uses "*ellos*," "*cobardes*" and "*inclinados*" it is clear that she is referring exclusively to males. In fact, the bravery (honor) of women (and the cowardice of men) is more than insinuated in the same article: "Por eso os acusamos y por eso hemos venido a ocupar vuestro puesto" (128). Gutiérrez de Mendoza is accusing men of not living up to their roles as men. They, Mexican men, the crouching heroes, have failed to fulfill their culturally given position as men, as defenders of themselves and, by extension, of their families, particularly women, described here as "personas perseguidas y amenazadas entre las que nos encontramos *nosotras*" (128, emphasis mine).

Gutiérrez de Mendoza's accusation is designed to *picar la cresta* (ruffle the feathers) of Mexican males. She intends to embarrass men for acting passively—or in a "womanly" manner—so that they take up arms against the Díaz dictatorship.

Gutiérrez de Mendoza repeats her strategy to shame men into action in other newspaper articles. In "¡Ecce hommo!" she uses the word "cobarde" to charge the dictatorship: "Después de todo esto viene la *cobardía* inaudita" (131) and in another article, "Cuando se muera," she denounces the cowardice of the people who simply take the abuse of the dictator: "¡*Cobardes*! Tantas veces hemos visto los rostros desencajados, las miradas furtivas, los labios trémulos, en los que se escapan temblando las palabras: 'Cuando se muera el General Díaz' " (145). As in the first example, by charging men with cowardice, Gutiérrez appears to reinforce established models of masculinity. But she is hoping to appeal to men's sense of honor, to their rightful, culturally assigned virility, to move them to action against the dictatorship.

In the same manner that Gutiérrez appeals to traditional ideas of masculinity to decry cowardice, to the idea of the fallen hero, she also appeals to the traditional concept of passivity to denounce it. As stated before, passivity is a plague in Gutiérrez de Mendoza's articles, especially when men, whose value as human beings resides precisely in their agency, suffer from it. Cowardice makes men passive, or *héroes agachados*. Mexican men, she stresses, are "16 millones de espectadores [que] contemplan impasibles esa lucha descomunal" (129). This comment is important because it highlights the precarious condition of men as nonparticipants (*espectadores*) in the Revolution, the political game that has the potential to liberate them or bind them even more, depending on its outcome. As we saw in the first part of this essay, Gutiérrez de Mendoza reaches to the myth of *el héroe agachado* to shame men into action. The fact that Mexican men are "inclinados," or bending over, allows the regime to trample them; it turns them into spectators. It also consigns them to the position of abject victims of the Revolution when they should be the protagonists.

In a manner similar to the Flores Magón brothers and Gutiérrez de Mendoza, Andrea Villarreal González also reaches for the guilt of *el héroe agachado* to shame men into action. In a letter introducing her newspaper, *La mujer moderna*, to her readers, she also accuses men of failing their traditional role as men, or defenders of home and nation. Whereas the thrust of Villarreal González's editorial is to present her newspaper as an advocate for women's rights, she stresses that women must leave their designated cultural space only because men have failed their role as men. She writes:

> Gritaremos si es preciso para que los hombres recuerden *lo que deben ser, sientan vergüenza* de su infamia actual y despedacen sus yugos. Si es necesario nuestras manos serán rudas para sacudir *los desmayados brazos de los tímidos* . . . Y, ya que muchos hombres *permanecen de rodillas*, nosotras nos levantaremos y haremos que ellos se pongan también de pie. (Lau and Ramos 193, my emphasis)

Clearly Villarreal appeals to traditional images of masculinity to justify the political involvement as women. Women, traditionally quiet, will shout (*gritare-*

*mos*) if necessary to shame men for their condition as *héroes agachados*, to remind men that they must act like men and abandon their passive condition: "para que sientan vergüenza de su infamia actual." The "*infamia actual,*" the passive behavior, is expressed in two ideas in the text: one, that men's arms are limp (*brazos desmayados*) and that they are kneeling heroes, or *héroes agachados*, (*de rodillas*). Women, therefore, will abandon their traditional roles to get men to act as men, to take the lead in the Revolution.

### Politics, Traditional Images, and Gender

We have seen how Gutiérrez de Mendoza and Villarreal González use the word "coward" and the image of *el héroe agachado* to rouse men's pride and coax them into joining the Revolution. However, there are larger implications suggested by the use of the image of the crouching hero as a double-edged sword that go beyond the mere reproduction of traditional images of femininity and masculinity for the purpose of inciting men into the battlefield. Both Villarreal González and Gutiérrez de Mendoza suggest that when men become effeminate and thus inactive *héroes agachados* they engage in a shameful act. However, both writers suggest that when women reverse traditional roles, that is, when they become active and take over the sword in the battlefield (literally or symbolically, through discourse, for example) to defend what men have failed to defend, their behavior—though nontraditional—is not only acceptable but also necessary, as Villarreal González states when she writes that women will scream, if necessary, to awaken men, to remind them about what they ought to be, and so that they feel embarrassed about their infamous behavior—their passivity and tolerance of abuse.

Comments such as those by Villarreal González, and Gutiérrez de Mendoza before her, are important in that they decry passivity both in men *and*—and this "and" is significant—in women, thus redefining femininity to include *activity*. Passivity in early twentieth-century México is a feminine virtue: "Ésta [Mexican woman] sigue siendo, casi siempre, una mujer colonial en las que se exaltan las virtudes pasivas, si es posible que la pasividad sea virtud" (Rivas Mercado 318).

The break with the traditional binary (male as activity and female as passivity) at the heart of gender ideology on which the activists engage by advocating for female political activity is significant because with it the *activistas* disrupt the notion of gender difference that relegates women to a passive role of the non-presence: the non-doing and therefore nonbeing. This non-presence is also what consigns women to the role of shadow of what is traditionally thought of as the legitimatizing subject: that which is male. By doing away with passivity for both genders, Gutiérrez de Mendoza and Villarreal González challenge women's cultural standing as the Other.

But in a culture such as the Mexican culture, where the highest and lowest representations of femininity—the Virgin of Guadalupe and la Malinche—are both defined by their passivity, challenging established articulations of femininity is not a task a woman does, consciously or unconsciously, openly and without difficulty.[4] In an autobiographical article, Gutiérrez de Mendoza describes how as a little girl she tried to read a piece of paper she had found on the ground: "I put all my attention in trying to decipher those enigmatic lines," she comments, but the letters "laughed at me," making the task impossible. She writes: "Y era tarea aquello . . . las letras se burlaban de mí diciéndome lo que querían y a fuerza de recorrer varias veces las que se agrupaban en una palabra, resultaba cada vez una palabra distinta . . . " (Mendieta Alatorre 16). Her frustration gives way to panic as a male voice asks her if she likes to read. She writes:

> Sentí que me hundía y que los troncos también se hundían en un inesperado cataclismo; *yo sabía que leer era un crimen* [my emphasis] y el que hablaba era nada menos que Don Felipe, el propietario de los troncos, de la hojarasca, de la tierra amontonada y por consiguiente, propietario también del papel impreso que yo trataba de descifrar. Creí que iba a fulminarme y fue tal mi espanto que sin ocultar siquiera el cuerpo del delito respondí maquinalmente: —Sí. (*Juana Belén* 16–17)

As the anecdote reveals, Gutiérrez de Mendoza understands reading as "a crime" for someone of her social status and gender. Reading and writing represents a social position inaccessible to her in her condition of a peasant girl. And she has been caught by "none other than Don Felipe, the owner of the tree trunks, of the leaves, of the piled up dirt and, hence, also *the owner of the printed paper that [she] was trying to decipher.*" She panics. She is aware of the cultural position allotted to her according to her class and gender. And, moreover, as a child, she knows not to go against authority. That is why she panics when Don Felipe finds her reading. She is poor, female, and young. Nevertheless, a benevolent patriarch in the tradition of other *letrados*, don Felipe decides to share his cultural privilege with Gutiérrez de Mendoza and convinces her parents to send her to school.

Ironically, and despite this paternalistic introduction to knowledge, writing becomes the weapon Gutiérrez de Mendoza uses against the establishment that Don Felipe represents and is part of, the Díaz government. Beginning in 1901, she launches her own written-word war against Díaz and any other politician she considers corrupt. Anecdotally, when she decides to write against the Díaz regime, her only possession is a herd of goats. She sells them to buy a printing press and initiate a 32-year journalistic career denouncing political abuse.

Thus, it is accurate to say that behind Gutiérrez de Mendoza's verbal flogging of men are Don Felipe's symbolic face and words. Her historical moment and cultural baggage does not allow for an openly postfeminist or even feminist position on her own behalf or on behalf of other women. Therefore, Gutiérrez de Mendoza has no choice but to take Don Felipe's words, like she has taken the education he facilitated, and expanded her definition of femininity with them to include political, civil and human rights activism. Gutiérrez de Mendoza's writing, though direct and daring, cannot help but be populated with "virile" images. These images pretend to appeal precisely to the virility of Mexican men, within or without the power structure, but also have the subversive potential to mobilize men and destabilize the political machine. The virile language and underlined subversive desire for action on Gutiérrez de Mendoza's part at once reproduce and expand traditional articulations of femininity.

Thus, whereas Gutiérrez de Mendoza clearly appeals to conventional gender ideology to shame men into action, she engages in double-voiced discourse when it comes to her articulation of femininity. When she advocates that women abandon their culturally revered position within the home and become politically active, she voices a defiant articulation of femininity at the same time that she encourages women to not abandon their position as mothers. To understand her position, and that of Villarreal González who also advocates for political involvement for women, but from the space of motherhood, one must understand the feminism practiced in countries with Latin roots which embrace sexual difference as an innate human characteristic. Although this type of feminism ascribes to women and men different roles, and indeed reproduces a gender ideology that has historically identified women with nature and men with culture, the theory can be considered feminism in that its adherents subvert traditional paradigms of gender by inverting "las conclusiones valorativas adscritas a los dos sexos" (Alda Blanco 26).

What this inversion of values that Alda Blanco observes means in the particular case of the Mexican writers that concern us is that they accept motherhood as part of this innate gender identity, but value it beyond its traditional worth. Like feminists before them, such as European feminists in the 1700s (Karen Offen 46), the *activistas* declare that a woman's main role may indeed be motherhood, but as mothers of the men who are to liberate the country from the despotic Díaz regime it is indeed their duty as mothers to defend their children, even if that defense comes in the form of political involvement and forces them to abandon traditional roles and spaces.[5]

The significance of the *activistas*' view of motherhood is that it allows them to (re)define the model in terms that do away with the notion of Mexican motherhood as an embodiment of *la Chingada,* or the passive notion of motherhood, proposed by Paz in *El Laberinto de la Soledad* (1959). Paz states that unlike the Spaniard, who is an *hijo de puta,* Mexican men are even worse off when it comes to their honor. "Para el español la deshonra consiste en ser hijo de una mujer que voluntariamente se entrega, una prostituta; para el mexicano, en ser fruto de una violación" (72). This distinction is important, according to Paz, because that means that the Mexican mother is not even a whore who participates voluntarily in the sexual act. She is a passive, violated nonbeing. Paz states that the passivity of *la Chingada* "es abyecta: no ofrece resistencia a la violencia, es un montón inerte de sangre, huesos y polvo . . . Pierde su nombre, no es nadie ya, se confunde con la nada, es la Nada . . . [y] el símbolo . . . es doña Malinche" (77).

Under the light of Paz's portrayal of Mexican motherhood, when Gutiérrez de Mendoza proposes active motherhood, she is in effect (already in the early 1900s, decades before Paz's assertions) advocating against the mythology of passive femininity that would become Paz's characterization of Mexican motherhood. By advocating that mothers become active members of society, that they fight back instead of "bending over" or accepting the given cultural role as *héroes agachados*, thus accepting the violation of their rights and those of their children, she does away with the characteristic that turns Mexican motherhood into a nonbeing, a limp sum of biological parts—a cluster of inert bones, blood, and dust: passivity.

Subsequent readings of the Gutiérrez de Mendoza texts reveal other levels of meaning related to the idea of women as defenders of nation that go beyond the textual expression of conventional conceptions of masculinity and femininity, again in a game of give-and-take between tradition and modernity. First, in a traditional fashion, Gutiérrez de Mendoza formulates the idea of the violated home (*el hogar violado*). Men have failed in their role as the protectors of the home in both their official (government) and personal (head of household) roles. The government has entered the home and violated it. "[N]*o ha respetado ni lo inviolable del hogar.*" Government, explains Gutiérrez de Mendoza, has entered the homes "*ultrajando lo inviolable: Nuestro hogar, lo sagrado, lo intocable, lo que respeta hasta el más salvaje, hasta el animal.*" Government, then, is yanking women out of their homes and incarcerating them, violating through this act the traditionally sacred space that is the home. There is no head of household to prevent this desecration. Men who do not take part in the violation of the home, but who support it by condoning it, are as guilty as those perpetrating the violation on the women/home/nation.

The idea of the violated home allows Gutiérrez de Mendoza a space of entrance into public discourse. If government is violating the home, and the men are allowing it, again, there is a void in the body—at the national and domestic level—that is supposed to protect women and by extension men, whose honor rests on protecting the women in their home. That void must be filled lest the home/country become a desecrated place. Since men, says Gutiérrez, have failed as guardians of their own honor by failing to protect the violation of the home, women must take the lead and defend their own homes. Through this defense, they symbolically defend the nation, thus engaging in a political and cultural role that expands the traditional role of women as political nonentities.

## Speaking though Father's Words?

Like any other text written from the interstice from where marginal subjects are forced to write, Gutiérrez de Mendoza's and Villarreal Gonzalez's texts have several levels of meaning. On a first reading, the image behind their mirror is no doubt that of the patriarch. Like the Flores Magón brothers, Gutiérrez de Mendoza and Villarreal González reproduce a linguistic and cultural paradigm in accordance with their historical moment and cultural upbringing. Men are the rightful defender of humanity and especially the defender of women, who become a metaphor for home and nation—whose fragility is unquestionable and who have been violated by the actions of the dictator and the inaction of the men. The home is a sacred place in the process of desecration by the abuses of the body politic and the inaction of the men who sit idle and watch from afar—unable to act from their culturally fatal position of *héroes agachados*, or emasculated men—instead of preventing the attack. For this reason, because men act in a cowardly manner and hesitate to defend women/home/nation, women must leave their assigned domestic roles and assume a position both *alien* and *complimentary* to their *natural* (biological) role as mothers of humanity: absent the protective father, they must venture beyond the home (alien) to protect their children (complimentary). This action itself suggests a contestatory position for women: protecting their homes *and* by extension—extension of their traditional roles, their physical and symbolic space—the nation as the home makes the nation, and the nation is indeed a home.

The crisis of masculinity exemplified by the figure of *el héroe agachado*, (real or imaginary), has created that void at a critical time in Mexican history when it is crucial that someone guard the home/nation from the abuses of the political elite. Men have abandoned the fight. The existence of a void implies the need for someone to fill the gap, to play the role abandoned by men. This opens a space for women to take action. And they do: by joining the struggle as soldiers, smugglers of weapons, messengers, or in any other capacity that they are needed. Gutiérrez de Mendoza and Villarreal González also see the rupture and join the Revolution in active roles. More significantly, the language denouncing men as weak also signals, for the activists, a discursive gap. This allows them a space, if limited and mediated by their gender and culture, to express their political ideas. They seize the opportunity and found newspapers where they decry the government's abuses *and* the perceived crisis in masculinity that they believe is ruining the country by allowing the dictator to pursue his agenda of repression. They may still have no political power in the form of the female vote or positions in the body politic, but the opportunity to fill the void they had detected opens the possibility of active involvement in the physical struggle and in the discursive debate through newspaper articles. More importantly, the *activistas* take the opportunity for expression, seizing with it the possibility of expanding women's voices beyond that of traditional domesticity.

Thus, Gutiérrez de Mendoza's and Villarreal González's texts, seemingly traditional, are in fact contestatory. They expresses political thought while appearing to accept and even repeat other traditional gender constructs, such as the idea that men are supposed to be the valiant guardians of the home. They use existing mythology of gender, such as the myth of the crouching hero, to cajole men into joining the Revolution. But Gutiérrez de Mendoza's and Villarreal González's appeals to traditional myths of gender, specifically to the myth of *el héroe agachado*, go beyond simply cajoling men into joining the Revolution. The women are deeply concerned with the politics of their country and their relationship to the marginalized masses, women, miners, campesinos, the indigenous population, and any other indigent group, as highlighted in the letter by Gutiérrez de Mendoza addressed to "to all Mexicans" cited previously (Mendieta Alatorre 128).

The aim of the *activistas* couldn't be clearer. They become politically active in their role as mothers. But they are not the passive mother, *la Chingada*, who will bend over and take the violation of her own rights and those of her children. And they will not tolerate that in their children either, male or female. They argue that since those in charge of defending the home/nation are incapable of defending their own rights, the *activistas* and others like them will rise to defend the rights (*la libertad,* in this case) of their children. In this sense, they transgress traditional models of femininity, which frown upon women speaking publicly about public issues. But, unable or unwilling to abandon their cultural home, they do so from prescribed spaces. By speaking through traditional gender discourse, the activists expand the domestic role of motherhood to include the very public space of political discourse and activity.

## Notes

[1] For the purpose of this paper, the Magonista press will be defined as articles published in the Flores Magón newspapers and in newspapers published by their followers.

[2] Cited in Bartra, 93.

[3] Most of Los Contemporáneos were born in the late 1800s and the early 1900s. Samuel Ramos, for example, was born in 1897.

[4] The passivity of the Virgin of Guadalupe reaches back to the original model of the Catholic Virgin, the Virgin Mary, the receptacle where God deposits his verb (action), his son, Jesus, to deliver him to humanity; and in the condemnation of Eve, the woman who dared defy God's will. Octavio Paz fully discusses the passivity of la Malinche in *El laberinto de la soledad* (1959).

[5] *In European Feminisms 1700-1950*, Offen quotes Charles-Irénée Castel, abbé de Saint Pierre, writing in 1730, about the importance of motherhood. The quote reads: "It is so important for a household to have a virtuous and intelligent mother [mere de famille] that I have willingly adopted the proverb 'Women make or break households.'" She also quotes Nicolas Baudeau, writing in 1762, who proposes a plan for national education that fully included female citizens: "We must propose as a fundamental maxim that the Daughters of the nation are destined to become within their class, *Citoyennes*, Wives, and Mothers" (46).

## Works Cited

Bartra, Roger. *La jaula de la melancolía*. (1987) México, D.F.: ESN: CONACULTA, 2002.

Blanco, Alda. *A las mujeres: Ensayos feministas de María Martínez Sierra*. España: Ediciones Instituto de Estudios Riojanos, 2003.

Gutiérrez de Mendoza, Juana Belén. "A los mexicanos." In Lao and Ramos, *Mujeres y Revolución, 1900–1917*.

______. "¡Ecce Homo!" In Lao and Ramos, *Mujeres y Revolución, 1900–1917*.

Lau, Ana and Carmen Ramos. *Mujeres y Revolución, 1900–1917*. México, D.F.: Instituto Nacional De Estudios Históricos de la Revolución Mexicana, 1993.

Mendieta Alatorre, Ángeles. *Juana Belén Gutiérrez de Mendoza (1875–1942). Extraordinaria Precursora de la Revolución Mexicana*. México: Impresores de Morelos, 1983.

______. *La mujer en la Revolución Mexicana*. México, D.F.: Talleres Gráficos de la Nación, 1961.

Offen, Karen. *European Feminisms 1700–1950. A Political History*. Stanford, California: Stanford UP, 2000.

Paz, Octavio. *El laberinto de la soledad*. (1959). México, D.F.: Fondo de Cultura Económica, 1979.

Rivas Mercado, Antonieta. *Obras completas de María Antonieta Rivas Mercado*. 1981. Ed. Luis Mario Schneider. México, D.F.: Secretaría de Educación Pública, 1987.

# Treacherous Women in the *crónicas* of Quezigno Gazavic: A Strategy in Creating Community

**GABRIELA BAEZA VENTURA**
University of Houston

During the period between World War I (1914–1918) and World War II (1939–1945) large waves of economic and political refugees from Mexico migrated to the United States as a consequence of the Mexican Revolution of 1910. Immigration increased even more in the 1920s given that living conditions worsened in Mexico and the United States was perceived as an avenue of prosperity in which employment was readily available in industry, mines, railroad and agriculture. The majority of Mexican citizens who migrated settled in the Southwest where they established barrios and *colonias*, which were ready markets for Spanish-language newspapers and magazines.

The U.S. Great Depression (1929–1941) reduced the employment available for Mexicans in the United States and culminated in episodes of forced repatriation affecting approximately 500,000 people of Mexican descent. As the Depression receded and World War II erupted, a shortage of unskilled labor encouraged renewed Mexican migration to the United States, which was formalized with the Bracero Program in 1942. New Mexican communities joined old Mexican-American towns in preparing immigrants from Mexico for life away from the homeland.

Spanish-language newspapers played a critical role in helping immigrants adjust to their new surroundings. Newspapers informed and supplied immigrants with news about their native land, helping them maintain ties to what was left behind, thus easing the immigrant transition from their native land to the new inhabited space. The phenomenon experienced by immigrants of finding themselves between two cultural spaces (here and there; *aquí y allá*) is the focus of this paper and is one of the central themes in Immigration Literature.

Immigration Literature was primarily written for economic refugees.[1] Its purpose was to ease the accommodation and transition of the newly arrived into the new country, but this did not translate to an acceptance of complete assimilation to U.S. culture.[2] Resistance to acculturation was common among immigrants, and newspapers often encouraged readers to preserve their original culture and they expressed concern about acceptance and adoption of North American values. In this spirit of resistance, Mexican newspapers in the United States advanced the ideology of "México de afuera," a type of imagined community, as we will see in this study, in which Mexico was presented as superior to the place left behind.[3]

Many *cronistas* who migrated to the United States from Mexico came from a journalist tradition and participated in identity politics and national imaginings. Aníbal González in *Journalism and the Development of Spanish American Narrative* pointed out that journalism had always gone hand in hand with the creation of nation:

> From the beginning, journalism was placed in the service of nation-building, although the often unruly, contentious nature of the independence-era periodicals would seem to belie this: Polemics was the order of the day, and, in the multitude of voices, conservatives as well as liberals made themselves heard. (15–16)

In his research of Hispanic-American journalism, González traced the history of the press and posited that in the first half of the nineteenth century, the press consisted of two currents: the economic and the mercantile. The production of newspapers was very limited. Newspapers were created solely for merchants and impresarios. Newspapers of that time were read at home, or at cafés. These newspapers printed news of the arrival or departure of freighters and of their shipment, as well as essays on economics, politics, medicine, antiques and natural history, letters to the editor, a few poems, governmental speeches and brief news on noteworthy events occurring throughout the world. They were printed with great difficulty and had limited circulation. They reflected the ideals and education fostered in the European Enlightment (16).

With the arrival of technological advances like the steam press and commercial innovations such as the "penny newspaper," the mass audience, the prestige and power of journalism rose, allowing it to grow considerably (17). Benedict Anderson, in his acclaimed book *Imagined Communities: Reflections on the Origin and Spread of Nationalism,* indicated that newspapers created an imagined community of the people who read them through provinciality and plurality. He argued that readers in Mexico, Buenos Aires and Bogotá, who knew little of each other, became aware of each other's existence in their respective spaces. It was, in this way, that a double nationalism developed in Latin America, rooted in a local one and another that enveloped all (61–65).

Carlos Monsiváis, in his study of the chronicle *A ustedes les consta,* also supported the idea that the newspaper was a significant tool in the creation of nation because it provided the chronicler the opportunity to unite a diverse community by entertaining and instructing.

> [ . . . ] el periódico, elemento constitutivo de la nación, representa y ordena las convicciones en pugna y es —no necesariamente en este orden— tribuna, escuela, ateneo, partido político, espacio de las bellas letras, foro agitativo, chantaje, novela por entregas. (19)

Monsiváis argued that *cronistas* used the newspaper as a forum for ideas as well.

Nicolás Kanellos' observations on the Hispanic press in the United States in *Hispanic Periodicals in the United States, Origins to 1960: A Brief History and Comprehensive Bibliography*, where he divides the press in the United States into three categories: exile, immigration and native, indicated that literary critics Lubomyr R. y Anna Wymar's definition of the ethnicity can be applied to the immigration press:

> It is by providing the sense of shared identity and common consciousness that the ethnic press serves as the cementing element within the community. The function of the press, as one of the major educational agents within the ethnic community, evolves from that of a primarily immigrant society to that of an established native American ethnic community. While the community still remains in its immigrant stage, the press primarily serves as the major tool of adjustment. By printing American news, describing the American way of life, and interpreting the conditions, customs, laws, and mores of the new society, the immigrant press eases the process of adjustment and consequently hastens the assimilative process. While the immigrant press acts as an agent of assimilation, at the same time it also functions as a force that retards assimilation. This latter role, the slowing of the assimilative process, results from the press's tendency to preserve the ethnic culture and identity by encouraging language retention, stimulating a continued interest in the country of origin, and sustaining involvement in ethnic community affairs within the host country. (18)

This definition was further supported by Robert E. Park in *The Immigrant Press and Its Control*, where he also noted that because the press slowed the process of assimilation through the predominant use of the native language, there was an increase in the need to interpret events from a point view that is particularly racial or nationalistic. This research, then, acknowledged that newspapers promoted and advanced nationalism.

Furthermore, Carlos E. Cortés's analysis of the Mexican-American press in the United States highlighted the importance of the press in reinforcing Mexican pride and nationalism. He suggested that even though newspapers maintained their own agenda, depending on the place of publication, they carried out three significant roles: 1) they preserve and transmit Mexican history and culture, 2) maintain and reinforce Spanish and 3) strengthen Mexican pride, cultural heritage, nationalism. As a result, the newspaper became the medium that allowed Mexican individuals to preserve their culture, history and language in foreign lands.[4]

In this way, it should not surprise us that the newspaper industry was the perfect tool for representatives of the "México de afuera" to promote a nationalistic agenda. Most intellectuals and elitist impresarios who headed newspapers and other cultural institutions in the U.S. Southwest of the early twentieth century reinforced this ideology that fostered the creation of an imagined community. The newspaper served as the medium that allowed them to reach their Mexican compatriots, to share with them the precepts of the ideology: preservation of Mexican culture and history, retention of Spanish and religion as well as strengthening of Mexican pride and nationalism. They believed that if the Mexican community in the United States observed these elements, they, as a whole, could recreate the Mexico that they took with them when they migrated.

Chroniclers were key participants in this enterprise because, as Monsiváis indicated, they guaranteed that "una colectividad pequeña, insegura de sus logros, incierta en su nacionalismo, vea en la crónica un espejo refulgente (ideal) de sus transformaciones y fijaciones" (26). Monsiváis noted that the primary purpose of chroniclers was to "contribuir a la forja de una nación describiéndola y, si se puede, moralizándola" (26). He went further by describing chroniclers as a sort of

> nacionalistas acérrimos porque desean la independencia y la grandeza de una colectividad . . . o porque anhelan el sello de identidad que los ampare, los singularice, los despoje de sujeciones y elimine sus ansiedades y su terror más profundo: ser testigos privilegiados de lo que no tiene ninguna importancia, narrar el proceso formativo de esta sociedad que nadie contempla. De allí, del miedo a la invisibilidad histórica, se desprende el sueño interminable en cuyo centro la Patria Agradecida bendice a quienes crean un país haciendo consciente una colectividad de la índole de sus tradiciones (que se evocan para declararlas obligatorias). (27)

Therefore, as they affirmed their nationality, the chronicles glossed an internal tourism and a "national philosophy." The chronicler undertook the responsibility of instructing all readers, they became "privileged witnesses" of the facts that no one cared about. In their desire to keep a national cohesion, Monsiváis noted that,

> si se quiere resistir a los invasores, eliminar o postergar a los reaccionarios y enseñar moderación y recato a los pudientes, se necesita—además de la burla como escuela de continencia—fortalecer a la Nación infundiéndole y aclarándole sus orgullos locales y regionales, recreando literariamente las formas de vida más ostensiblemente "mexicanas" y subrayando el desdén por la imitación de lo francés y la nostalgia servil de lo hispánico. (27)

The chronicler also needed a liberal ideology, the antagonism of conservative obsessions, and the joy at being an observer in the street so that he or she could produce a mirror in which the people (readers) were reflected. Monsiváis highlighted the mimetic foundation of the work:

> No estás leyendo. Estás frente a un retrato de tu país. Seas o no arquetipo catalogado, eres lector que se mueve entre arquetipos, y por tanto, existes doblemente: verifica (reflexivo) los alcances morales de la conducta ajena y diviértete (frívolo) con los excesos del pintoresquismo, la vulgaridad o la pretensión. Tales nostalgias del pasado y del presente permiten un acuerdo social sobre la "Esencia Mexicana", que empieza siendo un recuento de costumbres y deviene certidumbre metafísica. (30-1)

Regarding the journalist's position, Monsiváis noted that recognized journalists were always greeted, identified and celebrated because they knew how to write and they wrote for its audience, its readers. Readers demanded that they be interested in their lives, in their joy and sadness because without the reader, the writer does not exist. Therefore, journalists became interested in the lives of their readers and at the same time imparted morality to them (30). The chroniclers' primary role then was to legitimize their readers' existence in the place where they lived,

> que el lector se resigne a no vivir en París y columbre con alegría el chovinismo de sus nietos, a ellos (a lo mejor) les parecerá magnífico residir aquí. (30)

Monsiváis correctly indicated that the chronicle created a national identity, when he explained:

> así nos comportamos: ergo, esto somos de modo intransferible. Una tarea casi notorial unció la crónica a una idea fija: recobrar el Paraíso Perdido, el

> México que se disgregó para dar paso al México que se desvaneció para dejar sitio al México que está expirando. La crónica, correa transmisora de vigores antiguos y agonía inminentes. En la sociedad de masas que se inicia deja de importar la celebración de las costumbres [ . . . ] y el tema es lo borrado por o anulado por el tiempo, por el estallido demográfico, por la industrialización. El México que conocíamos ha desaparecido; el México que ignoramos nos rodea. [ . . . ] cronicar es insistir en la nobleza de nuestro pasado, recurso nacionalista que se opone a la norteamericanización del país, o disposición tradicionalista que repudia el caos y la subversión. (58)

Evidently this is repeated in the United States, where chronicles written by Mexican authors were used to articulate nationalist attitudes. Through them, the nationalist sentiment was fomented and the Mexican nation was recreated in the United States.

Kanellos, who supported Monsiváis' observations, added that the chronicle acquired an incomparable value in the United States because from a masked perspective, the moralizer had the freedom to sarcastically comment in first person on the customs and behaviors of a colony that was threatened by Anglo-Saxon culture.

In this manner, the immigrant press became a space in which chroniclers presented their moralizing doctrine in an effort to unite the Hispanic community under the ideology of the "México de afuera," creating a nation, an imaginary community. Readers not only learned about their native lands when they read the newspapers, they also received a dose of moral and cultural dogma and were encouraged to maintain their national identity to demonstrate that they were not acculturating. In order to achieve these objectives, the reader received countless pages in journals and magazines where they were told how to act and behave in the new country. Sometimes this information was introduced or presented through assigned columns such as "El buzón femenino" (Feminine mailbox)[5] of *El Cronista del Valle* (Brownsville, Texas) or through subtle editorials, jokes, anecdotes and chronicles.

Almost all literary genres were employed to propagate the ideology of the "México de afuera," but the *crónica*, a satirical commentary that was published weekly or daily on newspapers, depending on their run, was a preferred medium for many authors.

Hence, any person who did not share the ideology of the "México de afuera" was criticized. Women were often the target of the fiercest censure. They acquired a special focus as transmitters of values and cultural practices. Their image, in the literature of immigration, was pigeonholed into two stereotypes: ideal (*el ángel del hogar*) or treacherous (*pelonas, evas,* flappers).

Women's efforts to survive individually outside of their native homeland were devalued; they were also criticized for not maintaining traditions inherent to the Mexican race and for wanting to occupy positions generally designated to males or Anglo-American women. Thus, all women who did not conform to the "México de afuera" ideology short-circuited the nationalistic project of creating a community and the *cronista* had the civic responsibility of whipping the community into conformity through their writing.

Mary Louise Pratt, in her research on the poetry by Gertrudis Gómez de Avellaneda, who criticizes José María Heredia for his andocentric behavior, indicates that women are denied their citizenship because it is believed they are incapable of

> de mantener una conducta constante basada en principios generales —fue uno de los factores que invocaban para excluir a las mujeres de la ciudadanía. A través de los siglos, el monopolio político masculino se legitimaba atribuyendo a las mujeres un conjunto de defectos naturales que las incapacitaban para la ciudadanía— la incapacidad para el pensamiento abstracto, el emocionalismo, el particularismo, el infantilismo, etc. (263).

Pratt adds that women are also excluded from the community when they are not given historical agency, and she points out that she is assigned to spaces that exist "fuera de la ciudadanía y, más importante, fuera de la historia: allí nada cambia; todo es regido por la ley natural." (264) Therefore

> los papeles sociales legitimados para las mujeres se van limitando, en la ideología y en la práctica, a la reproducción social, centrada en la esfera doméstica y la maternidad. El trabajo de la mujer será reproductivo, en el sentido amplio de la palabra; económicamente ella será dependiente, o muy pobre; su valor social contingente: dependerá de su capacidad reproductora ejercida dentro de la familia patriarcal. (266)

This, too, can be seen in chroniclers who supported the ideology of the "México de afuera" when they assigned specific behaviors to women. Mexican women living in the United States were depicted as vulnerable to acculturation and therefore criticized so that they might reconsider and not abandon the Mexican community. The chronicler shared this threat with the immigrant audience who found itself in the ever-changing environment that allowed women to have more control over their lives and to obtain rights and privileges that would allow them to perform outside of their "traditional" norm. Countless chronicles and news on the influence of the terrible "flappers," women from the "Roaring Twenties" smoked in public and wore their hair short, and above-the-knee dresses, exemplified this situation.[6] Chroniclers were concerned that Mexican women who came to the United States and immediately adopted these activities and fashions were disrespectful of Mexican values and traditions. "México de afuera" supporters feared that Mexican women would desert their race, and chroniclers reinforced this fear by questioning and manipulating images of Mexican women that satirized and censured those who did not maintain their traditional roles.[7]

Ignacio G. Vázquez, wrote *crónicas* under the pseudonym of Quezigno Gazavic, and was preoccupied with the acculturation of Mexicans living in the United States, especially women. Although Vázquez's biographical data is very limited, in my research I discovered that his pseudonym is created with the letters in his "baptismal name," according to an article published in *El Heraldo Mexicano,* in San Antonio, Texas, on May 5, 1928. This same article reveals that Gazavic also wrote under the following pen names: Xavier de León and Lic. Sin Título. The first was used when he criticized religion aspects and the latter in his column dedicated to political criticism, aptly titled, "Tiros al blanco" (Target Shooting).

Gazavic published a weekly column titled "Tanasio y Ramona: Narración continuada y en verso de las pintorescas aventuras de dos sujetos 'de allá de casa'" in *El Heraldo Mexicano,* in San Antonio, Texas, in 1928. In this rhymed *crónica*, Quezigno delved into the despicable repercussions of a woman's betrayal of her husband who is left to suffer while she enjoys a new life in the United States with a new husband who cares not if she is unfaithful to him. This *crónica* followed a novelesque format in which the plot developed in weekly chapters and depicted characters just as they would appear or exist in their respective provincial communities.

Gazavic's *crónicas* representative of the "México de afuera" ideology, advocated and reinforced the preservation of Mexican traditions and culture; and encouraged Catholicism as the religion of choice for Mexicans. All these elements set the foundation for an imagined community in the United States. This ideology, shared by other *cronistas,* was the fundamental reason for which Gazavic appeared to quickly point out the repercussions of Americanization through the characters of Ramona and Tanasio.

The narration of this *crónica* is executed through Gazavic's three-fold observations as an insider, friend and *compadre* to Tanasio; a newspaper reporter who travels through South Texas in search of stories of Mexican immigrants in the United States to share with his readers; and through an epistolary component. What stands out is that readers only hear and know of Ramona through secondhand sources: letters that she writes to Tanasio and physical descriptions given by her husband and Gazavic.

In the following examples, you will see that Ramona embodies that which chroniclers repudiate in Mexican women, and Gazavic will focus on the behavior of women who like Ramona, are responsible for the suffering of their faithful and loving husbands. Ramona is primarily depicted as a sellout, a *renegada*, a *pocha*, a Mexican woman enamored with American ways that prefers material objects over her faithful husband. Gazavic presents readers with a mirror of what their lives are like in the United States. He portrays Ramona as a selfish person, who by nature only desires and never thinks of others. Repercussions of this representation is a warning to readers to be aware of the females who surround them who could give in to U.S. ways and fall into the trap that leads to Americanization. Gazavic's *crónicas* seem to posit one solution, to control women and isolate them from American influences because dangers lurk across the border, dangers that can overpower gullible Mexican citizens and put an end to the Mexican race in the United States if *mexicanas* leave their Mexican husbands for U.S. men.

As a "México de afuera" purveyor, Gazavic expressed his solidarity to Tanasio, who embodied Mexican males. They are left to suffer not only because they have been abandoned but also because their Mexican women have embraced a new identity: the American woman. For this reason, Tanasio is characterized as pure, innocent, honest, good and truly Mexican. The following quote reveals some of Gazavic's descriptions of both characters:

> Lo cierto es q' el buen Tanasio
> del mundo sólo conoce
> treinta leguas, y de pueblos,
> pares, sin llegar a doce.
> Casó con Ramona Paz,
> una "floja" de su tierra,
> malcriadota y rezongona
> que siempre le dio la guerra
> a pesar de su apellido,
> quien al fin se le "juyó"
> con un patán cuyo nombre
> Tanasio no conoció.
> Desconsolado Tanasio
> por la suerte "recochina"
> que tocó, según él,
> "con la perjuria y indina
> costilla" tomó desquite
> con el mescal y la parranda.

This description also reveals that from the onset, Ramona did not conform to her condition as woman and was always difficult to control. Ramona is described as a lazy, spoiled woman who gripes and was always a lot of trouble for her husband, who she leaves for an Anglo man. All adjectives used to describe her juxtapose all the negative qualities that she holds over those of the respected Mexican woman who is active, respectful, quiet and, above all, faithful. Therefore, in the tradition of the *crónica* as described by Monsiváis, Gazavic holds up a mirror for women who might emulate Ramona and for readers who should heed the warning and immediately restrain *mexicanas* from falling into American ways.

Later in the *crónica* we learn that Ramona is accused of leaving Tanasio for a blue-eyed, blond-haired gringo. Her treason forces her husband, a person who hardly knows anything that pertains to worldly matters, to leave his harmonious, edenic home in Mexico. Gazavic informs us that Tanasio has never attempted to wander outside his small town, by highlighting throughout several chronicles that he is a "poor, innocent man" who believes that Ramona was taken from him by force and the she will soon return to him, "Se jue porque la llevaron / y que no es remoto el día / golverá más que de prisa."

This strategy allows Gazavic to alert the reader of Tanasio's innocence by focusing on his inability to acknowledge and accept the fact that his wife has left him. On the one hand, this element in the *crónica* reasserts that women such as Ramona are easy preys of the tempting tentacles of U.S. life and are easily seduced. On the other, it highlights Ramona's lack of respect for her Mexican traditions and customs, after all, she leaves Tanasio, whom she is to love till death do them part.

In the *crónica* featured on the January 29, 1928, issue of *El Heraldo Mexicano*, Gazavic narrates how he and Tanasio become acquainted. Gazavic explains that as he walks into a pharmacy, he suddenly runs into an angry man who wants to buy *aguardiente*. The *cronista* immediately becomes interested in the man whom he describes as "inteligente y bien dado" although he is dirty and misshapen. The soon-to-be narrator approaches Tanasio and begins to interview him, telling him that he works as a reporter and that he will be discreet with anything that Tanasio tells him. Tanasio, who is quite devastated and only wants to drink to forget about Ramona, agrees to share his sad story with Gazavic, and he, in turn, with us. The story begins with Tanasio's reasoning for Ramona's treason:

porque era una inocentita;
pero el indino arrastrao
con su manera maldita
de adueñarse de lo ajeno,

me la golvió coquetona,
la engañó, y al poco tiempo,
¡pobrecita mi Ramona!
se me juyó sin remedio.

Gazavic indirectly criticizes the United States' imperialist attitudes over the rest of the world, as Ramona can be read as an embodiment of Mexico and the "Indino" (foreigner) the United States. Ramona, being a woman, was easily seduced by el *indino arrastrao* who taught her about being *coqueta,* a clear indication that women in the United States tend to worry more about engaging the male gaze through their coquettish behaviors. The readers, male and female, are then warned that they too can be seduced if they are not aware. The only solution in maintaining one's integrity is by following the precepts of the ideology of "México de afuera" where it is believed that they can remain as Mexican as when one first migrated to the United States.

After this interview, the reporter runs into the pharmacist who tells Gazavic a little more of Ramona's betrayal. The *cronista* is made privy to a letter that Ramona left Tanasio before departing so that he would not miss her. The letter reads:

"Tanasio" dice l'infame;
"Con todo pesar te dejo,
a pesar de mi querencia,
contrito todo y perplejo.
No creyas que voy armada:
La esperanza sólo llevo
De jallarme al otro lao
Algún chicloso mancebo.
Quién sabe si no lo jalle
tan al pelo cual lo quero:
grandotote y colorao
y de cabello muy güero. . ."
"Sí Tanasio, ya no puedo
más tiempo vivir contigo.
Las mujeres ansí semos:
pensamos con el ombligo:
es decir, con el estómago,
y el mío ya se arrugaba
de tanto tiempo que hacía
que ni un frijol le bailaba . . . (29 enero 1928)

The letter reflects Ramona's desire in wanting a better future as she chooses to leave for someone whom she is attracted to as well as provide for her. Within the ideology of "México de afuera," a true *mexicana* in this situation would never abandon her husband or her family. The fact that Ramona leaves to look for a "gringo" or Anglo-Saxon man as a husband, shatters the traditional myths and ideologies that stipulate that women shouid stay by their husband's side. Ramona shatters traditional cultural values, not to mention moral issues, and may be condemned by the newspaper readership that may not approve of her "liberal" behavior.

In another letter we discover that Ramona is living with a man who is not the one she eloped with. This fact allows Gazavic to focus on another negative element in women like Ramona: their inconsistent nature and lack of moral values. We know that Ramona left Tanasio no more than a few months ago and in that little time, she has cohabited with at least two different men. Ramona, perhaps innocently or cynically, does not think twice about confiding this to her ex-husband. She goes to the extreme of sending him a photo in one of the letters so that Tanasio can see how she lives in the United States. Tanasio describes the photograph in the following manner:

> vio en un retrato reciente
> que no sólo está pelona,
> sino que exhibe sus zancas
> "hast'onde llegan las ligas"
> usa choclos, tiene perro,
> y numerosas amigas
> "que l'acompañan al tiatro"
> y hasta un Fotingo muy feo
> modelo mil novecientos
> en el que sale a paseo . . . (22 enero 1928)

Evidently, Ramona has transformed into a full-fledged *pelona*—the Mexican-American version of the well-known "flapper:" the American woman of the "Roaring Twenties" who would cut her hair short and smoke in public. She is now a liberal *americana* who wears a short skirt, drives a car, goes out with female friends to the theater without a chaperone and even owns a dog. Gazavic points out that his good friend Tanasio, after looking at the photo and rereading the letter, began to cry uncontrollably, not understanding why such changes could bring his ex-wife so much pleasure and happiness. Tanasio's reaction, again, exemplifies the frustration experienced by other Mexicans who cannot understand the U.S. lifestyle.

"Ramona tiene un Johnny" (*El Heraldo Mexicano*, February 19, 1928) is the subtitle of the *crónica* in which Tanasio receives another letter from Ramona. In it she tells him that she knows that he is traveling through the United States. Gazavic makes the following comment before proceeding with the letter:

> Interpretamos la carta de Ramona, en asonantes,
> siquiera para evitar monotonías pedantes.
> Además, como es mujer, o se supone lo sea,
> sus cartas deben fingir belleza, a falta de idea.

This quote denotes the extent of Gazavic's criticism, where he now places Ramona's gender in question. He posits that she has lost her "woman" qualities, especially those that tie her to the Mexican community. He stresses that she is not intelligent because she lacks "idea" and will therefore worry more about her "fake beauty," characteristics attributed to acculturation.

When we finally get to the letter, we read that Ramona is worried and saddened by the fact that Tanasio is following in her footsteps because she knows that he probably does not understand "los mitotes y enrejidos destas tierras tan estrañas." Although she does not mention her return to Mexico—a specific characteristic of literature of immigration—she offers to go visit him.

The possible visit allows Gazavic to question Ramona and her new husband's morality. Johnny is the stereotypical Anglo-Saxon man who has fallen in love with a Mexican woman. We are told that he is a weak man who is easily controlled by Ramona. We are aware of this because she explains how she asked Johnny, in front of his cousin "que le emprestara la 'troca,'" to go see Tanasio in Laredo, to which her gringo replied affirmatively. Gazavic immediately points out the lack of self-respect that the gringo had by allowing his wife to place his honor in such a delicate predicament, and above all in front of his own family.

Although Johnny, who is truly "güeno," allows Ramona to visit Tanasio, she decides not to go:

> Qué caray, mi pobrecito Tanasio
> me duele el alma; pero este Johnny
> es un gringo grandotote que lo quero
> porque le gustan . . . de chivo los tamales
> que le merco, y si 'hace desentendido . . . '

Gazavic acutely demonstrates that the only man who women like Ramona can access is one who is weak, one who has neither honor nor self-respect and is all too willing to jeopardize his reputation by allowing his wife to visit her ex-husband. The criticism is further enhanced by Ramona's vernacular expression that references her adulterous attitude and his acceptance of this. Once again, Ramona is portrayed as a shameless woman who has no moral values.

Tanasio comments at the end that he does not understand very well why Ramona goes out with "yones"[8] (Johnnies) or why she speaks in those "jergas agringadas," which reinforces Ramona's acculturation. Her loss of tradition and language easily negates her Mexican identity, something that can occur to those who forget the precepts of the "México de afuera" ideology.

Quezigno Gazavic like many other *cronistas*, supported the ideology of "México de afuera" because it gave him the tools to create an imagined community within the United States that reinforced Mexican traditions and customs. Gazavic's *crónicas*, as seen, demonstrated what happens to Mexican women in the United States who betray this ideology. Women such as Ramona and others who fall prey to U.S. ways, short-circuit the creation of imagined communities that would safeguard Mexican values until they are taken back to Mexico.

## Notes

[1] For more information, see Robert E. Park, *The Immigrant Press and Its Control*. (Westport, CT: Greenwood, 1970).

[2] Some of the topics covered in literature of immigration focus on human and labor rights, mistreatment of laborers, racism, cultural issues and generational conflicts. Through these themes, authors voice the abuses and mistreatment immigrants experience in the foreign land. They also reflect on how family dynamics are affected by immigration through domestic dramas and generational conflicts.

[3] Although literature of immigration is inscribed in all the literary genres, it is particularly evident in the short stories and chronicles written in newspapers for the working class rather than in novels.

[4] Daniel Venegas illustrates this with the phrase that concludes *The Adventures of Don Chipote; or When Parrots Breastfeed*: "los mexicanos se harán ricos en los Estados Unidos: cuando los pericos mamen" (159) (Houston: Arte Público P, 1998).

[5] Juan Bruce Novoa analyzed *México de afuera* under a different light and believed that Mexican expatriates—and Mexican Americans—of the *México de afuera* began to see their creation of Mexico as more authentic than the real Mexico. Bruce-Novoa explains that while the exiles are not permitted back into their country,

> They dedicate themselves to justifying their existence in a dual manner: they manipulate the image and significance of their residence out-

side their country by discrediting what the homeland has become; and two, they set about proving that they are authentic bearers of true tradition of the homeland and even of the ideals of the attempted revolution [ . . . ] this exercise in self-justification leads to the claim that the homeland has actually moved with the exiles, that they have managed to bring it with them in some reduced form, and that if the opportunity should arise, they can take it back to replant it in the original garden of Eden (153).

[6] María Luisa Garza "Loreley" was assigned this column for her *crónicas* dealing with feminine issues. See Gabriela Baeza Ventura, *La imagen de la mujer en la crónica del México de afuera* (Mexico: In Extenso UACJ, 2006) and Juanita Luna Lawhn.

[7] Ibid.

[8] Juanita Luna Lawhn in "*El Regidor* and *La Prensa:* Impediments to Women's Self-Definition" noted the phallocentric attitude of the press in the Southwest by focusing on two San Antonio newspapers published in the early twentieth century. Both newspapers had Mexican exiles as directors. Both men considered themselves key figures in guiding Mexican nationals' intellectual and moral development in the United States. Both promoted the *México de afuera* ideology.

[9] Literature of immigration authors utilize neologisms and regional and popular dialects to underline the differences between characters, above all between México and the United States. See Kanellos, *Hispanic Periodicals.*

## Works Cited

Anderson, Benedict. *Imagined Communities. Reflections on the Origin and Spread of Nationalism.* London & New York: Verso, 1983.

Argudín, Yolanda. *Historia del periodismo en México desde el Virreinato hasta nuestros díaz.* Mexico: Panorama Editorial, 1997.

Bencomo, Anadeli. "La representación de lo popular-urbano en la crónica mexicana-contemporánea." *Revista de Estudios* 11 (1998): 191–201.

Bruce-Novoa, Juan. "La Prensa and the Chicano Community." *Americas Review* 17.3-4 (Winter 1989): 150–56.

Hobsbawm, E. J. *Naciones y Nacionalismo desde 1780.* Barcelona: Editorial Crítica, 1992.

Hoerder, Dirk, ed. *The Immigrant Labor Press in North America, 1840's-1970's.* Westport: Greenwood P, 1987.

Hunsacker, Steven V. *Autobiography & National Identity in the Americas.* Charlottesville & Illinois: UP Virginia, 1999.

Ibarra de Anda, F. *El periodismo en México: Lo que es lo que debe ser.* México: Imprenta Mundial, 1934.

Kanellos, Nicolás. "Cronistas and Satire in Early Twentieth Century Hispanic Newspapers." *Melus* 23.1 (1998): 3–25.

______. *Hispanic Periodicals in the United States: A Brief History and Comprehensive Bibliography.* Houston: Arte Público P, 2000.

______. "Orality and Hispanic Literature of the United States". *Redefining American Literary History.* Ed. A. LaVonne Brown Ruoff and Jerry W. Ward, Jr. New York: MLA, 1990. 115–123.

Lomas, Clara. "Resistencia cultural o apropiación ideológica: Visión de los años 20 en los cuadros costumbristas de Jorge Ulica." *Revista Chicano-Riqueña* 6.4 (otoño, 1978): 44–49.

Luna Lawhn, Juanita. "El Regidor and La Prensa: Impediments to Women's Self-Definition." *Third Women* 4.2 (1989): 134–42.

______. "Victorian Attitudes Affecting the Mexican Woman Writing in La Prensa during the 1900's and the Chicana in the 1980's." *Missions in Conflict: United States–Mexican Relations and Chicana Culture.* Ed. Juan Bruce-Novoa. Tübigen, Germany: Narr, 1986. 65–71.

Monsiváis, Carlos. *A ustedes les consta. Antología de la crónica en México.* México: Ediciones Era, 1980.

Paredes, Américo. *Folklore and Culture on the Texas-Mexican Border.* Austin: CMAS Books, 1993.

Paredes, Raymund A. "The Origins of Anti-Mexican Sentiment in the United States." *Spanish Borderlands Sourcebook.* Ed. David J. Weber. New York, London: Garland Publishing, 1991. 145–171.

Park, Robert E. *The Immigrant Press and Its Control.* Westport, CT: Greenwood, 1970.

Pearson, Edmund. *Dime Novels; or, Following an Old Trail in Popular Literature.* Port Washington: Kennikat P, 1968.

# Part III

## Amparo Ruiz de Burton Literature and History

# Building a Bridge to the Twentieth Century Ruiz de Burton's Novel Techne in *The Squatter and the Don*

**KEVIN ANZZOLIN**
University of Chicago

*Only when genius is married to science, can the biggest results be produced.*
*—Herbert Spencer*

Since the Recovering the U.S. Hispanic Literary Heritage Project republished María Amparo Ruiz de Burton's *The Squatter and the Don* in 1992, the novel has ridden upon a wave of trans-american and cultural studies, and continues to garner the attention of academics from a wide range of disciplines.[1] Ruiz de Burton had hoped that her novel—which dramatizes the territorial disputes between Anglo-American squatters and latifundist *californios* after the passing of the Treaty of Guadalupe Hidalgo in 1848—would lead to political and social change within the United States, specifically in regards to land rights. Even though literary success for Ruiz de Burton has come over one hundred years too late, her novel feels more prescient than ever: against the specter of a forever-burgeoning iron curtain stretching across the U.S.-Mexico border—a veritable colossus meant to establish not only the United States' national sovereignty but also the makeup of its cultural citizenry—criticism of *The Squatter and the Don* has finally begun to point the novel in inspiring new directions.

Until now, much of the criticism surrounding the text has dealt with the novel's treatment of race and the racial politics of its author.[2] Others have debated the book's place both within the Untied States' literary history, as well as within the literary history of Latin America.[3] For the contemporary critic, it seems that the destiny of Ruiz de Burton's impassioned but highly problematic novel lies in a slippery "third space" of discourse:[4] that is, while the novel evinces some Pan-Americanist sensibilities,[5] it most definitely isn't Post-Nationalist. Still other critics have parsed out the commonalities that Ruiz de Burton's novel shares with more canonical Latin American texts,[6] placing particular emphasis on the nation-building aspects of the novel, and invoking, accordingly, Doris Sommer's far-reaching thesis regarding the so-called national romances of 19th century Latin America.[7] Although my following comments are informed by these diverse treatments of *The Squatter and the Don*, I hope to open up the text to interpretive modes that have yet to be explored. More specifically, in the following pages, I will look at Ruiz de Burton's rather ingenious employment of what I will refer to here as "mechanical imagery."[8] My primary claim is that *The Squatter and the Don* (this national romance belonging to not one but rather, two nations) is an intimately technophillic text: the novel's use of "mechanical imagery" suggests that the systematic privation of technological know-how ultimately derails the *californio* plans for national assimilation and cultural reconciliation. That is, Ruiz de Burton's novel doesn't court the muses of national romance via a dialogical dance between eros and polis solely, but rather, it suggests the existence of a third character waiting in the wings, perhaps making possible the consolidation of America's imagined community. Here, I hope to show that the text is a failed foundational fiction, the product of a frustrated rendezvous between eros, polis, and also, techne.[9] These are the organizing elements posited in the text as fundamental to buttressing both nationhood and cultural citizenship; of these parts, technology is the idea most fervently fixated upon. Moreover, with *The Squatter and the Don*, imitation indeed proves to be the highest form of flattery possible, as the novel woos technological know-how by becoming itself a veritable archive—a database, really—consisting of very voluntary memories of disquieting injustices.

The author's use of mechanical imagery provides "the illusion of precision for expressing abstract relationships" (Heiple 10). Here, I will define "mechanical imagery" as any inclusion/mention in the text of technological and/or mechanical apparatuses. Originally employed by the late Daniel Heiple in his study of poetry in Golden Age Spain, "mechanical imagery" was used to talk about the inclusion of clocks, telescopes, etc, in peninsular verse. The mechanical imagery found in Ruiz de Burton's novel obviously includes items more appropriate for her nineteenth century: namely telephones, trains, and cameras. These technological innovations are what march America onward to the beat of an unquestionable telos in *The Squatter and the Don*. In the novel, technological talk operates at the level of rhetoric, event, and at times, even on a metaphorical plane. Written during a century that witnessed a veritable cavalcade of technological firsts, the novel is a panoramic snapshot of sorts, representing a singular historical moment in a very innovative time. Our author isn't just writing a novel. Rather, I claim that she is trying to make history and then capture it, archive it, and exhibit if for all of America to see. Ruiz de Burton is in the business of manufacturing memories.

Thus, by turning to particular scenes in *The Squatter and the Don* and exploring the specific mechanical imagery employed by the author, I propose that the novel should be comprehended as nothing short of a technological tool in and of itself, ultimately meant to better document the unfortunate but indisputable history of native *californios*. Not only are polis and eros constructed contiguously in our novel, but moreover, we will see how techne gets in the mix, making for an interesting (but ultimately failed) tripartite marriage between romance, civil society, and technological know-how.

While mechanical imagery runs throughout the text, one of the most interesting instances takes place around the middle of the novel. Here, Mercedes and Clarence are already young sweethearts in the first flings of love. Their initial attraction is finally solidified as something serious when Clarence divulges that he has *bought* a substantial quantity of Don Mariano's land, thereby proving that he isn't of the same ilk as his father: Clarence is clearly not just another ravenous squatter. He is, in fact, terribly wealthy, having made his millions by way of smart speculation and successful fact-finding missions. His relationship with Mercedes, in turn, would seem to be a match made in heaven. Indeed, she isn't just another pretty face: marrying her also makes good business sense for all parties involved. Clarence wilfully positions himself to be the Alamar family's inroad to full cultural citizenship, while Mercedes—trafficked between two men, a father and a lover—allows for the continued circulation of both financial and cultural capital.[10] It is at this rather hopeful moment in the novel that our power couple, Clarence and Mercedes, decide to take a train cross-country to the national capital, Washington, D.C. Here, not a small amount of their libidinal energies are cathected toward the United States' political epicenter, at this juncture in the novel, it would seem that all the proper elements are in place for writing a successful national romance. Their cross-country crusade intimates an apt dovetailing of eros and polis made possible by the motorized potentialities of techne. Mechanical imagery is always close at hand during this trip, and we would do well to detail our travelers' experience on the train.

On their way to Washington, neither Ruiz de Burton nor her Mercedes find themselves very far from the train-car window. The natural treasures of the American landscape spread out before them in the following way:

> The memory of the mirror lakes, with their gorgeous borders of green, their rich bouquets of fragrant azaleas and pond lilies, as well as the towering

> cliffs, the overpowering heights of the wonderful valley, made a *picture* to remain forevermore a cherished souvenir. (Ruiz de Burton 1997 153)

Both selfhood and nationhood are wrapped up tightly in this picture-perfect description: in the "mirror lakes" we see our distinctly American selves. The "towering cliffs" and "overpowering heights" instill in the viewer a sense of the sublime[11] and of the transcendent goals staked out in the vast American West. But these feelings of self and nationhood—Ruiz de Burton's real sense of red-blooded, American nationalism—can only be captured and digested through the lens of technological know-how, not by a painter's brush. In order to more faithfully document this Edenic scene and preserve for posterity a sense of a unified, national self, Ruiz de Burton naturally invokes one of the many technological innovations of the nineteenth century: the camera. In her mind's eye, Mercedes would very much like to take a picture of this idyllic scene so that it remains "forevermore a cherished souvenir" (Ruiz de Burton 1997 153). But although the mention of technological know-how is couched in rather laudatory terms, Mercedes' experience is ultimately a bittersweet one: very soon, all that her fellow *californios* will possess are memories and photographs of these places that they used to call their own. Thus, a tinge of melancholy hangs about this mechanical image, as Ruiz de Burton can already imagine what the future holds in store for the *californio* population of San Diego County.

In the novel, technology is represented as having an almost innate capacity to level the playing field, allowing for commerce, democracy, and memories to be cultivated in an egalitarian fashion. This is particularly true in terms of photographic technology. During these salad days of the camera—that is, in the 19$^{th}$ century—photography was forwarded as an unbiased medium of representation, while the photographer, similarly, "was thought to be an acute but non-interfering observer—a scribe, not a poet" (Sontag 75). Ralph Waldo Emerson even went so far as to suggest that photography was truly a "Republican style of painting" (Warner Marien 4). Simply said, for Ruiz de Burton, photography is a democratic art, making possible the documentation of real lives and true crimes. Her use of mechanical imagery would suggest that what you see is what you get or, as a Kodak ad from 1883 proclaimed: "You push the button, we'll do the rest." Invoking the camera is a claim of objectivity and a hope that the native *californios*' plight will live on in America's collective memory.[12] Thus, peering out comfortably from her train-car window, the lovely Mercedes is situated as an impartial observer both of American ideals and of America's errors. On one hand, photographic "proof" could scientifically demonstrate that native *californios* experience the same emotions as Anglo Americans, that they too have a deep sense of American ideals. On the other hand, photographs can easily be entered as evidence in legal disputes; therefore, the employment of mechanical imagery here points in divergent but not necessarily contradictory ways. Whether used to gauge *californio* feelings of national pride or to objectively justify their land rights, its function is unquestionably ingenious. Photography is cast as a legitimation tool par excellence for Mercedes as she makes her way across America.

When our loving couple finally arrives in Washington D.C., similar mechanical imagery is woven into the narrative, operating at both a rhetorical and an event level. Our travelers gain a sense that the political stakes of their journey are markedly higher here, as they now find themselves among the sacred grounds of the Capitol. Lauren Berlant has posited that a citizen's trip to the U.S.'s capital is a type of pilgrimage, testing the traveler's patriotic purchase.[13] Only those visitors whose demeanour and perspective suggest a sufficiently docile naiveté and an uncritical acceptance of U.S. hegemony will pass this patriotic litmus test. Here, the innocent, beautiful, and observant Mercedes, is most aptly coded with American patriotism. But that is not to say that these are stock characterizations, nor that the scene is devoid of deeper tensions and knotty cultural issues: Ruiz de Burton is indeed trying to prove a point. Mercedes is white, Christian, an upstanding citizen who loves America. But she is also a *californio*. The suggestion is that even native *californios* should be accepted as true Americans, and to that end, mechanical imagery—and technological know-how—need to be kept close at hand. We read the following:

> With Clarence by her side, Mercedes looked carefully at the city that like a magnificent picture lay there beneath them. She wished to carry it photographed in her memory. (Ruiz de Burton 1997 198)

Coded as an exemplary American citizen—good-hearted, a bit infantile, and willingly docile—Mercedes becomes the privileged harbinger of the technological know-how that could perhaps catapult the *californios* (whom she represents) into full cultural citizenship. Looking down upon the city of Washington from a panoramic vantage point,[14] Mercedes' photographic memory records a singular moment in American history: not only will the photograph she carries in her mind's eye sing the praises of America, but it will also record the crimes of U.S. legislators, who have turned a blind eye to squatter invasions of *californio* territory. The claim is that—perhaps via technological know-how, via a privileged way of objectively *seeing* the contemporary situation of the *californio* ranchers—socio-political and economic trends can be changed for the better. Indeed, seeing, as a metaphor for knowledge and lucidity, is one of the major organizing tropes of the novel, and from a creative standpoint, dovetails quite nicely with Ruiz de Burton's inclusion and appraisal of a relatively new technological innovation: photography. While Mercedes' eyes are remarked upon for their prettiness and their pristine blue clarity, Darrell, contrarily, is described as "blind" on account of his uncontrollable anger and his inability to see that squatters shouldn't have right to *californio* lands. Via photographic innovation, our author hopes that the reader may see "[c]omo en fotografía en un instante, todo lo que los Yankies nos han hecho sufrir a los Mexicanos" (Ruiz de Burton 2001, 117).

Photography is not, however, the only example of mechanical imagery we see employed in *The Squatter and the Don*. Both the telephone and the train are hallmarked in their own ways as being of utter importance to the *californio* cause: while the telephone functions on a more rhetorical level within the text, the train functions both at an event level and a metaphorical level. Ruiz de Burton's treatment of the telephone is especially enthusiastic but, not unlike the camera, it too is cloaked in somewhat melancholic tones. Ultimately, both images are described as extraordinary but frustrated means of communication. They come to epitomize the type of failed attempts at cross-cultural unity that Clarence and Mercedes—perhaps the novel's most highly symbolic characters—so fervently promote.

The inclusion of the telephone as a mechanical image at the very beginning of the novel (the technological tool is mentioned in the first paragraph of the second chapter) foreshadows the fact that any attempt at reconciliation between Anglo Americans and the native *californios* will necessarily come to nought. Posited in hypothetical terms, Ruiz de Burton sadly muses how telephonic technology—if it had reached the hinterlands of the American continent—could have given voice to the concerns of the silenced *californios. But even if the timbre of Ruiz de Burton's discussion of the telephone is rather sorrowful,* the actual capacity of the telephone, as an instance of mechanical imagery, is presented in absolutely glowing terms. The telephone forms part of a direct rhetorical discourse ingeniously placed (literally and figuratively) between squatter and don: again, while in the first chapter of the book we meet the Darrell family, a somewhat grungy bunch of squatters camping out in Alameda County, in the second chapter we meet the regal but notably perturbed Alamar family on their San Diego county ranch. The image of the telephone is placed squarely between the two men. With these two sides of the territorial dispute being illustrated in their respective, beginning chapters, Ruiz de Burton posits a hypothetical question: what if technological development in the United States was such that real conversing, even across immense distances were really quite easy? We are asked to consider the following hypothesis:

> If there had been such a thing as communicating by telephone in the days of '72, and there had been those magic wires spanning the distance between William Darrell's house in Alameda County and that of Don Mariano Alamar in San Diego County, with power to transmit the human voice for five hundred miles, a listener at either end would have heard various discussions upon the same subject, differentiated only by circumstances. (Ruiz de Burton 1997 62)

It is then suggested that perhaps these two men—even though ascribing to two entirely different views of land rights—could "[t]alk quite warmly of the same matter" (Ruiz de Burton 1997 63) if those magic telephone wires were indeed in place. Once again, technological innovation is put forth as an inroad to a deeper understanding and eventually to reconciliation between two distinct cultural groups.

We would do well to remember that Ruiz de Burton's very celebratory presentation of technology was—without a doubt—very much of her time, but probably wouldn't have been accepted as axiomatic by everyone. That is, a fair number of intellectuals of the nineteenth century feared technology's increasing foothold in a rapidly-modernizing society. While Edgar Alan Poe refused several times before finally consenting to pose for Civil War photographer Mathew Brady, Englishman Samuel Butler wrote the fantastic novel *Erewhon*, wherein machines—in keeping with the newly discovered possibilities of Darwinian evolution—nightmarishly morphed into intelligent, emotional beings. Particularly curious is Mark Twain's vitriolic dismissal of the telephone, a mechanical device that he feared would invade the most basic comfort of bourgeois life: the private household.[15] Simply said, Ruiz de Burton seems to very much disagree with these jaundiced perspectives, and offers a novel interpretation of technological advancement, which touches upon such important issues as nationhood, historical truth, and even memory itself. Telephonic technology in particular is heralded as yet another possible bridge between Anglo-American culture and the native *californio* population. It is presented as a means of communication between squatters and dons, as well as one way that the *californios* can better take part in the modern American socio-political landscape.

For our discussion of *The Squatter and the Don*'s technophillic inclinations to be complete, we must not forget the importance of the proposed railway system—the Texas-Pacific Express—which would stretch from the beleaguered, postbellum South to the *californio* communities of San Diego County. The ongoing drama of the railway forms an integral part of the plot; the train, as mechanical imagery, operates on both a rhetorical and an event level. Better said, not only is the train explicitly (or rather, rhetorically) proposed as a solution to the economic hardships in San Diego County and thus, as a means of saving the feudal lifestyle hitherto enjoyed by the native *californios*, it also operates as a symbol of transcontinental bonds and, ultimately, as a trope for cross-cultural understanding. Not unlike the proposed marriage between Clarence and Mercedes, the train system would join two different communities—the *californios* with the downtrodden South—in a financially beneficial union. Musings about the Texas-Pacific Line constantly "filled the minds and hearts of all the San Diego people" (Ruiz de Burton 1997 214). The text suggests that San Diego county and the South should be united financially, that they could help each other rise from a shared past of suffering, and that their "marriage" would be an economic boon for both regions. Together they could right the wrongs promulgated by a corrupt U.S. government that no longer ascribes to the enlightened ideals represented architectonically in the museum of values that is Washington, D.C. This train trope—which gestures strongly toward a cross-cultural and Trans-American connection—is effectively a knot, a tie that binds, a technologically savvy lasso, and which is at heart a mechanical image that echoes in subtle ways throughout the novel. This trope of unity is fundamental to understanding the rather novel techne Ruiz de Burton employs in writing *The Squatter and the Don.*

The author's craft really shines through when this knot metaphor is siphoned into smaller representations, particularly in chapter twenty-five, the eponymous "The Squatter and the Don." Here, we see the long-awaited meeting between the squatter—Mr. Darrell—and the Don—Don Mariano. After being brusquely pressed for information, Don Mariano reluctantly admits that he has indeed sold some of his land to Darrell's son, Clarence. Effectively, Clarence has gone against Darrell's wishes and undermined his father's authority. Darrell finally sees how he is perceived by others, especially by his own son: he is viewed as an economically impotent squatter, determined to rob Don Mariano's lands. Darrell becomes hostile toward Don Mariano, as well as towards the Don's two sons who are present, Gabriel and Victoriano. A brief skirmish ensues which ends with Darrell being tightly lassoed by the rope-wielding *californios*. Our image of union—this trope of cross-cultural connection that promises to be a veritable tie that binds—carries not a positive connotation here but rather, a negative one. Registering this scene from the flipside, the binding of Darrell coincides with the plight of the *californios* and indeed, all of San Diego County, which is being slowly straightjacketed into life-destroying isolation. In sum, this scene is most likely an ironic inversion of a traditional Mexican marriage ceremony, in which a rope is lassoed around the bride and groom in a figure-eight pattern. After the exchange of vows, the priest removes the lasso and presents it to the bride as a keepsake. Thus the skirmish scene employs the organizing 'loop' trope that runs throughout the novel (a symbol of the facilitated means of communication and connectivity that railways, telephones, and cameras all promise) but more pessimistically, also suggests that a true union between the two cultural groups represented may never be realized. However one unpacks the symbolic nuances of this particular scene, it aptly echoes the novel's intense inclusion of mechanical imagery.

At the end of this section, Darrell is finally untied and walks away, defeated by the *californios* and embarrassed by his own son. Upon arriving home, Darrell is doubly ridiculed by his own children; once again, more circular, 'lassoed' imagery is appropriated. Willie says to Clarence of their father:

> We have had a circus performance. Your father distinguished himself by performing in the tight rope with Don Gabriel—a very tight rope. (Ruiz de Burton 1997 246)

Soon after, Darrell queries his son, Clarence, regarding the veracity of Don Mariano's statements. Clarence admits that everything that has been said on the contested fields is indeed true: he has legally purchased large swaths of Don Mariano's territory, land that Mr. Darrell believes should be bequeathed to his family—effectively free of charge—by the U.S. government. After a heated discussion between father and son, Clarence leaves, uncertain as to where he will go. Before departing, he

> covered her [his mother's] face with kisses, while his own was bathed in tears. Without lifting his eyes or saying another word, he walked out into the darkness [where] [t]he delicious, fragrant air, loaded with the perfume of roses and honeysuckle and heliotrope, seemed to breathe a farewell caress over his heated brow, and the recollection of the loving care he had bestowed upon these flowers when he planted them to welcome his mother, flashed through his memory with a pang. He sighed and passed into the gloom. (Ruiz de Burton 1997 249-250)

At first glance, this passage seems unrelated to my previous claims regarding the vast amounts and subtle uses of mechanical imagery in *The Squatter and the Don*. I suggest, however, that it is in this passage that mechanical imagery is employed most subtly and most successfully. Here I propose that via clever wordplay revolving around the definition of "heliotrope," one can gauge how ironically charged mechanical imagery can be; in this passage a specific mechanical device is wrapped up in the messiest of family matters.

On a superficial level, we can all agree that a "heliotrope" is effectively a sunflower: in order for the process of photosynthesis to take place, it needs to crane its stem so as to follow the *helios*—that is, the sun.[16] A heliotrope isn't just a flower, however, it is also the name given to a mechanical device invented in the notably innovative nineteenth century. In 1820, while surveying land in

Hanover, Germany, scientist Karl Freidrich Gauss created a mechanical device that came to be known as the heliotrope, an instrument that reflects the sun's rays in order to better measure distances across terrain.[17] With the heliotrope, solar rays are projected in straight lines across land so plots of land can be more easily divided. My contention, therefore, is that this heliotrope is yet another mechanical image and ultimately points to a darkly ironic invocation of how Clarence made his millions: that is, we can assume that Clarence's land and mine speculations were waged, in part, by the application of this extraordinary mechanical device, the heliotrope. Like other mechanical imagery already seen in the text, the inclusion of the heliotrope here points in contradictory ways, paradoxically intimating the highest highs of Clarence's life during his lowest point in the novel. In this passage—not unlike the heliotrope itself—we too follow the trajectory of a *son*, although the scene is notably not a very sunny one: it is here when the reader of *The Squatter and the Don* finally captures how the story must necessarily end tragically. Ruiz de Burton's technique is quite finely tuned, invoking a past moment of levity and financial success during a full-on familial crisis. This sobering scene underscores the ramifications of the displaced patriarch and the impossibility of solving the Californian land disputes. Indeed, even technology itself, which normally conveys the increasingly complex possibilities of the forever new, is here lamented as if it were but another unrealized potentiality born in a more innocent, mythical time. For Ruiz de Burton, that which could best transform the conditions of her existence—namely technology—is the very thing that is most consistently denied. Finally, it shouldn't be surprising that it is during this final section of the book when we are told that Mr. Darrell, the novel's dethroned patriarch, has lost his "*train* of reasoning" (Ruiz de Burton 1997 228) (italics mine).

Mechanical imagery is truly one of novel's most ubiquitous organizing tropes: it works in small, subtle ways, permeating even the briefest of asides, being reworked and reproduced in echoic, almost micrological resonances throughout the text. It sneaks its way into everyday conversations, into images, and even into the flowers that Clarence plants for his mother. Nation-building and love-making are tricky businesses: Was Ruiz de Burton suggesting that only when paired with the most advanced examples of technological know-how could the precarious melding of eros and polis be feasible? Furthermore, if we concede that *The Squatter and the Don* does share certain thematic commonalities with those texts normally situated under the broad rubric of national romances of nineteenth century Latin America, we need wonder if similarly uncomfortable, tripartite marriages between eros, polis, and techne can be readily perceived in such foundational fictions. A brief survey of some of these national romances would seem to legitimate my somewhat open-ended query.

Worth mentioning is Cirilo Villaverde's *Cecilia Valdes, or Angel's Hill,* in which the much-anticipated union between Leonardo Gamboa and Isabel Ilincheta coincides not just with Christmas, but also with the inauguration of the steam engine in the sugar-producing *ingenio* they visit on holiday. After not so carefully considering the amorous options available to him, Leonardo unwisely chooses the voluptuous Cecilia Valdés over the depressingly dour Isabel. The breakdown of their relationship coincides with that of the steam engine, which explodes in a spectacular fashion: here, neither eros nor polis are actualized, and technological know-how ironically underscores the entire sad story.

Similar uses of mechanical imagery find their way into Clorinda Matto de Turner's *Torn from the Nest,* in which Don Fernando and his wife, Lucía, take a train to cosmopolitan Lima from their Peruvian village, Killac, in hopes of fleeing from insupportable government corruption and the unjust treatment of the indigenous population. This move to Lima would also make a long-awaited marriage between Manuel Marín and the indigenous Margarita all the more possible. Unfortunately, their train to Lima eventually derails in the mountains of Peru, having collided with a herd of cattle. Thus, Matto de Turner here dramatizes (indeed, very literally) a true clash of civilizations—or perhaps better said, a battle of epistemologies—in which eros and polis are derailed (once again) alongside our seemingly constant interloper, technological know-how. While my reading of this particular scene from *Torn from the Nest* would suggest the appropriateness of a rather simple truism—that is, "two's company, three's a crowd"—it remains intriguing that Matto de Turner, like Ruiz de Burton, can't resist talking through her national imaginings in terms of technology.

In closing, I suggest that it is not only important to note that "Ruiz de Burton writes her fiction in English, clearly meaning to target a U.S. audience" (Pita 2006 188), she also—like the majority of this Anglo-American reading public—thinks of technological know-how as being an almost supernatural force, deemed demonic by some, and absolutely divine by others. Written well before industrial technology became nearly synonymous with melting ice caps in the Arctic Circle and the brutal conditions of Fordism, *The Squatter and the Don* cajoles us to lay transcontinental railways, lasso ourselves in cross-cultural marriages, stretch telephone wires out across the country, and take photographs of beautiful, faraway places. *The Squatter and the Don* is a technophillic text that culls contemporary historical documentation via telephones, photographs, and efficient railway systems: indeed, these are all ways to better communicate, to collapse both space and time, to put facts into our contemporary archive, and thus showcase an alternative but indisputable history for all who wish to see it. So, even while writing from an odd third space—a *californio* woman caught on the wrong side of an illegitimately-constructed and hastily-established border—

Ruiz de Burton would seem to take up a theme longtime examined in Latin American letters: namely, she too participates in a seemingly endless search for cultural and historical authenticity via the archive. Of course, Ruiz de Burton doesn't merely seek out this archive—rather, she takes it upon herself to create it: the terribly novel techne *the text evinces* is, thus, the descriptive novel "of contemporary occurrences" itself. Indeed, no matter what literary tradition we situate *The Squatter and the Don* in, we can safely state that Ruiz de Burton's very particular understanding of technological know-how is intimately involved with the issues most important to her: nationhood, justice, and even love.

## Notes

[1] See Dworkin y Méndez and Lugo-Ortiz.

[2] See the works of Luis-Brown, John González, as well as those of Alemán for examples of a discussion of the racial politics of *The Squatter and the Don.*

[3] Both Saldívar (in his "Remapping American Cultural Studies) and De la Luz Montes work towards "collapsing borderlines and times" (De la Luz Montes 205).

[4] See Bhabha, who claims that this so-called "third space" is "a space of translation: a place of hybridity, figuratively speaking, where the construction of a political object that is new, neither one nor the other, properly alienates our political expectations . . . a space that can accept and regulate the differential structure of the moment of intervention without rushing to produce a unity of the social antagonism or contradiction" (Bhabha 25). Especially for the contemporary reader, I would claim that *The Squatter and the Don* and indeed, Ruiz de Burton herself, who has taken on almost larger than life proportions among some scholarly circles, inhabit this third space: What to do with Ruiz de Burton as she fights for issues and incarnates a political identity that the contemporary reader would register—more often than not—as summarily paradoxical? How can Ruiz de Burton fight for silenced, ghettoized voices from her distinctly upper crust vantage point?

[5] See the articles of both Sánchez and Pita in *José Martí's "Our América:" From National to Hemispheric Cultural Studies.*

[6] See Rodríguez

[7] See Sommer.

[8] I believe this term can be aptly applied to a discussion of Ruiz de Burton's novel. In *Mechanical Imagery in Spanish Golden Age Poetry*, the late peninsularist Daniel L. Heiple cogently argues that gentleman literati of Golden Age Spain maintained a highly problematic relationship with mechanical imagery—images of clocks, tools, etc. Such imagery was deemed unfit for the

loftiness of literature because mechanical devices for measurement and observation ultimately pointed to the loathsomeness of manual labor. For Heiple, this jaundiced attitude toward technology was a distinctly Spanish trait, reinforced by a domineering Catholic Church. The crux of Heiple's thesis is buttressed by the notion that technology and nationhood were intimately associated in the collective consciousness; mechanical imagery was problematic in relation to national integrity. If Daniel Heiple's literati of Golden Age Spain shunned technology and the mechanical imagery it inspired, I would suggest that not few of writers of nineteenth-century America loved it, employed it, wrapped it up in more intimate affairs, like nationhood, like lovemaking: indeed, in Ruiz de Burton's novel, technology can even play the part of matchmaker, setting up apt unions not just between human and machine, but also couplings across cultures, ethnic backgrounds, and religions.

[9] Nussbaum explains that for the Ancient Greeks, the idea of *techne* suggested a knowing and a know-how, a way to marshal today's knowledge into a proactive praxis so as to deal with tomorrow's problems. It is this etymological core that really shines through in the 19th century's gloss of 'technology'. Nussbaum goes on to propose that *tuche*, the contrary of *techne*, embodied that which is contingent, doubtful, and unpredictable: *tuche* is fortune, while *techne* is harnessed to counteract *tuche*'s sometimes devastating effects. Ruiz de Burton seeks this sense of technological know-how via her novel.

[10] Here I have in mind the groundbreaking study of Kosofsky Sedgwick, who claims that the consolidation of social and financial power is negotiated via an asymmetrical homosocial triangle. It would seem that Clarence, Don Mariano, and Mercedes are apt examples of the validity of said claim.

[11] See Burke's enthralling study of the idea of the sublime, which he describes as the following: "Whatever is fitted in any sort to excite the ideas of pain, and danger, that is to say, whatever is in any sort terrible, or is conversant about terrible objects, or operates in a manner analogous to terror, is a source of the sublime; that is, it is productive of the strongest emotion which the mind is capable of feeling. I say the strongest emotion, because I am satisfied the ideas of pain are much more powerful than those which enter on part of pleasure" (Burke 36). I suggest that pain is very much part of *The Squatter and the Don,* and using a sense of the sublime to describe America's vast hinterlands seems completely appropriate for Ruiz de Burton's project.

[12] Of course, by using "collective memory," I am suggesting that we couch this facet of Ruiz de Burton's use of mechanical imagery in Halbswach's study.

[13] See Berlant, who claims that the U.S. "produce[s] a special form of tyranny that makes citizens like children, infantilized, passive, and overdependent on the immense and tutelary power of the state" (Berlant 42).

[14] Meers explains how, in the nineteenth century, panoramic imaging was very popular. In America and in Europe, various exhibitions were set up in which the interior walls of cylindrical rooms were adorned with panoramic images, providing the visitor/viewer with the thrill of seeing far-away, exotic places in panoramic way.

[15] See Casson for this anecdote.

[16] "Helios" is, of course, the Greek word for "sun."

[17] See Hall's description of the instrument in his biography of Gauss.

## Bibliography

Alemán, Jesse. "Historical Amnesia and the Vanishing Mestiza: The Problem of Race in *The Squatter and the Don* and *Ramona.*" *Aztlán: A Journal of Chicano Studies*. 27.1 (2002 Spring): 59-69.

Berlant, Lauren. "The Theory of Infantile Citizenship." In *The Queen of America Goes to Washington City*. Durham, North Carolina: Duke UP, 1997.

Bhabha, Homi. *The Location of Culture.* London: Routledge, 1994.

Burke, Edmund. *A Philosophical Enquiry into the Origin of Our Ideas of the Sublime and Beautiful.* Notre Dame: U of Notre Dame P, 1967.

Casson, Herbert N. *The History of the Telephone*. Chicago: A.C. McClurg, 1910.

De la Luz Montes, Amelia María. "María Amparo Ruiz de Burton Negotiates American Literary Politics and Culture." In *Challenging Boundaries: Gender and Periodization*. Ed. Joyce W. Warren and Margaret Dickie. Athens, Georgia: U of Georgia P, 2000.

Dworkin y Méndez, Kenya and Agnes Lugo-Ortiz. "Introduction." *Recovering the U.S. Hispanic Literary Heritage, Vol. V*. Houston: Arte Público P, 2006. 1-22.

González, John M. "The Whitness of the Blush: The Cultural Politics of Racial Formation in *The Squatter and the Don.*" In *María Amparo Ruíz de Burton: Critical and Pedagogical Perspectives*. Ed. Anne Elizath Goldman. Lincoln, NE: U of Nebraska P, 2004.

Halbwachs, Maurice. *The Collective Memory.* Trans. Francis J. Ditter, Jr. and Vida Yazdi Ditter. New York: Harper and Row P, 1980.

Hall, Todd. *Carl Friedrich Gauss, a Biography*. Trans. Albert Froderberg. Cambridge, Massachusetts: 1970.

Heiple, Daniel. *Mechanical Imagery in Spanish Golden Age Poetry*. Madrid: José Porrua Turanzas, 1983.

Kosofky Sedgwick, Eve. *Between Men: English Literature and Male Homosocial Desire*. New York: Columbia UP, 1985.

Luis-Brown, David. "'White Slaves' and the 'Arrogant Mestiza': Reconfiguring Whiteness in *The Squatter and the Don and Ramona*." *American Literature*. 69.4 (1997): 813-839.

Meers, Nick. *Stretch: The World of Panoramic Photography*. Mies: Roto Vision, 2003.

Nussbaum, Martha C. *The Fragility of Goodness. Luck and Ethics in Greek Tragedy and Philosophy*. Cambridge: Cambridge University Press, 1986.

Pita, Beatrice. "Engendering Critique: Race, Class, and Gender in Ruiz de Burton and Martí." In *José Martí's "Our America:" From National to Hemispheric Cultural Studies*. Ed. Jeffrey Belnap and Raúl Fernández. Durham: Duke UP, 1998: 129-144.

______. "Ruiz de Burton's Questioning of "Manifest Destiny." In Dworkin y Méndez and Lugo-Ortiz.

Rodríguez, Arelene. "'In order to form a more perfect union': Interethnic/Interracial Romances, Unions, and Nation Formation in Helen Hunt Jackson, María Amparo Ruiz de Burton, Elizabeth Van Deusen, and Manuel Zeno Gandía." Diss. U of Massachusetts, 2004.

Ruiz de Burton, María Amparo. *Conflicts of Interest: The Letters of María Amparo Ruiz de Burton*. Ed. Rosaura Sánchez and Beatrice Pita. Houston, Texas: Arte Público P, 2001.

______. *The Squatter and the Don*. Ed. Rosaura Sánchez and Beatrice Pita. Houston, Texas: Arte Público P, 1997.

Saldívar, José David. *Border Matters: Remapping American Cultural Studies*. Los Angeles: U of California P, 1997.

Sánchez, Rosaura. "Dismantling the Colossus: Martí and Ruiz de Burton on the Formulation of Anglo América." In *José Martí's "Our America:" From National to Hemispheric Cultural Studies*. Ed. Jeffrey Belnap and Raúl Fernández. Durham: Duke UP, 1998: 115-128.

______, and Pita, Beatrice. "Introduction." In Ruiz de Burton, María Amparo. *Who Would Have Thought it?* Ed. Rosaura Sánchez and Beatrice Pita. Houston, Texas: Arte Público P, 1995.

Sommer, Doris. *Foundational Fictions: The National Romances of Latin America*. Berkeley, California: U of California P, 1991.

Sontag, Susan. *On Photography*. New York: Farrar, Straus and Giroux, 1977.

Warner Marien, Mary. *Photography and its Critics*. Cambridge: Cambridge UP, 1997.

# Irony and Laughter in Ruiz de Burton's Public Sphere

**TIMOTHY P. GASTER**
University of Chicago

Since Rosaura Sánchez and Beatrice Pita's recovery of *The Squatter and the Don* from American literary heritage's lost and found in the early 90s, much scholarship has focused on questions of cultural politics, land struggle and conquest, nationhood, gender, and race when talking about the text, thereby contributing to a reconceptualization of not only how we talk about identities and modernity but also about how we "map" cultural studies in general in this country.[1] Though we should applaud these contributions, I also believe that in order to accord the text its rightful place in the American literary tradition it would only be right to treat the text how other texts have been treated historically: as a literary work first and foremost. By this I don't intend to ignore the historical context that informs this literary artifact nor do I want to claim that such a distinction between literary and historical texts is necessary. Rather, I think it is time we also pay attention to the literary merits of the work. Hence, I will approach the text first from a literary perspective, so secondly it may inform us of the historical. In the end, by doing a close reading of certain aspects of the novel I hope to show nuances of Ruiz de Burton's "reception" of the invading Anglo "modernization" project that occurs in her homeland of California in the late nineteenth century.

The one specific element of the modernization project I am concerned with is participation in a public sphere. My objective is to consider the moments in *The Squatter and the Don* where there is what appears to be a fictional model of what I will be calling a public sphere and to see how this can inform us of Ruiz de Burton's own personal ideas about civil participation in the democratic process of modern societies. What I will be analyzing in the text is not an actual public sphere, but rather encounters of community that prefigure a public sphere. What I am referring to are the meetings that take place in the novel between the heads of community where these men begin to organize themselves based on common economic needs in order to eventually state their rights against governing authorities. Based on Habermas's study *The Structural Transformation of the Public Sphere,* we see "public sphere" defined as,

> the sphere of private people coming together as a public; they soon claimed the public sphere regulated from above against the public authorities themselves, to engage them in debate over the general rules governing relations in the basically privatized but publicly relevant sphere of commodity exchange and social labor. (27)

My study revolves around what I am calling a public sphere because it is in those moments of community meeting wherein lies an element that has been largely overlooked in the novel up till now. That element is the function of laughter. I believe laughter and a critique of Washington's public sphere are intricately entwined in the text. What I intend to demonstrate is how Ruiz de Burton implicitly critiques the large, real-life models of the public sphere from Washington (which so effectively excluded the *californio* voice), by making the fictional model of community encounters (the public sphere) in the text a mirror of the processes of the official model in Washington and by causing this reflection to crack under counterhegemonic forces of carnivalesque irony and laughter. Ruiz de Burton's critique can be read in her dismantling of the textual model through laughter.

Based on a close reading of the moments of laughter in the novel, I find that they inform us of two dimensions. First of all, laughter doesn't just parallel another movement in the novel—the movement of the *californio* population from landowners to a popular, working class—but it actually acts as the device that *represents* this change. Based on and referring to Bakhtin's idea of carnavalesque laughter as representative of the popular, folk culture inverting and making ambivalent the official institutions of the high culture, we are able to see in *The Squatter* similar distinctions of popular versus high culture and their corresponding asymmetries of power relations, depending on how and by whom laughter is being used. For the *californio* Dons, laughter will be the mark of a new status in a new society: from the aristocrat to the peasant who wields laughter as a tool of defense.

This leads us to the second function of laughter prevalent in the novel. Thinking again along Bakhtinian lines, laughter works as the medium through which this change of power is critiqued and challenged. In a carnivalesque moment, roles and hierarchies are inverted and the popular masses that have inverted themselves into the ruling order's role not only laugh in general but laugh directly at those in power. And as Bakhtin emphasizes on the role of laughter in his seminal study on Rabelais, "Laughter liberates not only from external censorship but first of all from the great interior censor; it liberates from the fear that developed in man during thousands of years: fear of the sacred, of prohibitions, of the past, *of power*" (94, emphasis is mine). Laughter in the carnival works as a means of creating an ambivalent world where norms, privileges, and prohibitions become suspended along with the differences between official and popular culture. The implications of this temporary ambivalent world for the battle between official culture and popular culture after the carnival is explained quite well in Renate Lachmann's essay, "Bakhtin and Carnival: Culture as Counter-Culture":

> The provocative, mirthful inversion of prevailing institutions and their hierarchy as staged in the carnival offers a permanent alternative to official culture—even if it ultimately leaves everything as it was before. It is this *irrepressible, unsilenceable* energy issuing from the carnival's alternative appeal—and not so much the particular manifestations of folk cultural practice—that disrupts official, institutionalized culture. (125, emphasis is mine)

This "irrepressible, unsilenceable energy" has significant implications for our study regarding a public sphere where community members come together to have their voices heard. In fact, it is at the very first meeting of the San Diego citizens (where we get a first glimpse of what could be considered the prefiguration of a public sphere), that we already encounter Ruiz de Burton's preoccupation with the restrictive practices that occur in "public" dialogue on issues of the community. In Chapter V the Don organizes a meeting to talk to the squatters to propose a deal that could save their cattle and help them make a more secure and profitable living. The narrator provides us the particulars of who can attend. "The heads of families all came—the male heads, be it understood—as the squatters did not make any pretense to regard female opinion with any more respect than other men" (Ruiz de Burton 84). Bracketing off of "the male heads" from the main sentence along with the emphatic statement "be it understood" do nothing less than demonstrate that Ruiz de Burton doesn't think too highly of this practice of exclusion. Perhaps even more revelatory of Ruiz de Burton's criticism is the fact that she directs it solely at the squatters. It is they and not the Don (even though he is the person that proposed the meeting in the first place), that she singles out specifically for not respecting the opinions of women. It is these two elements, the occlusion of participation in dialogue (repressing and silencing the energy of others) and the Anglo squatters who do the occluding, that form the heart of Ruiz de Burton's concerns in this novel.

The question is what literary tools/weapons does she employ to critique and combat these two forces? Or in Bakhtinian terminology, what alternative does she provide to this official culture of suppression?

The answer to these questions can be found in the atmosphere that surrounds this very same first meeting of the male heads of community. In a description of the those attending the meeting we see, "At ten minutes to two, Señor Alamar, accompanied by Mr. Mechlin, arrived. . . . Clarence, Romeo, Tom and Jack sat together in a corner, conversing in low tones, while Gasbang was entertaining his guests with some broad anecdotes, which brought forth peals of laughter" (85). Given that this joking occurs just as the Don is arriving, it is not hard to imagine the derogatory and racial nature of these jokes. Whether this joking is noticed by the Don or not, the text doesn't make explicit. However, shortly after this, when the Don is going to begin to propose that the squatters fence in their land, it would seem the laughter caused by the Don's statements not only works to defend himself against some of the squatters like Gasbang but actually causes them pain. In response to the Don's statement that he will not keep the men very long, one of the squatters, Miller, responds, "Only let us out in time to bring the milch cows home, before night comes on." To this the Don replies laughing, "Exactly, we want to look after our cows, too." And laughing: "All saw the fine irony of the rejoinder and laughed heartily. Miller *scratched his ear as if he had felt the retort there* . . ." (86, emphasis is mine). Obviously the laughter caused by the Don's statement does more than just act as an effort to create a light atmosphere. It also has direct physical implications. Here we have an early indication of the power that laughter can have as a liberating force from power and tyranny of which Bakhtin speaks. The meeting starts with Gasbang telling wry anecdotes, gaining peals of laughter from the likes of Mr. Matthews, and now the Don mollifies any threats through laughter also. The Don has turned the laughter of the squatters into a weapon for his own use directed toward those same that were only moments ago probably laughing at him. It has become a battle of who can defend himself best, with humor and laughter as the weapon of choice.

Looking at it from the perspective of laughter, it may not be, then, too much of a stretch to consider this first instance of public meeting as representing a carnivalesque moment. In addition to the moments of laughter that permeate the entire scene, there is a play of role inversions that takes place the moment the Don arrives at the meeting. We see the Don and his son described as English gentlemen: "'They look like Englishmen,' was Clarence's next observation. 'Yes, particularly Victoriano; he is so light he looks more like a German too, I think,' said Romeo" (85). Here, the obvious irony is that they are not Englishmen and weren't expected to appear like those old white authors of the Magna

Carta. There is a play of expectations, and roles seem to be reversed. It is ironic in this scene that the actual descendents of Englishmen (the squatters) look like ruffians and the supposed barbaric Mexicans look like Englishmen.

Another indication of role reversals appears when we take into consideration what the Don proposes at the meeting. His intention is to create a political economy in the San Diego Valley that would suit all settlers' needs, including his own. Interestingly, what he proposes is actually an inversion of a metaphor for civilization and barbarism. The Don suggests that the squatters fence in their land. The fence works as a metaphor for civilization. It protects the civilized from the wild, barbarous element that could come from outside. The fact that this is actually proposed by the Don, the one who in an Anglo's eyes should represent the barbarous, and then it is rejected by the squatters, the supposedly "civilized" ones, should seem to the reader to go against expectations. It is ironic that the squatters, who consider themselves so superior to the Mexicans, would reject the very object that represents, in the western world, civilization: the fence.[2] Again, expectations are played with and the roles become reversed. The Don seems to be in the position of the high culture.

However, a doubt could be raised here. If the Don actually represents the high, official culture and not the popular culture, how can he form part of the popular culture at the same time that he uses the carnivalesque to mollify power? The Don *is* a Mexican aristocrat, and it is highly doubtful that Ruiz de Burton would be suggesting that he be anything but this. So the question is, are the squatters representative of the popular culture of which Bakhtin speaks and do they, with their sneering jokes and laughter, actually liberate themselves from the power of an aristocratic class represented by the Don? Or is it the Don that does this? And if so, how?

It is true that the Don reverts to laughter seemingly to protect himself from the possible threats of the squatters. However, this laughter could be considered in terms of what Bakhtin has referred to as a degradation of the carnivalesque devices of the masses. In analyzing the reception and history of the grotesque in Rabelais within the literary genres, Bakhtin states that all these genres "had a more or less oppositional character that permitted the grotesque to enter their sphere, while still remaining within the limits of official culture; therefore the nature of laughter and of the grotesque was transformed and degraded" (103). Lachmann clarifies the implications of this historical change in the reception of Rabelais from the literary realm to the cultural: "In other words, the misunderstanding of Rabelais's novel is the result of a waning carnivalesque consciousness that is expressed in the reduction of the carnival to innocuous revelry, in its puritanization, and in *its usurpation by bourgeois culture*" (121, emphasis is mine). Again, could the Don's laughter be a case of usurpation by the aristocratic class in order to transform and degrade the subversive carnivalesque efforts of the squatters?

In order to answer this, it is necessary to consider the power dynamics that are at play in this first meeting. We can decipher the power dynamics by examining closely what language is used and by whom at the meeting. When the Don first arrives looking so gentlemanly and English, he does so in silence. Then, when the Don addresses the others he politely begs pardon for his "poor" English. "'If you don't understand me I will repeat my words until I make my meaning clear, but I hope you will ask me to repeat them; or perhaps, some one of these young gentlemen will do me the kindness to be my interpreter,' said he" (Ruiz de Burton 86). We can see the irony in this comment because obviously, if he can speak this well in English, he doesn't need an interpreter. However, we must take into consideration that although a reader could interpret this statement of his as humorous or ironic, the truth is that he *has* to attach this disclaimer to his speech.[3] He needs a disclaimer because although he is the planner of the meeting, the language and the power relation inherent in this meeting from the beginning is foreign to him. He is forced to communicate in a foreign tongue (though he does it fluently), and, more importantly, he knows from the beginning that he is in a position of subordination; hence, his ironic but sincere apology for any mistakes he may make in *their* language. The terms on which he will have to negotiate are already determined by the "dominating" Anglo culture.

This point is further exemplified if we compare it with the use of Spanish at this first meeting. When the Don proposes that the farmers switch to cattle ranching, Mr. Matthews is the first to react, "'I don't want any cattle. I ain't no *vaquero* to go *busquering* around and *lassoing* cattle. I'll *lasso* myself; what do I know about whirling a *lariat*?' said Matthews" (89, emphasis in original). Given the emphasis placed on the words, it would seem quite evident that Mr. Matthews uses the Spanish in jest: to make light not only of the Don's offer but also his Spanish presence. Even more important, however, is Mr. Matthews's statement mixed with Spanish words that is given without a disclaimer. Whereas the Don feels conscientious about his possible failures in English and needs to apologize, the English-speaking squatter can butcher and make fun of Spanish without it even occurring to him that not only might he need to give a disclaimer like the Don does but also that he may be offending someone. Hence, the ironic fact that the first Spanish vocabulary words in the novel are mixed in with a white squatter's speech, confirms not only that the first meeting is an event where all roles are inverted but also that the squatters can feel easy about using Spanish without having to apologize for how they may use it or how it may sound.

Thus going back to the question of how Ruiz de Burton might be representing the Don at this stage in the novel and whether his use of laughter is to usurp or subvert, it would seem evident that the Don's status is changing from Mexican aristocrat to Mexican peasant in an Anglo society. Analyzing the power dynamics of language use in this "contact zone" allows us to verify the status of each player in this realm and from here we can match the laughter they employ with this status in order to reveal its mechanisms and functions. Hence, it would seem the squatters' laughter (or lack of it considering nobody found Mr. Matthews's comment funny) is more representative of the aristocrats wanting to protect the institution through usurpation of the laughter from "below." And the Don may come into the meeting looking more the part of the traditional aristocrat, but as we can see how he needs to apologize and defend himself with humor, the laughter he provokes is turning more toward that of the role of the peasant. The laughter that the Don resorts to has marked a change in the Don's stature in his quickly changing community, as is confirmed by his timid use of English. Hence we have a first meeting that it is marked by ambivalence, inversions of power, and especially laughter.

In addition to Mr. Matthews's use of Spanish in the quote above, there is also an interesting allusion to him lassoing himself. Mr. Matthews being the butt of a joke involving imagery of horses and ropes recalls an earlier episode in the novel. In that episode Clarence Darrell, recruiting people to go to the meeting that the Don is organizing, meets with young Romeo who explains to Clarence how he got his stake of land. Romeo explains how he jumped the claim that the older Mr. Matthews had to the land by building a fence around it.[4] In the retelling of the events, Romeo's father defends his son when Mr. Matthews shows up to reclaim his land. The dialogue is as follows:

> Mr. Matthews says, "He's jumped my claim." "Now don't be silly," said Father, leaning on his rifle. "It is painful to my feelings to hear a grey-headed man talk like a child. You might have put tewnty [sic] notices—what of that? The law don't allow any circus performances like that, and if it did, you ain't a good enough performer to ride two horses at once." (82)[5]

Here we have an allusion to the circus and the rather humorous image of Mr. Matthews riding two horses at the same time. This episode is of interest because the telling of it occurs right before the official meeting between the Don and the squatters. And now during the actual meeting we have the very same Mr. Matthews making allusions to himself being lassoed. Furthermore, this episode and statement prefigure the tragic episode where Mr. Darrell will be the butt of a joke by being lassoed like an animal later, in Chapter XXV. And quite ironically, the very person who will provoke this joke is Mr. Matthews himself. With these repetitions and images of fences and ropes, we begin to get the sense of circularity, something that goes full circle in order to close itself in or to close someone out. I will return to this point later, but first we must see how these community meetings evolve.

The community meetings (what we are calling the public sphere), turn into a public sphere that excludes the man who brought it into being: the Don himself. The moment of the novel when the law has decided that the Don's land is rightfully his is exactly when the public sphere becomes stronger among the squatters, and only the squatters. We can add the Don to the list of occluded, alongside the women. When the Don has had to start running his cattle out to the mountains because the shootings have increased, the squatters begin to gather at Mr. Darrell's house with more frequency. The settlers, with lawyers in attendance, start going to Mr. Darrell's house in order to discuss issues always related to the Don. They begin making plans on how they can fight for their land rights in the courts, not just against the Don but also against the U.S. government and its laws.

Hence, we see the definite seedlings of a public sphere here. What is interesting to note, though, is that there is less subversive laughter in these meetings. The tone of the meetings has become serious, and the laughter that caused the inversion of roles of power and ambivalence before are now lacking. The only inversion of hierarchies is the continuation of the banter between the younger generations and the older men, especially between Romeo, the ever-loyal supporter of the Don, and Mr. Matthews, the Don's biggest adversary. When they meet to discuss how the government is settling on the titles of the land, Romeo and Mr. Matthews go at each other. Romeo starts, "'What makes you think so? Did you ever shoot any of the Don's cattle [ . . . ] The boys, the young men laughed. Matthews arose, too angry to remain quiet. 'Next time I come to talk business—serious business—with men, the men of my own age—I don't want to be twitted by any youngster.'" Romeo gives another reply to this remark which sends Mr. Matthews running out the door. "The shout of laughter that followed these words was too much for Matthews. The banging of doors as he left as the only answer he deigned to give" (211). Although in this instance it is Mr. Matthews who leaves, we understand that there is the threat that the exclusiveness of the membership in this public sphere (just with regard to the women and the Spanish speakers), could become even stricter: elimination by age also. The only element remaining at this moment that inverts the roles and opens the possibility for a plurality in the dialogue is the burlesque bantering of Romeo, who, with the weapon of humor, laughs at the laughers.

Furthermore, although the jokes up to this point almost always had a direct effect on one individual, as we just saw with Romeo and Mr. Matthews, the overall effect of the humor always worked against the power itself inherent in the meetings (as we can see how the joking and Mr. Matthews's leaving disrupts the whole proceedings). However, as the meetings become even more exclusive, this ability is diminished. Now the jokes must be directed at the "club" mostly from the outside as opposed to from within. For example, in the following discussion we see Victoriano, Everett, and Mercedes talking about the meetings that are being held at the Darrell house:

> "Where is the colony?" Mercedes asked. "That is the new name for the large room next to the dining room, which Clarence said he built for a *'growlery.'* Alice called it a *'squattery'* because Father always receives settlers there; but Mother changed the name to *'colony,'* to make it less offensive, and because the talk there is always about locating, or surveying, or fencing land—always land—as it would be in a new colony," Everett explained. (215, emphasis in original)

As we see here, the mother's preoccupation with calling it the "colony" instead of a "squattery" does very little to hide the fact that they are making fun of these meetings and the power mechanisms that they represent. But at this point the joking from the outside does not disrupt the meetings. The fact that it is the meetings specifically that they talk about and not specific members is important to note, though, because this points to the idea that what concerns Ruiz de Burton is not an individual but what this individual can represent. But what they need is something that can symbolically embody this institution. What will allow the carnivalesque power of laughter to work again even from the outside is an object that embodies for the occluded masses the power of the institution. In the following scenes we will see what this embodiment is and how this attack is carried out, which will have implications for Ruiz de Burton's larger concern: the public sphere in Washington.

As mentioned earlier, the person who foreshadows the moment when Mr. Darrell eventually ends up lassoing himself is Mr. Matthews. In one of the colony meetings, Everett eavesdrops on the proceedings as we read,

> He heard them laughing at some of Gasbang's coarse, vulgar jokes, and then all sat down. After some desultory talk, Matthews, evidently anxious to begin at what they had to state said: 'I am afraid, neighbor Darrell, that somebody has been fooling you and laughing at you, or if not, then the thing will look as if you yourself had been fooling us and laughing at us. This we can hardly believe.' (226)

Mr. Darrell replies gruffly, "I don't understand you . . . I am not given to joking or laughing much, and I never knew anybody dared to laugh at me" (226). Again the scene is framed by Gasbang's coarse jokes, but then we see the preoccupation of Mr. Darrell with being made fun of. And the idea that he doesn't joke or laugh much reminds us of what Bakhtin says about (medieval) official institutions: "As opposed to laughter, medieval seriousness was infused with elements of fear, weakness, humility, submission, falsehood, hypocrisy, or on the other hand with violence, intimidation, threats, prohibitions. As a spokesman of power, seriousness terrorized, demanded, and forbade" (94).

This last quote encapsulates quite nicely all the emotions and actions that Mr. Darrell will experience when he goes to encounter those who are supposedly laughing at him: the Don and his family. It would seem that Mr. Darrell is the ultimate manifestation of power, and he is about to exercise his tyranny. As the well-intentioned irony of Ruiz de Burton demonstrates though, laughter will have the last laugh. The lassoing of Mr. Darrell is probably the most humorous scene of the novel.

The importance of this scene is reflected in the fact that it takes place in the chapter that shares the same title as the novel itself. Mr. Darrell goes out on horse to confront the Don about Clarence buying the farm from him, when Mr. Darrell literally attacks the Don. Referring to Bakhtin's description of medieval seriousness, Mr. Darrell's fear, weakness, falsehood, and hypocrisy spur his violent behavior, which is intended to intimidate so the Don will become humiliated and submissive. Mr. Darrell tries to whip the Don. A scuttle ensues and Mr. Darrell is quickly lassoed by the Don. Then, as Everett and Victoriano are trying to help Mr. Darrell off the horse, they almost keel over from laughter. "But Victoriano had suppressed his desire to laugh too long, and now his risibility was *beyond control*. Everett was overcome in the same manner, so that he hung on Victoriano's shoulder, shaking with *ill-suppressed* laughter" (Ruiz de Burton 232, emphasis is mine).

The emphasis given in the prior passage is to show the power of laughter as something that is beyond control and something that cannot be suppressed, as expressed explicitly in the text. The power of laughter has come to invert the ultimate power, and it can't be stopped. And, if Mr. Darrell is the ultimate power of the meetings, representing the official institutions that unleash their power on the masses, then his body could be considered the U.S. government—the American land/body, an allegory for the governing bodies of the land. His *body* is the *body* of land over which the Anglos and Mexicans are fighting, and whose ultimate destiny is in the hands of the governing *bodies* of Washington. From here we can see that there is a struggle for the protection against being made fun of played out over this body. Mr. Darrell's body as a metaphor for the congressional body, the official institution at which nobody laughs, has been overcome and criticized through laughter and the physical representation of the rope.

It is actually the rope that connects the body of Mr. Darrell to the local public sphere and the public sphere in Washington: Congress. This idea is given validity when later in the novel Mr. Darrell explains to Clarence what happened when he was lassoed: "We have had *circus performances*. Your father distinguished himself by performing in the tight rope, with Don Gabriel—a very tight rope,' he said, making a *semicircular sign around his body* with both hands . . .'" (246, emphasis is mine). The image of the semicircle and being roped off is reinforced again later when Mrs. Darrell, the only woman to ever dare try to speak in the public sphere, shows up at the colony: "Mrs. Darrell walked in and, bowing to the astonished squatters, came slowly forward and stood about the middle of the *semicircle, though outside of it*" (235, emphasis is mine).

This circularity can also be related to the circle that surrounds the representatives in Washington, i.e. the circularity (dome shape) of the congressional buildings visited by Mercedes. In Chapter XXI, "Looking at the Receding Dome," we witness Mercedes telling her friend George that she "wanted to go to the dome of the Capitol, and see Washington City from that elevated place" (198). There are many curious points in this episode and passage that would lead the reader to believe that the visit to the "dome," rather than being just a sightseeing trip, carries much symbolic significance for the text as a whole. Calling it a "receding" dome, the overemphasis in calling it a "dome," and calling Washington "Washington City" all tend to point to the circularity of the institutions that promulgate laws but which at the same time contrast starkly with the multidimensional shape of the Washington where for the "Californians the view of that city of proud and symmetric proportions, with its radiating avenues lost in diminishing distances, its little triangular parks and haughty edifices, all making a picturesque *ensemble*, was most pleasing and startling" (198, emphasis in original). It would seem the circular Capitol doesn't share the quality of being an ensemble as the city does. It would seem the circularity of the Capitol is like the rope around Mr. Darrell's body and like the imaginary semicircle surrounding the "club." Each one acts as a barrier to keep others out.

The rope, which represents how the public sphere has excluded others from the democratic process, is activated in the scene where Mr. Darrell is lassoed by those very same ones who were excluded. They invert the rope (the weapon of repression) and lasso the representational body. So the circle that once kept the marginal voices out is ironically now used to strangle the body that allows itself to be manipulated by forces from within that are implicit in this segregation of voices. The squatters who claim to be protecting Mr. Darrell from being laughed at are like the congressmen and senators who corrupt the governing bodies by lying to keep power in its exclusive place: within the circle. As we have seen, it was Mr. Matthews who was first seen as a circus performer riding two horses at a time right before the first big meeting where the two cultures came into contact for the first time. Then in that meeting Mr. Matthews prefigured the lassoing of Mr. Darrell by talking of himself being lassoed. And now it is Mr. Darrell, whom "nobody laughs at," that by being duped by Mr. Matthews became lassoed. Again the circularity of this motion is noteworthy. All revolves around the meetings and Mr. Darrell's body. The circle of the lasso correlates to the circle formed in the public sphere which in turn corresponds to the dome of Washington, all three representing the circular shape of a circus. Hence, what is most important about this scene is the laughter that accompanies the inversion of the role of the rope. The lassoing forms part of a carnivalesque performance where the irrepressible, unsilenceable, beyond-control laughter creates a moment where all prohibitions and norms are suspended and there is liberation from fear and power. And shortly after the roping of Mr. Darrell's body we witness the appearance of a woman at the meetings for the first time.

But the carnival and laughter fully employed by the Don don't just act as a weapon of aperture in dialogue, they also mark the Don's complete conversion into the peasant class. This change, though, is not accepted so easily as is evidenced by the Don's and Victoriano's reaction to something that happens in the moment Mr. Darrell is lassoed. Everett and Victoriano are laughing uncontrollably and then suddenly two Indian "vaqueros" show up and begin to laugh also. The two "vaqueros" begin to shout in markedly informal Spanish "'¡Apa! Viejo escuata o cabestreaas o te orcas,' [6] cried one."

This is contrasted with Victoriano,

> "¿Qué es eso? ¿A qué vienen acá? ¿Quién los convida? ¡Cállense la boca, no sean malcriados, váyanse!"[7] said Victoriano, turning to them in great indignation. This rebuke and imperative order silenced them immediately, and not understanding why these gentlemen were having all the fun, and did not laugh, nor wished anyone else to laugh, quietly turned away. (231)

As if the fact that they are Indian "vaqueros" didn't signal enough the class they belonged to, Ruiz de Burton provides an obvious contrast between the "correct, proper" Spanish of Victoriano juxtaposed alongside the informal speech of the "vaqueros." But even more interesting is the reaction of Victoriano. Till this moment Victoriano and Everett had been laughing uncontrollably. Now in a very threatening tone, they tell the "vaqueros" to shut up. Could this not be a clearer indication of the transition from aristocrat to peasant? In the moment that Victoriano recognizes that his laughter is the same laughter as that used by the popular culture he not only stops his own laughter but he threatens the poor "vaqueros." Victoriano's emphasis on "proper" Spanish in this moment, in addition to his telling them to shut up, is obviously an overcompensating effect or reaction caused by fear. This fear surges from the fact that he has come face to face with his future. He and his family are from this moment on members of the peasant class. And, as if their use of laughter to combat the new power in town wasn't proof enough, the Don's statement to Mr. Darrell just before the latter attacks him should leave no doubt: "'Good afternoon, Mr. Darrell,' said Don Mariano, pleasantly. 'You see we are Clarence's *vaqueros* now'" (229, emphasis in original).

In conclusion, we see that the micro–public sphere formed by men with business concerns in the valley of San Diego functions as an analogy of the larger public sphere of the United States which dictated the policy toward the rights of the *californios*. This sphere started in a carnivalesque atmosphere of irony and laughter where all those who would be affected by the policies, except the women, were able to express their opinions. Then, through further exclusion, this sphere eventually began getting smaller, to the point where the only inverting of hierarchy was between the younger settlers and the older squatters. Finally, all dissenting voices were at risk of being canceled out completely, and the carnivalesque tactics were launched from the outside, not against specific members in general from within, but through metaphors against the one body that represent the representative body itself, the one body that nobody supposedly laughs at: Mr. Darrell. Through our analysis of how the public sphere has been portrayed in the novel in relation to irony and humor, we have been able to see how Ruiz de Burton critiqued an aspect of the invading modernization program of the Anglos: the public sphere that did not include the opinions and concerns of the Mexican population of California. The fact that her analogy of the public sphere gets converted into a boys' club is her way of critiquing the same boys' club that runs the show in Washington. Through carnivalesque maneuvers she was able to create, even if only temporarily on paper, the moment in a public sphere which would combat the asymmetric relations of power and include the concerns of the *californios*. Like this, we can trace Ruiz de Burton's critique of the public sphere.

## Notes

[1] See for example, de la Luz Montes, Amelia María and Anne Elizabeth Goldman. *María Amparo Ruiz de Burton: Critical and Pedagogical Perspectives*. Lincoln: U of Nebraska P, 2004. Belnap, Jeffrey and Raúl Fernández. *José Martí's 'Our America': From National to Hemispheric Cultural Studies*. Durham: Duke UP, 1998.

[2] See *Dreamtime: Concerning the Boundary between Wilderness and Civilization*, by Hans Peter Duerr, for a discussion of the metaphor of the fence as boundary between civilization and wilderness in western societies.

[3] It should be noted that if the reader were to consider the Don's statement here as ironic or humorous, it would not be so in the Bakhtinian carnivalesque

sense. It would be more of a tongue-in-cheek or sarcastic comment. But as we will show, this interpretation is not very likely.

[4] Again we see the metaphor of the fence, that as we will see later literally *surrounds or encircles* the meeting.

[5] A continuation of the dialogue shows just how important the fence is. "What the devil is this?' said he, and began to swear a perfect blue streak. Then he took a hammer from his wagon and began hammering. 'I jumped up, took my rifle and halloed to him, as if I didn't know him, 'Who is there, hammering my fence?' 'Your fence?' said he; 'your fence?' 'Yes, sir, mine. I located here yesterday.'" Since it is a squatter keeping another squatter out with a fence, the fence again being the metaphor for civilization, we would appear to be confronted with a conflict of what or who is "civilized" within the squatter community.

[6] "'Giddap! old Squatter, either you give into the halter or you choke'" [escuata]=Spanish loan word for "squatter" (350).

[7] "What's this? What are you doing here? Who invited you? Shut up. Don't be discourteous. Go away!'" (350).

## Bibliography


Bakhtin, Mikhail. *Rabelais and His World.* Trans. Hélène Iswolsky. Bloomington: Indiana UP, 1984.

Belnap, Jeffrey and Raúl Fernández. *José Martí's 'Our America': From National to Hemispheric Cultural Studies.* Durham: Duke UP, 1998.

De la Luz Montes, Amelia María. "María Amparo Ruiz de Burton Negotiates American Literary Politics and Culture." In *Challenging Boundaries: Gender and Periodization.* Ed. Joyce W. Warren and Margaret Dickie. Athens: U of Georgia P, 2000.

______, Amelia María and Anne Elizabeth Goldman. *María Amparo Ruiz de Burton: Critical and Pedagogical Perspectives.* Lincoln: U of Nebraska P, 2004.

Duerr, Hans Peter. *Dreamtime: Concerning the Boundary between Wilderness and Civilization.* Trans. Felicitas Goodman. Oxford: Basil Blakewell, 1985.

Habermas, Jürgen. *The Structural Transformation of the Public Sphere: An Inquiry into a Category of Bourgeois Society.* Trans. Thomas Burger and Frederick Lawrence. Cambridge: MIT P, 1989.

Lachmann, Renate, Raoul Eshelman, and Marc Davis. "Bakhtin and Carnival: Culture as Counter-Culture." *Cultural Critique* 11 (Winter 1988): 115–152.

Ruiz de Burton, María Amparo. *The Squatter and the Don.* Ed. Rosaura Sánchez and Beatrice Pita. Houston: Arte Público P, 1992.

Shevtsova, Maria, "Dialogism in the Novel and Bakhtin's Theory of Culture." *New Literary History*, 23, (Summer, 1992): 747–763.

# The Interior Frontier Man: *The Squatter and the Don*, the Conquest of Manhood and the Making of Mexican-American Literature

**ALBERTO VARON**
University of Texas at Austin

Don Mariano Alamar in María Amparo Ruiz de Burton's *The Squatter and the Don* (1885) might qualify as one literary example of what Scott Sandage has recently called "born losers" in American history, figures of failure to be contrasted with the entrepreneurial spirit of the American frontiersman (Sandage). In contrast to the young Clarence who succeeds in business and eventually marries the Don's daughter Mercedes, Don Mariano witnesses the rapid decline of his fortunes, the maiming of one son, and the reduction of the other to manual labor before his own ignominious death. Such figures of masculine failure have been obscured from the annals of American historical and literary scholarship, which has preferred to rivet attention on the male who leaves the binding apron strings of the domestic hearth and sets out to master the frontier. Indeed, works like R. W. B. Lewis's *American Adam*, Perry Miller's *Errand into the Wilderness*, and Henry Nash Smith's *Virgin Land* have installed this myth of American manhood as one of the foundations of American literary criticism. This version of American masculinity, as Jane Tompkins argues, is characterized by the "anaesthetization of the hero," "the ethic of self-denial," and the "mortification of feeling—both the need to mortify feeling and the effect of having done so" (214–15). Rugged, determined, and undeterred, the frontiersman, in these accounts, is utterly devoid of feeling and without sentiment. Lacking the privilege of self-mastery and anesthetic composure, the failed male—who often expresses feeling in ways the frontiersman cannot—challenges prevailing conceptions of manhood. As Glenn Hendler and others have recently proposed, there is a "critical unwillingness to imagine the American man of sentiment, as if this subject position is too paradoxical, too unstable, too threatening to discuss" (7). In this paper, I argue that Don Mariano represents the other man of the American frontier—an interior frontier man—and that this figure assists us in rethinking the genealogy of Chicano literature, one that, as Ramón Saldívar has argued, has been at least partly characterized by a dialectic of patriarchy and defeat.

The very title of Ruiz de Burton's novel—*The Squatter and the Don*—indicates the contest between two forms of masculinity in what was to become the American Southwest. While the "squatter" here is the familiar American frontiersman, it is important to remember that the Don was also a frontiersman of the Spanish and then Mexican borderlands, part of a tradition of men who inhabited the regions from Texas to California long before the eastward migration of Anglos. The Don, however, was markedly different from the squatter in terms of class and religion. The hidalgo and ranchero social structure, which centered on the family, codified a distinctive version of masculinity. This masculine form is at times equally as antifeminine as its American counterpart, but at others is more sentimentally self-aware. The Mexican-American male represents an alternate masculinity on the frontier—a figure to contend with and an Other to the American settler. The American frontiersman necessitated the defeat of the Mexican male in order to assert his presence and thereby assure the Anglo-American supremacy in the domestic colonial endeavor. While in reality the Mexican male existed as an alternate form of masculinity, for the national imaginary of the American West he existed only as an object of the frontier, not as a participant in the collective experience of nation building.

The hinge of feeling and sentiment, the interior frontier man, positions the U.S.-Mexican male not only in opposition to but also in dialogue with the American male. Through a willingness to display sentiment, the interior frontier man enters into a discursive arena, one that implicates him politically and one that is denied by most literary renderings of the frontier man. Sentiment further connects the interior frontier man to the discursive communities of the American East Coast, which stand apart from images of the West in which he lived. It is to these East Coast communities, the seat of American politics, that Ruiz de Burton in many ways addresses her novel and that overtly concern her other novel, *Who Would Have Thought It?* Affective display perhaps more closely aligns the U.S.-Mexican male with the situation of the U.S.-Mexican woman than usually thought.[1] Ruiz de Burton's interior frontier man typifies a sentimental manhood through which the future figures of masculinity, particularly the *corrido* hero, can be understood. As a descendant of the interior frontier man, the *corrido* hero becomes more than an instance of resistant masculinity, challenging Anglo hegemony; the corrido hero becomes a man of feeling, one with a complex interior organization and authentic sentiments.

Yet, although a figure of resistance and, as I have suggested, a sentimental man, the *corrido* hero embodies many of the same traits as the American frontiersman. Both accounts of masculinity rely on images of independent opposition to seemingly unconquerable odds. Both masculinities accentuate the hero's determination in pursuit of a cause significant beyond the man himself, either Mexican-American culture or the collective national vision of Manifest Destiny. The *corrido* hero parallels the frontiersman in his resistance to forces which seek to destroy them, either the influx of a colonizing power, the power of Mother Nature, or simply the power of mothers (the feminine) more generally.[2] However, while "cultural homogeneity, isolation, and a patriarchal, traditional way of life made the existence of a native folk balladry possible," the border region was one of continual conflict—between the Spanish settlers and the indigenous peoples, between the Spanish and burgeoning Mexican nation, and between Mexican communities and Anglo settlers (Paredes 241). The *corrido* often blurred historical fact regarding the typically male hero, giving way to a depersonalized mythical retelling of the hero's life in order to emphasize resistance to the colonizing forces that disrupted the established way of life. While violence was an intricate part of the frontiersman's narrative, Américo Paredes explains that "the peaceful hero minding his own business is essential to the concept of the Border hero" (111). The frontier male is seen as a master of the forms of violence as a means to an end, exemplified in the almost affectionate relationship between the hero and his gun. In the *corrido*, violence is always a reactionary force, where violence forces an individual to transcend himself, to become something he is not. The difference helps account for the variation between the types of masculinity available on the western frontier.

In "The Borderlands of Culture," Ramón Saldívar examines identity formation in Américo Paredes' *George Washington Gómez* and hones in on the way that the title character's culturally charged name, Gualinto, interpellates the protagonist as colonial, hybrid subject. Saldívar asserts that Paredes' novel provides a "prefigurative instance of the state of Chicano literature and the Chicano subject at the end of the twentieth century" in that the identity Gualinto rejects at the novel's end, one that dates back to pre–Guadalupe Hidalgo society and directs its gaze southward toward Mexico, does not account for the markedly different position of the Chicano in American society ("Borderlands of Culture: Américo Paredes's *George Washington Gómez* and Chicano Literature at the End of the Twentieth Century" 274). During the Chicano movement, the Mexican-American male was coping with a tradition of resistance to American influence under a self-imposed rubric of cultural isolation; this tradition overtly appears in the *corrido*. According to Saldívar, the *corrido* form "[links] ideologies of resistance and historical agency with ideologies of masculinity" and "while the corrido links patriarchy and resistance, it also unconsciously joins patriarchal authority and defeat, since in the songs of border conflict the hero is invariably killed, captured, or exiled from his home" ("Borderlands of Culture: Américo Paredes's *George Washington Gómez* and Chicano Literature at the End of the Twentieth Century" 288).

The introduction of Ruiz de Burton's text into American studies forces scholars to reconsider the trajectory of Mexican-American literature and compounds Saldívar's claim in several ways. First, while Saldívar convincingly argues for Paredes' "prefigurative" portrayal of Chicano identity, Ruiz de Burton's novel allows us to reconsider and extend some of his insights about the significance of gender in the formation of Mexican-American identity. While Saldívar does state that "gender is articulated through and through with questions of identity formation and the creation of stable subject positions," he pays little attention to the psychological consequence of gender categories (and its affiliated political reverberations), specifically masculinity, to a Mexican-American subject who bears the emotional baggage of machismo and the ranchero social system ("Borderlands of Culture: Américo Paredes's *George Washington Gómez* and Chicano Literature at the End of the Twentieth Century" 287). Although *corrido* masculinity weaves itself through *George Washington Gómez* at a variety of levels, it remains unclear how masculinity impacts the novel's identity choice and its function as "an early expression of the now widely explored complexities of Chicana and Chicano subject identity" (of which gender is in the forefront) ("Borderlands of Culture: Américo Paredes's *George Washington Gómez* and Chicano Literature at the End of the Twentieth Century" 289). Second, while *George Washington Gómez* provides a locus from which to leap forward to chart Chicano identity, Saldívar overlooks the history of Mexican Americans prior to Paredes' novel. The tumultuous social and political climate leading up to the Paredes' novel is indelibly marked by the tumultuous social and political climate that precedes it, a climate that includes both the effects of the Mexican Revolution that haunt the novel and the history of resistance and defeat that coalesces in the cultural institution of the *corrido*.

As in *George Washington Gómez*, questions of identity and subject formation are integral to *The Squatter and the Don*, with some pronounced differences. Writing half a century apart, the two authors approached their texts with a decidedly different agenda.[3] If we take Ruiz de Burton's novel, which places us earlier in history, as the starting point of Chicano literary identity, we can use gender identity in her novel to more accurately map the changing role of U.S. Mexicans in American society. Ruiz de Burton provides us with a critical and foundational account of Mexican-American masculinity written by a Mexican-American woman, one that provides an opportunity to see the ways in which men's identities are imbricated with women's. Ruiz de Burton relies heavily on her male characters to plead her case to a largely female reading public (disguising her novel as historical romance). The masculinity she describes and which I argue guides U.S-Mexican subject formation until the middle of the twentieth century advances the American colonization of the Mexican male in its very efforts to defend their cause. In the final section of this paper, I draw upon the understanding of masculinity that *The Squatter and the Don* affords to demonstrate how the interior frontier man also allows us to reframe a masculine figure commonly regarded as inaugurating the Chicano literary tradition. In José Antonio Villarreal's *Pocho* (1959), the male protagonist wrestles with his contradictory emotional impulses and influences as he straddles two cultures. Richard Rubio struggles to understand his feelings of powerlessness and his desire for sovereignty and self-affirmation. These feelings then are transferred onto his sexuality, and played out through the space of his body.

**Ruiz de Burton and Gender Nostalgia**

*The Squatter and the Don* was among the first and most significant works republished by the Recovering the U.S. Hispanic Literary Project. The recovery of these works has presented considerable challenges and opportunities for scholars. In order to approach the multitude of—and often conflicting themes in—Ruiz de Burton's writings, it is necessary, as Jose Aranda Jr. has postulated, to "[move] scholarship beyond counter-nationalist arguments that conceive Chicano/a culture and history in strict opposition to U.S. and Western cultures by insisting on the need to formulate histories and analyses that place some people of Mexican descent at the center of discourses more typically associated with Anglo-America" ("Contradictory Impulses: María Amparo Ruiz De Burton, Resistance Theory, and the Politics of Chicano/a Studies" 554). Ruiz de Burton uses "ethno-racial romance" as a "solution to the sociosexual conflict" that depicts the U.S. Mexican's desire to carve out a social niche in dominant, white American society, however problematic that solution may be (Alemán 108). She optimistically seeks to establish a U.S. social and cultural locus for the *californios* through the symbolic unions of Mercedes and Clarence in her novel *The Squatter and The Don*. In doing so, she draws upon the conventions of the sentimental novel and the Latin American historical romance.

Like the sensational literature popular during the late nineteenth century, Ruiz de Burton's text "promotes competing ideologies of heroic masculinity and mobilizes representations of women's bodies as symbols of race and nation" (Streeby 32). Ruiz de Burton similarly activates the male body as a symbol of the nascent Mexican-American social group. In her novel, the patriarchal leader must surrender, through death or social incapacitation, to the forces conspiring to end a certain social order. The loss of Mexican patriarchy and that which the father figure represents suggest an emphasis on the shift in masculinity as inextricably bound to the configuration of Mexican-American culture. Don Mariano is described as the emotional center of the Alamar family; all family decisions, whether business or intimate, must gain his approval. He is described as noble, intelligent, compassionate, and even in the face of adversity, when others "forget your dignity, I do not" (Ruiz de Burton 230). He is a gentleman in every way. Don Mariano, who alone "clearly identifies himself as Mexican," represents the prototypical Mexican male, a site of absolute virtue and adherence to the past, virtually unflawed but ultimately doomed (Sánchez and Pita 38). As such, Don Mariano's body functions as a symbol of Mexican-American masculinity.

These virtues, however, prove ineffectual in a landscape that witnesses the encroachment of U.S. capitalism, here figured in the form of the growing railroad industry. In *The Squatter and the Don*, Mexican culture must turn to Clarence, the American male skilled in the laws of the market, to resolve its crisis and guarantee the continuance of Mexican generations. Clarence is able to bridge the gap between the squatters and the Alamars precisely because of his capacity to display sentiment. His sensitivity to the *californio* plight and his willingness to look past the absolutes of the colonizing narrative make him better suited to adapt to the novel's social realities. Clarence deviates from the image of a wholly American frontiersman and is rewarded by capitalist success. In his conquest of the emerging capitalist economy, Clarence also exhibits a liminal mode of citizenship that mediates between Don Mariano's feudal hacienda heritage and American liberal capitalism, to which I will return below.

Toward the end of the novel, Clarence is forced to leave the region, unable to resolve his dual allegiance to his family and the Alamars, who both have made claims on the same piece of land. Don Mariano's daughter Mercedes is heartbroken and his two sons are wounded, Gabriel from the perils of working-class labor, and Victoriano made lame by the land which for a century had nurtured the family. The broken home is too much for Don Mariano to bear, and shortly thereafter he dies. On his deathbed, he asks his family to "tell Clarence I bless him with my last breath" (Ruiz de Burton 304). That the two central male characters are denied a *despedida*, a formal parting, underscores the link between them as the divergence in character—Don Mariano as an artifact of the past and Clarence as a herald of the future—is left unresolved. Don Mariano's passing occurs in the narrative concurrently with Clarence's return. The Don's death, then, marks a new beginning. Don Mariano's last thoughts are with Clarence, and Clarence's first words upon his return from exile end with him "[pacing] the floor in great agitation . . . for they knew he was thinking that never again, in this world, would he see his noble friend, Don Mariano" (320). The text depicts in vivid detail the moment of Mariano's death, the "last few aspirations [that] followed that last sigh, and all was over—his noble soul had passed away" (304). The emphasis on the finality of the moment, the passing of the figure of familial cohesion, only further accentuates Don Mariano as a symbol of Mexican masculinity. His death occurs as a public event, as the entire family gathers around the bedside, as the Don "looked again to see whether every one of his family was there; he forgot no one," which further elevates the patriarch's demise from an instance of family mourning to a defining moment in the community. All that the Don represented, the good and stability ascribed to the Mexican male, fades with the dissolution of his body, and "the memory of [Don Mariano] made most subjects most painful" (328).

It is important to note the public character of Don Mariano's death scene. Historically the division between public and private spheres has been delimited by gender. In his influential discussion of the advent of the public sphere in eighteenth-century Europe, Habermas explains how the public emerged in coffeehouses and salons that in the process differentiated the space of the home and of public gatherings as gender marked. Identity that was developed in the home is then rehearsed in public.[4] Through the process of reading and critique, "privatized individuals coming together to form a public . . . formed the public sphere of a rational-critical debate in the world of letters within which the subjectivity originating in the interiority of the conjugal family, by communicating itself, attained clarity about itself" (Habermas 51). The distinction later taken up by American studies scholars as a model through which to explore literary genres within nineteenth-century American literature, a division that is often class-marked between high and low literatures, has more recently been disputed through great work done by many scholars, particularly through feminist critique of the separate spheres model, to better understand the influence of the so-called male and female literatures that crossed public and private distinctions.

Both in Don Mariano's inclusive, enveloping gaze and in the impact his death has on the community, Ruiz de Burton puts pressure on the boundaries between public and private spaces. Don Mariano's funeral scene takes place in the most intimate of spaces, the bedroom of the family home, but the "scene of grief, of heart-rending agony" has public consequences that extend far beyond the private home. From his demise ensues the disintegration of the Alamar family. Crucial to an understanding of this scene is the way that public and private "are the very scene of selfhood and scarcely indistinguishable from the experience of gender and sexuality" (Warner 24). Public enactment of privately constructed masculinity in the figure of the patriarch was one of the cornerstones of *californio* society prior to the U.S. incursion. Mariano Guadalupe Vallejo, one of Ruiz de Burton's closest friends and most frequent correspondents, "posits pre-1848 *californio* society as a 'true community' in the sense of one held together by manners and morals deriving from a commonly held view of reality . . . with the idea of a 'patriarchal,' 'healthy,' 'moral' Californio community subverted by the (corrupting) capitalist forces" (Pérez 45). Masculinity occupied a visible, multivalent public space on the hacienda; the buildings themselves "that make up the whole of the hacienda are arranged sequentially from public spaces to the most private— those reserved for the owner, his family, and his guests. Areas serving as a backdrop for the relationship of the landowner and his workers, such as the office and the chapel, are strategically placed between public and private areas" (Nierman and Vallejo 19).[5] In his multiple roles, the patriarch inhabits his public self nearly simultaneously with his private persona. In this "true community," the patriarch embodies and all but erases the distinction between public and private. Private concerns directly impact public life, and the family as community becomes implicated in social political debates. By blending public and private, Ruiz de Burton's novel creates a space that allows mobility between otherwise static gender spheres that positions *californio* masculinity as emotive or interior and thereby opens a connection to its American counterpart, as described above.

At the moment of gender bequeathal, when masculine identity passes from the Mexican to the Mexican American, Don Mariano and Clarence can be read conjointly, as the reincarnation of Californian (and by association, Mexican) identity in its new Mexican-American form. Don Mariano's death symbolically silences the heroic Mexican male and ends aristocratic, hidalgo culture. The ranchero hero's masculinity, to reemerge in a new heroic form in the *corrido,* has now abandoned Mexican culture and been transformed and entrusted to the American male. But for this substitution to take place, Clarence himself must first turn against his father, rupturing his own patriarchal lineage. In a heated exchange between father and son, Clarence realizes that Mr. Darrell angrily "[insulted] me under the shelter of your paternal privileges. You have been taunting me until I can bear it no longer. I suppose you wish to drive me from your house." Clarence storms from home, "never to enter it again," and wonders "could he claim to be a gentleman, being the son of that rough?" (Ruiz de Burton 249–50). The concern for gentility acknowledges Clarence's cognizance of the responsibility he assumes. By severing the line between himself and his father, Clarence allows the possibility of affiliating himself with the Alamars, an act that his marriage to Mercedes confirms. Simultaneously, the new alliance allows the Alamars to lay claim to an American future through the male body of the only squatter with a rightful claim to the land, both economic and patrilineal.

While the passing of the patriarch is inevitable as it predicts the conquest of Mexican Americans, Ruiz de Burton essentially martyrs the Mexican male. Clarence arrives too late to see Don Mariano, but inherits his legacy. He "felt deeply Don Mariano's death," and newly acquired filial bonds, "as a slight reparation for [the] cruelty" of the squatters (and by their association with the American government), required he treat the family "as kind as if you were her own child" (331). The burden and authority of the family patriarch and of the quintessential male has been transferred to the cultural outsider. Clarence must interiorize his masculinity by adopting Don Mariano's cultural and familial role in order to meld his conception of loyalty and morality with the cultural obligations that Don Mariano's death bestows on him. The process becomes particularly crucial given the failed utopian ending, where *californio* society seems doomed because of the loss of class status and land rights. In the narrative logic of the novel, Clarence's refusal to incorporate aspects of Mexican-American masculinity could result in the disappearance of *californio* society.[6] Without an heir, the patriarchal society would, out of necessity, conform to Anglo dominance. Clarence—both in his relations with Don Mariano and through his marriage to Mercedes—suggests news horizons for a Mexican-American future, a future where new forms of resistance and cultural life will be possible.

Here, Clarence exemplifies the forms of liberal publicity that characterize late nineteenth-century society, with its emphasis on social decorum, civility, and rules of conduct for social interaction, and which are at play in Ruiz de Burton's first novel *Who Would Have Thought It?* Clarence's insistence on gentility in his behavior, his gratitude for the Don's hospitality, and his resistance to the antagonism of the squatters situate him within the norms of publicity extant in the realm of westward-driven, expanding capitalism. Clarence's victory in the novel confirms this mode of public identity while at the same time questioning its inclusiveness and functionality as the requisite form of public identity to national citizenship. The relation between Clarence and Don Mariano provokes a different interpretation of the public self. In some measure typical of the liberal publicity of early capitalist society and a necessary entry point for U.S. Mexicans into American society, Clarence also represents a transitional public self. Clarence threatens the Don's public self and so moves *californio* society away from its historical stability towards a tectonic collision of two distinct modes of production. However, as a foil to the Don, Clarence represents a markedly different liberal publicity.

Clarence is thrust at the novel's end into a comparison with the elite of San Francisco, where a railroad magnate is hosting "'The Great Nob Hill Silver

Wedding Ball' of one of San Francisco's millionaires" and the host delivers a speech on his rags-to-riches success. Mrs. Grundy, a marginal character who merely functions to enable Dona Josefa's capitalist critique, "ascertained who were to be the best-dressed ladies, what their pedigree was, and how their money had been made" before she agrees to attend the ball (334). The penultimate chapter of the novel abounds with allusions to the performance of public belonging.[7] The point about criteria for social inclusion and the association with capitalist progress underscore the interdependence between a public and political and economic inclusion. Clarence is included in this society by his access to capital but is conspicuously absent from the social scene. This can be partially accounted for by the way that he represents a new form of citizenship and publicity, a citizenship dependent on his ability to perform new norms of masculinity that traverse disparate social and cultural arenas. The interiority of Clarence's publicity empowers him to straddle American and *californio* society, the geocultural space between east and west, and the historical change which moves U.S.-Mexican society from the hacienda to liberal capitalism.

If as Glenn Hendler states, "the novel [functions] as an instrument of subject formation," then the loss of the patriarchal figure so emblematic of Mexican hidalgo society that Ruiz de Burton portrays must be read as a symptom of a social reconfiguration with which nineteenth-century Mexican Americans were grappling (Hendler 22). Ruiz de Burton may have failed to secure a place for Mexican Americans in the developing U.S. social hierarchy (as some have convincingly argued), but she succeeded in establishing, in Don Mariano, a figure which later Mexican Americans would both mourn and attempt to recuperate.[8] If "what the novel does support is a political future where the civic ethos of an evolving, educated Californian citizenry takes as its founding mythos a nostalgic embrace of Californio ranch culture," then, as I demonstrate in my reading of Don Mariano's death, Ruiz de Burton's idealization of gender locates male identity outside of the individual or community, and places it in an imaginary past, in a cultural memory (Aranda "Returning California to the People" 15). After the death of Don Mariano, the specter of his presence becomes the point of desired but unattainable return. His memory can only be retained "with loving tenderness and ever-living regret," but has no contemporary agency or potency (Ruiz de Burton 329). Since the formation of identity is one that must occur within an individual or cultural body, then the placement of masculinity on an imaginary fringe sustains social dislocation. The traditional male figure was shattered by the colonization of California society and later reconfigured through its literary enactment in an idealized form, such as the archetype found in the *corrido*, creating what I term "gender nostalgia." Since the post–Guadalupe Hidalgo Mexican male is unable to live up to the expectations of an idealized past (the sociopolitical realities of nineteenth- and twentieth-century Mexican Americans make it impossible), his conception of self cannot exist; it must remain imaginary. Gender identity reacts by becoming internalized, as demonstrated in later sexual behavior and gender relationships, in order to compensate. Not until Chicano literature of the mid-twentieth century revives this version of masculinity can he reimagine and reassert himself as a Mexican American, and thus a part of U.S. society.

I argue that from Ruiz de Burton through most of the first half of the twentieth century, U.S. Mexicans confronted a crisis of how to imagine an agentive Mexican-American masculinity. Masculinity becomes for the individual male subject a source of great distress, as he tries to continue the tradition of resistance without a clear target to oppose, since he is now part of the very society he opposes. In order to express his gender publicly, he must enter into the very institutions that created his quandary. For instance, in order to exhibit the resilient bravery that helped Mexican males survive the frontier, the twentieth-century Mexican American must join the U.S. Army. Since the U.S.-Mexican social structure inherited from Spanish Mexico becomes disintegrated in the mid to late nineteenth century, it operates entirely as an imagined past, a wholly interiorized space of resistance and longing. Following Ruiz de Burton, masculinity is constructed around the idealized male precedent for both the individual and the community. During this period, Mexican-American masculinity becomes latent, something that would only find expression later, after the catalyst of the Mexican Revolution and the exhaustion of other attempts to attain the rights of full cultural citizenship in the United States. As a result, the once proud, outspoken, authoritative Mexican male became subverted, destabilized, and forced to internalize gender identity. Since gender roles are one of the integral ways by which societies organize themselves, then the disruption of U.S.-Mexican masculinity has profound implications for the Mexican-American community generally. Unwilling to relinquish its tradition and not yet able to reorder the social imagination, Mexican masculinity succumbed to, as Dana Nelson argues, the notion of "national white manhood" and its exclusion of the Other. Consequently, the cultural solidarity that unified Mexican-American males in the period of the Chicano movement was so slow to develop and an unsated nostalgia for gender persisted.

**Sexuality and Sovereignty**

Ramón Saldívar calls *Pocho* "the 'beginning' of the Chicano novel," a novel that has provided some measure of coherence to the Chicano literary tradition. If *Pocho* is a novel that looks both at the present and forward to the future, we can also, in light of the crisis of masculinity we detected in *The Squatter and the Don*, see that it looks backward.[9] Gender nostalgia projects the self into cultural memory, where it attempts to discover coherence in the gendered forms of the past to contrast with a feeling of incoherence in the present. Villarreal's novel, located geographically in California but in a radically different sociopolitical environment than Ruiz de Burton's, contends with two actualities. On the one hand, the novel appears after the hope of full citizenship in American society via Mexican-American participation in World War II failed to materialize. On the other, the protagonist finds himself unable to live up to the obsolete moral and cultural codes of his father, a figure aligned with the resistant heroics of the *corrido* hero. While Clarence in *The Squatter and the Don* was able to synthesize these two masculine forms—the official masculinity of the nation with Mexican-American masculinity—Richard Rubio, *Pocho's* young hero, finds those forms distant even as he longs for the mastery and social relevancy that they promise. Richard is emotionally isolated, and his frustrated attempts to secure stable masculine gender markers are registered in his sexuality and sexual acts.

In his development, Richard's sexual acts are limited to self-gratification, to masturbation, often performed with his male friends. As George Mosse has noted, masturbation, insofar as it is not procreative and can distract young men and women from a range of sexual norms, has historically been regarded as not only a threat to the health of the child but also to the health of the nation (Mosse). Richard seems to regard sexuality in this normative manner, imagining it as having consequences that extend beyond himself. Specifically, he links his sexual acts with his father's authority. Initially, Richard "sensed that for him there was something unnatural in the act—not morally or physically wrong but wrong in a manner he did not wholly understand" and thus hesitated to participate with the other boys, but eventually caves to his physical urges (Villarreal 113). A few days following the initial encounter, Richard's father becomes suddenly ill. Richard is afraid that the exercise of his sexuality has caused his father's sickness. He repents, but immediately upon his father's recovery, "Richard did it three times to make up for what he had missed" (114). The narrative conflation of internalized sexuality and the malady of the paternal figure is particularly revealing. Unable to express his fears and confusion verbally, Richard must find a physical outlet for the cultural demands which gender, through his father, has imposed. At some level Richard is aware that he will never be able to live up to the "hero's unwavering commitment to his communal identity" which Juan Rubio represents, and it is through his internalized sexuality, and the implied refusal of traditional gender roles, that Richard is able to express these frustrations (Saldívar *Chicano Narrative : The Dialectics of Difference* 62).

At the same time, however, Richard's masturbatory episodes demonstrate his attempts to fulfill the self-sovereignty and command that he detects in his father's masculinity. Robert McKee Irwin argues, "the fact that one can play-act, can experiment with gendered scripts that he or she has not assimilated as part of his or her identity . . . points to the possibility of agency, an ability to resist and perhaps even subvert, an ability that helps account for historic change" (Irwin 22). In light of the gender nostalgia and the history of an interiorized frontier man that Richard inherits, sexuality becomes an accessible outlet for the internalized masculinity. Feeling guilty about his acts, Richard eventually confesses to a priest, yet another version of patriarchal authority. Noting that he "derived great pleasure at the confessional," Richard finally explains, "I do it in my mind" (Villarreal 115). Masturbation becomes a convenient expression for interiorized masculinity precisely because it demonstrates a kind of interior sovereignty. More importantly, masturbation allows the individual an outlet for the expression of sexual identity while maintaining control over the body, subjectivity, and over patriarchal succession and lineage; the self-gratifying sexual act grants the subject total dominion over his identity. While this self-sovereignty may be homologous with the father's early masculine glory, these masturbatory scenes, often occurring amongst other boys, refuse to reproduce exactly the father's path, instead producing horizontal lines of connection among the boys themselves. Sexuality becomes a socially symbolic act, at once a resistance to the resistance masculinity of previous generations that have proven ineffectual in securing citizenship and a space for the improvisation of future formations of masculinity.

The novel as a whole is explicitly concerned with the generational gap between those U.S. Mexicans that see themselves as diasporic Mexicans in the United States and those negotiating a Mexican-American identity. Juan Rubio claims to be "happy, except when I remember" (131). He orients himself to the past that requires him, in the novel's present, to deny that past. What throughout the novel was nostalgia for a glorious past has now exhausted itself of its political potentiality. Richard is acutely sensitive to the rupture between his own future social needs and his father's: "and Richard knew that although his father was not one of the vanquished, as he claimed, there was little resistance left" (131). Juan Rubio's internal conflict between imagined and lived reality was one of struggle, a struggle ultimately against self-actualization. Richard then determinedly seeks a determinate American social and Mexican cultural space, but is hindered by his inability to use sexuality to project himself into a participatory public.[10] Where interiority grants Clarence access into various publics in Ruiz de Burton's nineteenth-century California, a similar interiority becomes detrimental to the development of Richard's public self in *Pocho*'s early-to mid-twentieth-century California, and in its national repercussions.

As Saldívar notes at the conclusions of his analysis of *George Washington Gómez,* "through these effects we also glimpse the heterogeneous arenas through which future Chicano subjectivities might yet emerge into the realm of history" (Saldívar "Borderlands of Culture: Américo Paredes' *George Washington Gómez* and Chicano Literature at the End of the Twentieth Century" 289). Further study into Mexican-American literary history and its relation to American history will allow for a more nuanced understanding of both the current state of Chicano literature and the historical influence of Mexican Americans on the American West. The Mexican-American male that emerges out of literature of Ruiz de Burton's *The Squatter and the Don* (and later reveals itself in *Pocho*, oft regarded as the literary provenance of the Chicano movement) offers an alternative to the frontier man typical of the U.S. national imaginary since the mid-nineteenth century. Thus, the Mexican-American male represents, in several ways, an interior frontier man. He is interior in the abstract geographic sense as he was bound on one end by American civilization on the other by Mexican territory. The Mexican-American male was socially interior as he became subsumed by U.S. society and forced to reconstruct himself as proletariat Other within dominant society. And third, his gender identity was forced to internalize and thus existed within the physical or psychological interior of his body alone.

The interiority of the Mexican-American male becomes particularly germane to future considerations of the impact that American and Mexican masculinities have had on one another, as I have argued here. As one scholar has suggested, "the romance of Aztlan, then, and Chicano nationalism by extension, is the erasure of criollo origins in favor of a romanticized national unity that eliminates a nineteenth-century Mexican and Mexican American past incongruous with twentieth-century Chicano ideologies" (Ruiz 117). While this may hold true, a fuller understanding of the way American, Mexican, and Mexican-American communities interacted is necessary to draw out the complexities of nineteenth- and early twentieth-century culture. Taken conjointly, American and Mexican-American literary masculinities may provide a more complete account of the dynamic nature of nineteenth-century American society and how the nation functioned as a network of cultural exchange therefore finding a historical place for Mexican Americans in the literary future of American studies.

## Notes

[1] There has been a good deal of criticism written on Ruiz de Burton's literary practice as participating in the popular genre of novels of domesticity which

activates norms of affect to achieve a sympathetic response from the reader to mobilize a political initiative.

[2] The frontier male was in many ways the antithesis of the model of femininity described in novels and stories of domesticity. Where these models of femininity stress norms of affect as an avenue toward social change, the frontier hero critiques this model as lacking the physical strength and emotional commitment necessary to pursue the national objective of westward expansion.

[3] Ruiz de Burton's *The Squatter and the Don* was originally published in California in 1885, nearly forty years after the Treaty of Guadalupe Hidalgo created Mexican Americans as a minority group. Her novel was to disappear from print and critical attention until its rediscovery in 1992 as part of the Recovering the U.S. Hispanic Literary Heritage Project. The Paredes' novel was written sometime in the late 1930s, but remained unpublished until 1990.

[4] Interestingly, and by comparison, in Jovita Gonzalez's novel *Caballero* there is less of a division between public and private spaces. At least on the hacienda, where public identity is more similar to the performative nature of monarchic rule where ritual and ceremony distinguish authority, the depiction of masculinity is more rigid and less adaptable to changing social conditions. When the family moves to Monterrey, unable to develop a public self, the family dissolves and is absorbed by American cultural forces.

[5] This beautiful architectural study of the hacienda describes the way that the structure and edifices were designed to complement the social needs of the community.

[6] As the embodiment of the national gender transition, Clarence functions as both the ideal Mexican-American male and as a symbol of the Mexican defeat. This conflicted nature carries over into Chicano masculinity's concern with the duality of identity.

[7] Ruiz de Burton's final chapter, "Out with the Invader," clearly positions her novel in a political context. In the chapter, Ruiz de Burton abandons her fictional character for a historical diatribe against Mr. Huntington and other political and economic figures whose intrigues resulted in the seizure of *californio* lands. She concludes the novel by identifying the aristocratic *californio* population as "white slaves," further stressing the conflict between incompatible social forces.

[8] Ruiz de Burton idealizes both Don Mariano and Clarence but in slightly different ways. Don Mariano represents the apogee of Mexican aristocracy in America. Clarence, through his ability to bridge both cultures, is idealized in that he is able to negotiate both worlds as part of his identity, and not as a conflict within it.

[9] A similar argument for the internalization of gender identity can be made in Jovita Gonzalez's *Caballero*, Paredes' *George Washington Gómez*, and Maria Cristina Mena's short story *The Education of Popo*.

[10] Quite poignantly, in this same exchange, Juan Rubio tells his son that "you are a man, and it is good, because to a Mexican being *that* is the most important thing. If you are a man, your life is half-lived; what follows does not really matter." This only underscores the importance, and the frustration, of relying upon a gendered identity to situate oneself as social being.

## Bibliography

Alemán, Jesse. "'Thank God, Lolita Is Away from Those Horrid Savages': The Politics of Whiteness in *Who Would Have Thought It.*" in *María Amparo Ruiz De Burton: Critical and Pedagogical Perspectives.* Ed. Amelia Maria de la Luz Monte and Anne Elizabeth Goldman. Lincoln, NE: U of Nebraska P, 2004.

Aranda, José F. "Contradictory Impulses: María Amparo Ruiz De Burton, Resistance Theory, and the Politics of Chicano/a Studies." *American Literature* 70 (1998): 551–79.

______. "Returning California to the People." In *María Amparo Ruiz De Burton: Critical and Pedagogical Perspectives.* Eds. Amelia Maria de la Luz Montes and Anne E. Goldman. Lincoln, NE: U of Nebraska P, 2004.

Chapman, Mary, and Glenn Hendler. *Sentimental Men: Masculinity and the Politics of Affect in American Culture*. U of California P, 1999.

Habermas, Jurgen. *Structural Transformation of the Public Sphere: An Inquiry into the Category of Bourgeois Society*. Trans. Thomas Burger and Frederick Lawrence. Cambridge: MIT P, 1989.

Hendler, Glenn. *Public Sentiments: Structures of Feeling in Nineteenth-Century American Literature*. Chapel Hill: U of North Carolina P, 2001.

Irwin, Robert McKee. *Mexican Masculinities*. Cultural Studies of the Americas vol. 11. Minneapolis: U of Minnesota P, 2003.

Mosse, George. *Nationalism and Sexuality: Respectability and Abnormal Sexuality in Modern Europe*. New York: Howard Fertig, 1985.

Nierman, Daniel, and Ernesto H. Vallejo. *The Hacienda in Mexico*. Trans. Mardith Schuetz-Miller. Austin: U of Texas P, 2003.

Paredes, Américo. *With His Pistol in His Hand: A Border Ballad and Its Hero*. Austin: U of Texas P, 1958.

Pérez, Vincent. *Remembering the Hacienda: History and Memory in the Mexican American Southwest*. College Station: Texas A&M UP, 2006.

Ruiz de Burton, María Amparo *The Squatter and the Don*. Eds. Rosaura Sánchez and Beatrice Pita. Houston: Arte Público P, 1992.

Ruiz, Julie. "Captive Identities." In *María Amparo Ruiz De Burton: Critical and Pedagogical Perspectives*. Eds. Amelia Maria de la Luz Montes and Anne E. Goldman. Lincoln, NE: U of Nebraska P, 2004.

Saldívar, Ramón. "Borderlands of Culture: Américo Paredes's *George Washington Gómez* and Chicano Literature at the End of the Twentieth Century." *American Literary History* 5.2 (1993): 272–93.

______. *Chicano Narrative : The Dialectics of Difference*. The Wisconsin Project on American Writers;. Madison, WI: U of Wisconsin P, 1990.

Sánchez, Rosaura, and Beatrice Pita. "Introduction." In *The Squatter and the Don*. Houston: Arte Publico P, 1997.

Sandage, Scott. *Born Losers: A History of Failure in America*. Cambridge, MA: Harvard UP, 2005.

Streeby, Shelley. *American Sensations: Class, Empire, and the Production of Popular Culture*. Berkeley: U of California P, 2002.

Tompkins, Jane P. *West of Everything: The Inner Life of Westerns*. New York: Oxford UP, 1992.

Villarreal, Jose Antonio. *Pocho*. New York: Anchor Books, 1959.

Warner, Michael. *Publics and Counterpublics*. Brooklyn, NY: Zone Books, 2002.

# Part IV

## Language Representation and Translation

# Representations of Language in Three Early Novels by U.S. Latinos

MARÍA IRENE MOYNA
Texas A&M University

## Introduction

This study considers the strategies used by three bilingual authors to represent bilingualism in their literary production. It thus ties in with two related but distinct issues: the literary production of bilinguals and the representation of languages in literature. The two topics are often related in practice, because bilingual authors frequently write about their linguistic and ethnic backgrounds through the medium of their two codes. They are separate topics, however, in that theoretically one need not be bilingual to represent another language for character or atmosphere building, nor is it requisite for bilingual authors to produce only code-mixed prose.

As bilinguals, Ruiz de Burton, Venegas, and González had at their disposal two linguistic codes to express themselves. In that sense, this study provides a historical antecedent to a growing literature that focuses on the writing of contemporary bilinguals. In particular, it comes to expand on the study of Spanish-English written code mixing as analyzed by Montes Alcalá for nonliterary prose, Keller and Nuessel for literature in general, Cortés Conde and Boxer and Callahan for prose, Valdés Fallis and Mendieta-Lombardo and Cintron for prose, and Pfaff and Chávez for drama.

The works of our three authors also constitute examples of the literary representation of linguistic varieties in prose, as each one reflects patterns of language use among different populations: *californios* faced with an Anglo invasion and concomitant land loss, working-class Mexicans forced into economic exile in the United States, and Tejanos on the verge of contact with Anglos in the Rio Grande Valley. In that sense, this study is a contribution to the broader issue of linguistic representation in literature, explored in works which deal with foreign speech, bilingual speakers, and contact varieties by Azevedo, Callahan, Coll, and Hess, among others.

For the specific topic of Spanish-English mixing in the United States, studies have focused on literature written since the 1960s, partly because of the saliency of the phenomenon today, and partly, one suspects, due to the unavailability of earlier texts. Some exceptions are found in the World War I *corridos* mentioned in Martínez and Lomelí (287), and even earlier antecedents of Nahuatl-Spanish and English-Spanish mixing in Mexican literature appear in Leal (93). The present study thus comes to fill the gap by covering three earlier works, allowing us to look back on the emergence of this phenomenon. By doing this, it shows that strategies of language representation are inextricably linked with the conditions of literary production, including the type of audience targeted and the overarching narrative and ideological purposes of each author. A contribution of this paper is therefore to show that language representation is not random but results from the interplay between a prevalent power structure and an author's specific narrative and ideological purposes.

## Authors and Their Works

With this in mind, let us now briefly introduce the three authors, paying special attention to their linguistic and educational backgrounds, when such information is available. The circumstances of each novel's production and publication are also highlighted, since that may have influenced their portrayals of language.[1]

Our first author, María Amparo Ruiz de Burton, was born and raised in an upper-class family in Baja California and came to Alta California at the time of annexation, where she married an American officer she had met in La Paz. She became fully literate in English while she lived in California and the East Coast, where her husband was stationed during the War of Secession. After she became a widow, she returned to San Diego to fight for recognition of her land titles and attempt several business ventures.

*The Squatter and the Don* was Ruiz de Burton's second novel. Its main themes were the plight of landed *californios* and the deleterious effects of bad legislation and corrupt capitalism. Set against this political and social backdrop, the main plot is a love story between a *californio* girl, Mercedes Alamar, and Clarence Darrell, the son of an Anglo settler. Ruiz de Burton pursued two main purposes with the publication of her book. On the one hand, she had an ideological aim, i.e., to bring the plight of land litigation faced by *californios* to the public eye and convince the Anglo majority of their unfair treatment. She also attempted to achieve commercial success, which would help overcome her ever-precarious financial situation. If she was to reach her goals, she had to earn her share of the linguistic marketplace, as defined by Bourdieu, by writing in English to appeal to Anglos, but simultaneously including Spanish to portray *californios*.

Our second author, Daniel Venegas, was very popular in his day, yet very little biographical information is available about him. A little more is known about his literary endeavors, thanks to the fact that he published a humorous weekly, *El Malcriado*, in Los Angeles between 1924 and 1929, and wrote popular plays advertised and reviewed in local papers between 1924 and 1933. His productions enjoyed success among popular audiences since they chronicled life in the American metropolis among the humblest social groups, i.e., the Mexican immigrant workers, and did so in their own popular language.

*Las aventuras de don Chipote o cuando los pericos mamen,* in particular, was published in installments by *El Heraldo* of Los Angeles in 1928. Written in Spanish in the picaresque tradition, its main theme was the denunciation of the ill-treatment of working-class Mexicans in the United States. It is narrated as the satirical saga of a Mexican who comes to the United States following dreams of prosperity but instead falls victim to the rapaciousness of others and his own gullibility. The narrative follows the main character, Don Chipote, from the Mexican interior to El Paso, Los Angeles, and back to Mexico, where he arrives poorer but wiser than he was when he left. With its publication, Venegas attempted to show the importance of preserving "el México de afuera," maintaining loyalty to the mother country even outside its borders, and to alert Mexicans against the dangers of believing the myth of the American Dream and becoming absorbed into mainstream culture.

Our last author, Jovita González, was born in the Rio Grande Valley, in the town of Roma, Texas, in 1904. Raised in a prominent Tejano family where Spanish was the only language spoken, she educated herself in her native language and later in English. Overcoming the hurdles of her gender and minority status, she would eventually become a teacher of Spanish and would work in South Texas. In the early 1930s she was granted a master's degree by the University of Texas–Austin for her research on border folklore. Throughout her life she continued to be actively involved in teaching and folklore research along the border (González: ix–xiii, Chase: 122–126).

*Dew on the Thorn* was written between 1926 and 1940, and published posthumously after painstaking editorial work by José Limón. It describes traditional life along the Mexican-American border and the incipient changes brought about by the arrival of Anglos in the early twentieth century. The plot is a series of loosely connected vignettes which serve as the vehicle to retell numerous border folktales, many of which González had published separately.

Although all three writers were working in the American Southwest and combined Spanish and English in some way, each one had distinct narrative aims. For Ruiz de Burton, the literary challenge was to find a way to portray bilingualism positively without alienating the mainly monolingual English-speaking intended audience. For González, who also attempted to reach monolingual English speakers, the main goal was to represent faithfully the Tejano culture and folklore she had laboriously researched. Finally, Venegas shared argumentative and didactic aims with Ruiz de Burton and González, but he chose satire to reach his working class audience.

## Language Representation

In this section, each of the three novels is described in terms of how language is portrayed, including the frequency of mixing and the social and stylistic varieties of language represented, as well as the specific strategies employed to incorporate each of the codes in the text.

### *The Squatter and the Don*

In general, Spanish in *The Squatter and the Don* is scarce: in a novel that runs over three hundred pages in its modern edition, there are some eighty-two clear examples of Spanish or references to Spanish use, i.e., about one case every three and a half pages. In general, the language is more frequent in descriptive or narrative passages that evoke the *californio* environment and lifestyle, and particularly so in dialogue, while it is totally absent from discursive and argumentative passages.

Spanish is not simply a vehicle to depict the linguistic minority: it is used by *californios* and Anglos alike, especially by highly educated Anglos who have become accepted members of the local ranchero elite. Thus, Ruiz de Burton tacitly recognized that the value of a language is dependent on the value of those who speak it (Bourdieu: 22). For Spanish to be socially valued, it had to be associated with cosmopolitanism and divested of any traces of subordinate identity. In fact, all upper-class protagonists speak both English and Spanish, one of which they have learned as adults, thus eliciting metalinguistic comments about their proficiency and their efforts at language mastery (1).

1. Don Mariano excused himself for not speaking English more fluently. "If you don't understand me I will repeat my words until I make my meaning clear, but I hope you will ask me to repeat them; or perhaps, some of these young gentlemen will do me the kindness to be my interpreter," said he.
   [. . . ]

"You speak very good English, Señor. We understand you perfectly. You do not require an interpreter," Clarence said. (86)[2]

2. When for months past he had thought, time and again, of a probable interview with Doña Josefa, he had imagined himself talking to that queenly lady in his most stately Spanish. But now he had taken hold of Cervantes' language – I may say, jumped into it [ . . . ] (170)

Ruiz de Burton strived to show her upper-class characters as speakers of the standard variety (cf. the reference to Peninsular Spanish in 2). As if to underscore the cosmopolitan value of Spanish, other languages of high prestige (French and Latin, in particular) also make an appearance in the novel (3).

3. "The fact of the matter is that you will attract me always, no matter under what desguise," he whispered to Mercedes.
   "*Pas si bête*," she answered, stammering fearfully, and looking the prettier for it. (202)

On the other hand, monolingualism in nonstandard varieties is an undesirable trait of the lower-class antagonists. For example, the ignorant squatters only speak a nonstandard variety of English, peppered with bastardized Spanish borrowings. In an exchange between squatter Mathews and Don Mariano (4), the latter echoes the former but in the process corrects some of his borrowings and avoids nonstandard verbs.

4. "I don't want any cattle. I ain't no *vaquero* to go *busquering* around and *lassoing* cattle. I'll *lasso* myself; what do I know about whirling a *lariat*?" said Mathews.
   [ . . . ]
   "You will not have to be a *vaquero*. I don't go *busquering* around *lassoing*, unless I wish to do so," said the Don. "You can hire an Indian boy to do that part. They know how to handle *la reata* and *echar el lazo* to perfection . . . " (89–90)

Likewise, the native California Indians, who are portrayed negatively as lazy and indolent and thus constitute a second type of antagonists, are presented as speaking Spanish exclusively. Worse still, Indians often speak Spanish in contexts where it is impolite and inappropriate to do so. For example, in (5), which comes at the end of a scene where the Alamar men have lassoed old Darrell to prevent him from injuring Don Mariano, the Indian hands laugh at the sight of the old gringo riding on his horse, tied up and helpless. Note that in their mocking comments, they use excessively informal *tuteo* forms, inappropriate to address an older person of a higher class, and nonstandard expressions (the borrowing *escuata*—'squatter,' the form *orcas* for *ahorcas*—'you choke'). Although he himself is responsible for Darrell's present state, Victoriano Alamar is not tolerant toward this outburst of disrespectful mirth in Spanish, thus showing that unlike the Indian hands he minds his manners.

> 5. *"¡Apa! Viejo escuata o cabestreas o te orcas,"* cried one.
> *"No le afloje patroncito Gabriel,"* said the other. [ . . . ]
> *"¡Apriétate, viejo! ¡apriétate, míralo! ¡ya se ladea!"* cried again one *vaquero.*
> *"Creo que el viejo escuata va chispo,"* said the other.
> *"¿Qué es eso? ¿A qué vienen acá? ¿Quién los convida? ¡Cállense la boca, no sean malcriados, váyanse!"* said Victoriano, turning to them in great indignation. (231)

When incorporating Spanish into the English text, Ruiz de Burton was mindful of the linguistic limitations of Anglo readers and careful that Spanish would not affect comprehensibility. For that she resorted to meta-switches, i.e., explicit references to the code used without any overt shift in language, thus requiring no linguistic adjustment from readers other that their suspension of disbelief (Azevedo: 70). To the examples mentioned above (cf. 1,2), we could add others where Ruiz de Burton took pains to underscore the *californios*' knowledge and appreciation of both Spanish and English (6).

> 6. "Why don't you talk like Gabriel? He always uses good language—in Spanish or in English," Carlota added. (109)

When Spanish actually appears in the text it is in the form of lexemes, phrases, or interjections which Ruiz de Burton chose among those already quite well-known by California Anglos in the second half of the nineteenth century. Spanish tends to cluster around topics relating to the old economic order of extensive ranching, where English is indebted to Spanish throughout the Southwest. There are words that refer to architecture (*rancho, pueblo, corral, patio*), the people involved in ranching (*patrón, vaquero, mayordomo*), and related instruments and activities (*lazo, reata, venta)*. Other sources of Spanish words are cooking and everyday habits (e.g., *siesta*), family relationships, and titles (*hermanita, patroncito, señoritas, don/doña*). The common currency of many of these words and expressions can be corroborated by contrasting them against cowboy terms in Adams's cowboy lingo dictionary, and Stewart's compilation of word lists published in nineteenth-century California newspapers for the benefit of newly arrived Anglos.

Ruiz de Burton normally preferred to present these borrowings in their original spelling and morphology. Thus, for example, she overwhelmingly favored the spelling *lazo* over *lasso, lariat* normally appears as *(la) reata*, and the plural form of *corral* appears as *corrales* rather than *corrals*. This strategy, which could be called 'eye code–switching' (cf. the notion of eye dialect in Traugott and Pratt 339), served a dual goal, aligned with both Ruiz de Burton's literary and ideological purposes. On the other hand, it was a nonintrusive way to make the presence of Spanish felt, by foreignizing her text without impeding comprehension. On the other hand, eye code–switching shows that the author was protective of the integrity of Spanish and refused to nativize it, a sign of her linguistic pride and of the status she wished Spanish to be granted in the United States as a language of privilege and culture on an equal footing with English.

Ruiz de Burton occasionally indulged in bilingual humor, subtly suggesting the superiority of bilingual readers who would appreciate it. For instance, in (7), a pun based on the relationship between the noun *merced* 'mercy' and the proper name *Mercedes* is attributed to a non-native speaker of Spanish, underscoring that sophisticated bilingual humor need not be an ethnic marker and that the in-group was in fact a bilingual elite made up of *californios* and Anglos alike.

7. "Be merciful, remember your name is Mercedes," said poor, embarrassed Bob. (204)

To summarize, Ruiz de Burton's approach to bilingualism is conflictive. On the one hand, she presents cosmopolitanism as the ideal of high culture and she paints a positive picture of Anglo and *californio* bilinguals as educated, well-bred, and sophisticated. They are fluent in two standard varieties and capable of making and understanding jokes, idioms, puns, and other verbal play in both languages. On the other hand, anticipating a monolingual readership who might be prejudiced against Spanish and certainly not very proficient in it, she submitted to their limitations by using Spanish sparingly, choosing lexemes they were likely to understand.

### *Las aventuras de don Chipote, o cuando los pericos mamen*

Daniel Venegas's novel was written in Spanish but mirrors *The Squatter and the Don* in the sense that English is scarce and its density varies by text type and locale. As one would expect, it is more frequent in dialogue and in references to the United States, and less so in passages that relate to Mexico. However, unlike *The Squatter and the Don*, protagonists in *Don Chipote* are far from being depicted as elite bilinguals. For example, his antihero, Don Chipote, is a monolingual speaker oblivious to his new linguistic milieu (8). Spanish speakers belong to the lowest ranks of their own social hierarchy and are thus restricted to the nonstandard linguistic varieties, including rural dialect and urban *caló* (Kanellos 1984: 361).

> 8. —Mire usté, amo, para que mi compañero no se vaya solo, he decidido irme con él, de modo que deme mi tiempo en seguida.
> El mayordomo se quedó como antes y después, pues no entendía español sino tanto como Policarpo entendía inglés. (79)

Upon their arrival in the United States, the immigrants come into contact with equally uneducated Anglos, who are in a slightly higher position in the labor system. Their power is often manifested through abusive language which is lost on the characters but not on the readers. For example, in (9), Don Chipote's naïve interpretations of what his boss really calls him and his friend Policarpo are comedic because the writer and readers are fully aware of the meaning of *gaideme* (<goddammit), and *sanabagan* (<son of a gun). Yet, Don Chipote's blissful ignorance protects him against the sting of these insults, neutralizing them.

> 9. [ . . . ] Como no puede decir mi nombre me dice Chipoto y a Policarpo le dice Polocarpo, pero esto de vez en cuando, pues desde que entramos al trabajo hasta que salimos nos habla por un apodo muy chistoso que yo no entiendo bien, creo que es "gaideme" "sanabagan." Yo creo que nos habla así porque nuestros nombres no los puede pronunciar. (69)

Although Venegas's antihero is solidly monolingual and remains so throughout his American experience, there are some characters who speak or claim to speak English. Their depiction allows us to compare Venegas's views on bilingualism with those of Ruiz de Burton. In *Las aventuras*, Mexicans who have become acculturated to the United States and learned English are not examples to be emulated but tend to be derided. Their accommodation to the majority language is interpreted at best as humorously pretentious, as when Policarpo inappropriately flaunts his knowledge of English by code switching, much to the puzzlement of Don Chipote (10).

> 10. —¿De modo que tú ganabas seis de los de aquí?
> —Seguro que yes.
> —¿Y qué es eso de yes? —preguntó don Chipote con la boca abierta cada vez más.
> —¡Ah, esquiusme! —dijo Pitacio— se me olvidaba que ustedes no le saben nada a la tatacha del toquinglés y yo ya les estaba hablando en eso. Pos mire —prosiguió—, eso de yes, quiere decir como si dijéramos sí en nuestra lengua. (22)

The presentation of non-Spanish-speaking ethnic Mexicans is much less humorous and tolerant, especially since it is assumed that they probably know Spanish and are unhelpful to their compatriots rather than revealing their own identity (11).

11. [ . . . ] pronto detuvieron a un sujeto que por su color parecía mexicano. [ . . . ]

—Oiga, jefecito; dispense su mercé; ¿no quiere decirnos dónde podemos jayar trabajo?

A lo que el interpelado contestó poniendo una cara de desentendido:

—Juat du yu sei? Ai du no tok spanish.

[ . . . ] ¿Podrá haber más maldad que la de estos malditos, que por pasar por gringos, se niegan a hablar su propio idioma renegando del país donde nacieron? Creo que no. (45)

An examination of the strategies used in *Las aventuras* to represent English shows some commonalities with *The Squatter*. For example, there are frequent metalinguistic comments (12), which refer not to language proficiency, but rather lack thereof, resulting in humorous misunderstandings.

12. Cuando llegó su turno, se dejó ir como gato al bofe y allí fueron los aprietos, pues no entendió nada de lo que le dijeron por lo que hubo que llamar a un intérprete y con su ayuda, supo el empleado que se llamaba Chipote de Jesús María Domínguez, que no sabía leer ni escribir y que no traía con qué pagar. (30)

The different cultural value of Spanish and English in the United States is apparent in the lack of parallelism between borrowings in *Las aventuras* and those in *The Squatter*. Here English clusters around topics relating to the new industrial landscape, such as the railway (*suplai*—"supply," *traque*—"track," *dipo*—"depot"), new foods and drinks (*jamaneg*—"ham and egg," *jaqueques*—"hot cakes," *saida*—"cider"), and urban landmarks (*postofe*—"post office," *cho*—"show"). There is also incipient evidence of morphological adaptation of these borrowings to Spanish, prefiguring one of the most creative and maligned features of modern U.S. Spanish: *puchar* (to push), *troca* (truck, and its diminutive *troquecito).*

Another comic device used by Venegas is the representation of interlanguage, i.e., the simplified version of English that immigrants produce (13). For example, Spanish sound-symbol correspondences reflect non-native pronunciation and structures and show that English is filtered through the perception of Spanish speakers who have acquired the language orally with no formal instruction. This treatment of orthography is diametrically opposed to the respectful preservation of spelling in *The Squatter.*

13. Inmediatamente Policarpo tomó aire de sabio y, queriendo presumirle a don Chipote que ya sabía inglés, pidió la orden en esta forma: "Gimi cofi y donas." Como el mesero le preguntara a don Chipote qué le servía, este peló los ojos, pero su parna estaba listo y dijo: "Gifi sem tu, sabe," con lo que quedó muy pagado de su sabiduría y don Chipote asombrado de lo que sabía su cuate en tan poco tiempo. (102)

To summarize, for Venegas, English was an inevitable extraneous element for Mexicans in the United States, but one which threatened to weaken their unity and cultural identity. His novel was written for an audience who spoke at least some English, since a great deal of the humor is based on understanding what Chipote and Policarpo do not. On the other hand, it presents a distorted and deformed English, which helps to divest it of its voice of authority (Bourdieu: 20). By becoming a humorous device, its symbolic power is weakened and the myth of the American dream is deconstructed (cf. Baeza Ventura: 147).

*Dew on the Thorn*

Our last novel posed a complex discursive problem to its author, who was trying to be ethnographically and culturally accurate even as she represented a monolingual Spanish-speaking community to a mostly monolingual English-speaking readership.[3] Although it is never stated explicitly, it is understood that in this novel English is a fiction: whenever it appears in the mouths of the characters, it "stands" for Spanish. Additionally, of our three authors González is the one who used the secondary language most frequently. Like Ruiz de Burton and Venegas, she makes use of it mostly in dialogue, but not a page goes by without some example of Spanish in the narrative and descriptive passages as well.

As far as language proficiency goes, the overwhelming majority of the characters are monolingual Spanish speakers, regardless of class. Those who know English are singled out by this fact, and they are invariably men who have learned it by moving away. In the case of upper-class men, the migration may be for the express purpose of acquiring English (14), while for the working class, it is often prompted by the need to find employment (15). The acquisition of English is a matter of much discussion, including references to popular beliefs that it can be facilitated by adoption of other Anglo traits, such as changes in diet (17). González, ever the ethnographer, missed no opportunity to underscore the unity between language and culture.

14. "If Ramón will let me, I'd like to take him home with me, teach him the classics, and send him to the American school to learn English." (166)

15. [Pedro, the *venadero*] was a traveled man, had seen the world, spoke English, and knew many stories with which he entertained his listeners on winter nights. (77)

16. He had been told that if he ate salt pork he would soon learn to speak English. Bah! What a lie! He had eaten it three times a day and had only learned to say "Yes." (77)

Spanish is spoken in all its sociolinguistic and stylistic richness. For example, the upper classes use the standard variety, which is taught in the local school (17). The teacher, a Mexican, has been employed to educate the local boys, in particular the *hacendado* children, and is a well-respected member of the community. At least at the outset of the novel, education in the Spanish standard is all that is necessary for the local gentry. As Anglos start to impinge on the life of the valley, however, English comes to be seen as a necessary complement.

17. The mornings were usually devoted to reading from books of travel, writing, arithmetic, and grammar. The last subject was especially stressed. "A gentleman is recognized by the language he uses, and you as such, must use only the best Spanish," he insisted. (144)

On the other hand, there is also evidence of nonstandard varieties (18). Interestingly, the existence of an indigenous servant population adds nonnative speakers to the linguistic mix and requires González to suggest, through the medium of English, the features of their Spanish-based interlanguage (19).

18. Now followed the usual "*puema*" used for such occasions. (105)

19. "Singing, master?" repeated Ambrosio again in surprise. "I no sing. Ambrosio think," he answered [ . . . ] "That no singing, master," he continued. "Ambrosio think aloud. He think he is Aztec warrior. Spring come soon, cactus bloom, flowers will smell and Ambrosio think of his home in far Xochimilco." (123)

Turning now to the specific textual strategies used to represent language, González also employs meta-switches, but because the novel has established Spanish as the unmarked code of choice, comments about language performance or proficiency refer to English. Like in *The Squatter and the Don,* countless rural terms are borrowed from Spanish for cattle ranching, architecture, social customs, dress, cooking, and food. To these one must add many local terms for plants (*cenizo*—"gray Texas shrub," *nopal*—"cactus," *maguey*), animals (*javalinas*—"wild boars," *zenzontle*—"mocking bird") meteorology (*hielo prieto*—"black frost"), and occupations (*huellero*—"tracker," *venadero*—"deer hunter"). There are also frequent references to Catholic rites (*nacimiento*—"nativity scene," *Angelitos de Dios*—"God's little angels," *Ave María*—"Hail Mary"). Both of these new semantic fields of borrowing show González' willingness to embrace the mestizo border culture, something which sets her apart from Ruiz de Burton's attempts at whitening her *californio* characters.

Two additional strategies are unique to González among our three writers, and in line with her didactic purposes. The first one is the rather systematic use of translations and explanations side by side with Spanish terms (20, 21). In this category we can include the numerous songs and poems that González presents only in English translation.

20. "Oh, just for *un tiempecito*, a very short time." (60)

21. Stone benches, called *pollitos* because they were attached and formed part of the house, were on either side of the main door. (17)

Secondly, González foreignizes her English by calquing Spanish word order or employing unusual proverbs, translated word for word from Spanish. Thus, for example, in (22) the highly marked word order imitates the much freer syntactic possibilities of Spanish. In (23), the Spanish speaker will not fail to recognize some version of the saying *Tanto va el cántaro a la fuente que al fin se rompe*, but monolingual English speakers will be surprised by the novel phrasing to express the inevitability of a result after constant repetition of a process.

22. [ . . . ] "not a bit of wood have I in the house. Hard enough it is to start a fire with green mesquite wood, but much harder will it be tomorrow when the wood is wet." (122)

23. "Who is he?"
"That's Don Luis."
"The one who used to write love letters?"
"*El mismísimo*, the very same. Caught at last!"
"You mean married?"
"Yes—*¡Pobre hombre!*—He is not much pleased about it, though. However, he has no one to blame but himself; so many trips takes the water jug to the well that it ends by being broken,' is the saying [ . . . ]." (130)

To summarize, González understood that bilingualism was a necessary step for Mexican Americans to preserve their culture and make it known to mainstream Americans. Knowledge of English was essential to exercise linguistic and cultural rights, so that the integrity of the border community could only be guaranteed if some external influence was permitted. The irony of having to "become Americans in order to remain Mexicans" (González: 154) was not lost on her. She also recognized the unity of language and culture, and the inevitability of bilingualism leading to biculturalism. At the end of her novel, the children's voices in the yard shout out home runs and Spanish interjections alternatively, a poignant metaphor for the hybridization that is sweeping their valley.

### Conclusions

Ruiz de Burton, Venegas, and González employed some common strategies to depict their bilingual worlds. They all expressed awareness of the issue of language contact and made metalinguistic references to language use and proficiency. In their choice of strategies to represent language, they used lexeme borrowing more than other types of language mixing. However, these three authors were moved by different views about the legitimacy and value of the two languages. One embraced balanced, elite, Spanish-English bilingualism, another one rejected it as a tool of exploitation and abuse, and the last one saw English as a necessary means to preserve a Spanish-based culture. This study has shown that individual authors' language choices can best be assessed in the context of the environment that motivated them and of each author's specific aims. In order to bring out the diversity of the Hispanic experience in the United States, the analysis of code mixing in large literary corpora must be accompanied by microanalyses of individual authors such as the one attempted here.

## Notes

[1] For fuller biographies and appraisal of each author's literary impact, readers are directed to a growing literature. For Ruiz de Burton, one can consult works by Crawford, Oden, Luis-Brown, Aranda, Goldman, Montes, Montes and Goldman, Pita, Alemán, and Ruiz de Burton's own correspondence, published and edited by Sánchez and Pita. Venegas has been the object of fewer studies, but some important analyses are found in work by Baeza Ventura, Childers, González-Berry and Rodríguez, and Kanellos. For González, one can recommend articles by Limón, Reyna, and the doctoral dissertations of Cotera, López, López-Peláez Casellas, and Velásquez Treviño.

[2] All page numbers in the examples refer to the editions cited.

[3] The fact that the novel was never published and the audience never materialized does not eliminate the certainty that González had an audience in mind when she wrote the manuscript, and that she anticipated it to be mostly monolingual.

## Works Cited

Adams, Ramón F. *Cowboy Lingo*. Boston: Houghton Mifflin, 1936.

Alemán, Jesse. "Historical Amnesia and the Vanishing Mestiza: The Problem of Race in *The Squatter and the Don* and *Ramona*." *Aztlán*. 27 (2002) : 59–93.

Aranda Jr., José F. "Contradictory Impulses: María Amparo Ruiz de Burton, Resistance Theory, and the Politics of Chicano/a Studies." *American Literature*. 70 (1998): 551–579.

Azevedo, Milton M. "Linguistic aspects of the representation of foreigner talk in Brazilian literature." *Sintagma* 4 (1992): 69–76.

______. "Considerations on Literary Dialect in Spanish and Portuguese." *Hispania* 85 (2002): 505–515.

Baeza Ventura, Gabriela. "El aspecto carnavalesco en *Las aventuras de don Chipote, o cuando los pericos mamen*." In *Recovering the U.S. Hispanic Literary Heritage. Volume IV*. Eds. José F. Aranda, Jr. and Silvio Torres-Saillant. Houston: Arte Público P, 2002. 145–152.

Bourdieu, Pierre. "L'économie des échanges linguistiques." *Langue française*. 33 (1977):17–34.

Callahan, Laura. "Metalinguistic References in a Spanish/English Corpus." *Hispania*. 84 (2001): 417–427.

______. "The Matrix Language Frame Model and Spanish/English Codeswitching in Fiction." *Language and Communication*. 22 (2002): 1–16.

______. *Spanish/English Codeswitching in a Written Corpus*. Amsterdam: John Benjamins, 2004.

Chase, Cida S. "Jovita González de Mireles." *Dictionary of Literary Biography. Volume 122: Chicano Writers*. Second series. Eds. Francisco A. Lomelí and Carl R. Shirley. Detroit: Bruccoli Clark Layman, 1992. 122–126.

Childers, William. "Chicanoizing Don Quixote: For Luis Andrés Murillo." *Aztlán*. 27 (2002): 87–117.

Coll, Magdalena. "La narrativa de Saúl Ibargoyen Islas como representación literaria de una frontera lingüística." *Hispania* 80 (1997): 745–752.

Cortés Conde, Florencia y Diana Boxer. "Bilingual Word-Play in Literary Discourse: The Creation of Relational Identity." *Language and Literature*. 11 (2002): 137–151.

Cotera, María Eugenia. *Native Speakers: Locating Early Expressions of US Third World Feminist Discourse: A Comparative Analysis of the Ethnographic and Literary Writing of Ella Cara Deloria and Jovita González*. Diss, Stanford U., 2001.

Crawford, Kathleen. "María Amparo Ruiz de Burton: The General's Lady." *Journal of San Diego History*. 30 (1984): 198–211.

Goldman, Anne E. "'I Think Our Romance is Spoiled,'" or, Crossing Genres: California History in Helen Hunt Jackson's *Ramona* and María Amparo Ruiz de Burton's *The Squatter and the Don*." In *Over The Edge: Remapping The American West*. Eds. Valerie J. Matsumoto and Blake Allmendinger. Berkeley: U of California P, 1999. 65–84.

González, Jovita. *Dew on the Thorn*. Ed. José Limón. Houston: Arte Público P, 1997.

González-Berry, Erlinda, and Alfred Rodríguez. "*Las aventuras de don Chipote*: De lo quijotesco a lo carnavalesco." *Cuadernos Americanos*. 55 (1996): 110–117.

Gutiérrez, Ramón, and Genaro Padilla, Eds. *Recovering the U.S. Hispanic literary heritage.* Houston: Arte Público P, 1993.

Hess, Natalie. "Code Switching and Style Shifting as Markers of Liminality in Literature." *Language and Literature*. 5 (1996): 5–18.

Kanellos, Nicolás. "*Las aventuras de don Chipote*, obra precursora de la novela chicana." *Hispania*. 67 (1984): 358–363.

Keller, Gary D. "The Literary Stratagems Available to the Bilingual Chicano Writer." In *The Identification and Analysis of Chicano Literature*. Ed. Francisco Jiménez. New York: Bilingual P/Editorial Bilingüe, 1979. 263–316

Leal, Luis. "Truth-Telling Tongues: Early Chicano Poetry." In *Recovering the U.S. Hispanic literary heritage.* Volume I. Eds. Ramón Gutiérrez y Genaro Padilla. Houston: Arte Público P, 1993. 91–105.

Limón, José E. "Folklore, Gendered Repression, and Cultural Critique: The Case of Jovita González." *Texas Studies in Literature and Language*. 35 (1993): 453–473.

López, Shirley. *Remembering the Brave Women: Chicana Literature on the Texas-Mexico Border, 1900–1950.* Diss., U. of Iowa, 2004.

López-Peláez Casellas, Milagros. *Jovita González's "Dew on the Thorn": A Chicana Response to Patriarchy.* Diss., Arizona State U., 2003.

Luis-Brown, David. "'White Slaves' and the 'Arrogant Mestiza'": Reconfiguring Whiteness in *The Squatter and the Don* and *Ramona*." *American Literature.* 69 (1997): 813–839.

Martínez, Julio A., and Francisco A. Lomelí. *Chicano Literature. A Reference Guide*. Westport: Greenwood P, 1985.

Mendieta-Lombardo, Eva, and Zaida A. Cintron. "Marked and Unmarked Choices of Code Switching in Bilingual Poetry." *Hispania.* 78 (1995): 565–572.

Montes, Amelia María de la Luz. *"Es Necesario Mirar Bien": Letter Making, Fiction Writing, and American Nationhood in the Nineteenth Century.* Diss., U. of Denver, 2000.

______. "María Amparo Ruiz de Burton Negotiates American Literary Politics and Culture." In *Challenging Boundaries: Gender and Periodization*. Eds. Joyce Warren and Margaret Dickie. Athens: U of Georgia P, 2000. 202–225.

______ and Anne E. Goldman (eds.). *María Amparo Ruiz de Burton: Critical and Pedagogical Perspectives*. Lincoln: U of Nebraska P, 2004.

Montes Alcalá, Cecilia. "Written Codeswitching: Powerful Bilingual Images." *Codeswitching Worldwide*. Ed. R. Jacobson. Berlin: Mouton de Gruyter, 2001. 193–219.

______. "Oral vs. Written Code-switching Contexts in English-Spanish Bilingual Narratives." *La lingüística aplicada a finales del siglo XX*. Vol. 2. Eds. Isabel de la Cruz Cabanillas, Carmen Santamaría, Cristina Tejedor, and Carmen Valero. Alcalá de Henares: Universidad de Alcalá, 2001. 715–720.

______. "Dear Amigo": Exploring Code-switching in Personal Letters. In *Selected Proceedings of the Second Workshop on Spanish Sociolinguistics*. Eds. Lotfi Sayahi and Maurice Westmoreland. Somerville, MA: Cascadilla, 2005. 102–108.

Oden, Frederick B. *The Maid of Monterey. The Life of María Amparo Ruiz de Burton, 1832–1895*. Thesis, U. of San Diego, 1992.

Nuessel, Frank. "Bilingualism, Code-Switching and Lexical Borrowing in Hispanic Literature." *Languages Across Borders: Selected Papers From the International Conference of the American Society of Geolinguistics, October 17-18, 2000.* Eds. Leonard R. N. Ashley and Wayne H. Finke. East Rockaway, NY: Cummings & Hathaway, 2000. 71–84.

Pfaff, Carol and Laura Chávez. "Spanish-English Code-switching: Literary Reflections of Natural Discourse." In *Missions in Conflict: Essays on the U.S.-Mexican Relations and Chicano Culture*. Eds. Renate von Bardeleben, Dietrich Briesemeister, and Juan Bruce-Novoa. Tübingen: Gunter Narr, 1986. 229–254.

Pita, Beatrice. "Trials and Tribulations: The Life and Works of María Amparo Ruiz de Burton." In *U.S. Latino Literature*. Eds. Harold Augenbraum and Margarite Fernández-Olmos. Westport: Greenwood P, 2000. 11–19.

Reyna, Sergio. "Jovita González y su obra folclórico-literaria: Reconstrucción de la historia cultural méxico-americana." In *Recovering the U.S. Hispanic Literary Heritage. Volume IV*. Eds. José F. Aranda, Jr. and Silvio Torres-Saillant. Houston: Arte Público, 2002. 184–200.

Ruiz de Burton, María Amparo. 1885. *The Squatter and the Don*. 2nd edition. Introduction and notes by Rosaura Sánchez and Beatrice Pita. Houston: Arte Público P, 1997.

______. *Conflicts of Interest: The Letters of María Amparo Ruiz de Burton*. Eds. Rosaura Sánchez and Beatrice Pita. Houston: Arte Público P, 2001.

Stewart, George R. "Two Spanish Word Lists from California in 1857." *American Speech.* 16 (1941): 260–269.

Traugott, Elizabeth C., and Mary Louise Pratt. *Linguistics for Students of Literature*. New York: Harcourt Brace Jovanovich, 1980.

Valdés Fallis, Guadalupe. "Code-Switching in Bilingual Chicano Poetry." *Hispania* 59 (1976): 877–886.

Velásquez Treviño, Gloria Louise. *Cultural Ambivalence in Early Chicana Prose Fiction*. Diss., Stanford U., 1986.

Venegas, Daniel. 1928. *Las aventuras de don Chipote, o cuando los pericos mamen.* Ed. Nicolás Kanellos. Houston: Arte Público P, 1999.

# "Keeping it Real": The Translation of *El sol de Texas*

**ETHRIAM CASH BRAMMER DE GONZALES**
Wayne State University

It is a commonly held belief among literary translators that one should render a specific literary form in a source language as the same form in the target language: e.g. a sonnet as a sonnet, a villanelle as a villanelle, a novel as a novel, etc. This sounds somewhat elementary, but it is unfortunately quite common to see Spanish and Italian sonnets from the Renaissance converted into some sort of modernistic cross-genre prose poem when English translators privilege literal sense over the aesthetic sensibilities communicated by this kind of traditional verse form. In the article "Building a Translation, The Reconstruction Business: Poem 145 of Sor Juana Inés de la Cruz," renowned literary translator Margaret Sayers Peden chastises a number of English translators for ignoring rhyme and meter when translating the seventeenth-century Mexican poet's sonnets. Sayers Peden begins her article by likening the craft of translation to working with ice cubes: first, one must melt the original ice cube down to its water base; some molecules are lost due to evaporation; others are gained through condensation; but, in the end, when it is time to reconstitute, or "reconstruct," the ice cube in a new tray, one would like it to still look like an ice cube, not melted ice and not a popsicle (13). A sonnet in translation should still be a sonnet, not an unrhymed, nonmetrical prose poem.

Similarly, when attempting to adhere to Dryden's eighth "commandment" of translation (Thou shalt "[m]ake the author speak the contemporary English he would have spoken") (via Steiner 28), translators of historical literary texts often struggle to find linguistic equivalences from within the same historical time period as the original in order to more faithfully render a work, without doing it so much that the translation becomes inaccessible for the target audience. Therefore, for one translating Cervantes, for example, the intermittent application of a kind of Shakespearian English lexicon—sprinkling a "thy" or "thou" here or there—would seem justified, because the two writers were more or less contemporaries and many of the cultural realities of the historical period in Europe (following the gestalt theory of translation) would be similar, if not the same, even though the two lived in different parts of Europe and spoke different European tongues. However, the English translator of *El Cid* should think twice before attempting to render the Spanish epic in the Old English of *Beowulf,* because the majority of people who read in English today still wouldn't be able to access the translation, thus defeating the whole purpose of translation in the first place. Again, an ice cube to an ice cube, not an ice sculpture—regardless of how impressive such a Herculean effort might represent.

And so, if a translator needs to render a form as a form, a genre as a genre and a historical period as a historical period, then to properly translate a text like Conrado Espinosa's *El sol de Texas* (1926), an example of the Mexican/American realist/naturalist novel, he or she should render the work in the voice of an American realist/naturalist from the early part of the twentieth century.

But first things first. The translator must clearly establish that the work is, in fact, a Mexican and/or American realist and/or naturalist novel, especially in light of the text's frequent references to Catholic religious practice which seem to run contrary to the "objective" and "scientific" aesthetic principals developed by the founders of the naturalist movement, like Émile Zola (1840–1902).

## Nec Verbum Verbo: On the Teeter-totter with Espinosa, Balzac and Zola

At the 2005 American Literary Translators Association (ALTA) conference in Montreal, Quebec, renowned Sicilian translator Gaetano Cipolla made the analogy that translation is like riding on a teeter-totter with the author of the original text: up and down you go, sometimes better, sometimes worse, but always trying to maintain a certain balance and equilibrium within a given domain for the faithful representation of the text in the target language. If this is true, then establishing a work's historical period and the literary conventions of its time seems like a good way of making sure that you are hopping on the right teeter-totter to begin with.

Because literary translation is the translation of culture as much as written text, it is important to note that, though originally written and published in San Antonio, Texas, *El sol de Texas* is a work written in Spanish by a Mexican author, Conrado Espinosa (1897–1977), who eventually returned to his country of origin. Therefore, in order to clearly establish that *El sol de Texas* is, indeed, a work of Mexican/American realism/naturalism, one should look at both the

Mexican *and* American definitions of the period, perhaps even privileging the evolution of realism and naturalism within the Mexican or Spanish-American literary traditions, as it is clearly a more evident influence on Espinosa's work, especially when one considers the fact that the author was a journalist in Mexico before ever moving to the United States and, in the text itself, he makes numerous references to important works of Spanish literature, like *Don Quixote*.

Although pinning down exact definitions for literary periods can sometimes be a tricky business, we do know that realism as a literary movement begins in France with the work of Honoré de Balzac (1799–1850), and the naturalists subsequently emerge as an extension of realism beginning with the writing of Zola; however, because currents in American realism at times run parallel to modernist developments as well, when trying to define realism in the United States chronology seems to take a backseat to the definable characteristics, themes and literary conventions of the realists and naturalists themselves. Looking at the definition put forth and validated by two of the preeminent scholars on American realism and naturalism, Donald Pizer more or less agrees with George J. Becker's three criteria for American realism as outlined in Becker's foundational article written for the *Modern Language Quarterly*:

> a. The first is verisimilitude of detail derived from observation and documentation.
> b. The second is an effort to approach the norm of experience—that is, a reliance upon the representative rather than the exceptional plot, setting, and character.
> c. The last is an objective, so far as an artist can achieve objectivity, rather than a subjective or idealistic view of human nature and experience. (Pizer 3-4)

Pizer then goes on to argue that the traditional definition of naturalism as realism with a touch of philosophical determinism is problematic, because it seems to exclude more works that could otherwise be seen as part of the naturalist movement in the United States (12). He modifies the aforementioned traditional definition, by suggesting two "tensions":

> a. The first tension is that between the subject matter of the naturalistic novel and the concept of man which emerges from this subject matter. The naturalist populates his novel primarily from the lower middle class or the lower class. His characters are the poor, the uneducated, the unsophisticated. His fictional world is that of the commonplace and unheroic . . . But . . . [a] naturalistic novel is . . . only an extension of realism in the sense that both modes often deal with the local and contemporary. The naturalist, however, discovers in this material the extraordinary and excessive in human nature.

> b. The second tension involves the theme of the naturalistic novel. The naturalist often describes his characters as though they are conditioned and controlled by environment, heredity, instinct or chance. But he also suggests a compensating humanistic value in his characters or their fates which affirms the significance of the individual and of his life. The tension here is that between the naturalist's desire to represent in fiction the new, discomforting truths which he has found in the ideas and life of his late nineteenth century world, and also his desire to find some meaning in experience which reasserts the validity of the human enterprise. (12–13)

Now that we know how realism and naturalism manifested themselves in the United States when Conrado Espinosa was writing his novel in San Antonio, we should also take a look at how realism and naturalism evolved in Mexico and the rest of Spanish America during the same time period, because it seems a reasonable conjecture that Espinosa's gaze was probably cast more to the south, landing upon literary figures like Federico Gamboa (1864–1939), Mexico's most recognized naturalist writer, rather than northward toward the works of Frank Norris (1870–1902) or Theodor Dreiser (1871–1945).

The debate in Spanish America seems to be quite different from the way realism and naturalism have been constructed in places like France, Britain and the United States. In the introduction to his section entitled "Costumbrismo en transición romántico-realista," which outlines the history of the realist/naturalist novel in "Hispanoamérica," Manuel Antonio Arango L. seems to suggest that realism is little more than a brief, though necessary, transitional period which helps bridge the gap between the romantic and nativistic (local custom) literary traditions and the modernistic writing which develops later in Spanish America. He argues that it's difficult to determine a precise historical framework for realism and naturalism in Spanish America because one can often see works which employ techniques generally associated with these artistic movements fused with romantic, nativistic and modernistic elements as well (139). The idea that Spanish-American realism and naturalism is a kind of aesthetic *mestizaje*, or hybrid, blended with the earlier romantic and *costumbrista* traditions, as well as forecasting future modernist literary movements, seems to be echoed in the comments made by Gamboa himself, when he states, "Si con esta profesión de fe literario resulto en las filas de naturalismo, *naturalista* me quedo, o *verista o realista*, o lo que sea" (García Barragán 49). Aesthetic purity and theoretical homogeneity seem less important to the Spanish-American writer when adopting realist and naturalist techniques in the same work where one can still see an emphasis placed on local custom as well as the use of more romantic literary devices such as allegory and extended metaphor. In the end, this fuzzier, more opaque and more ambiguous approach to literary definition actually helps the Spanish-American realist/naturalist escape the kinds of theoretical traps and contradictions which are often cited in the works of Balzac and Zola when they, in fact, employ writing strategies—like grand, overarching, extended metaphors—which work to undermine the very aesthetic principals they have originated.

In the end, Arango L. essentially collapses the two categories when exploring realist and naturalist writing throughout Spanish America, prefacing his discussion by citing Mexican literary scholar Joaquina Navarro's fairly extensive definition for these characteristics as seen in the Spanish American realist novel:

> a. La labor del novelista realista será mostrar todo lo más que pueda de los sucesos comunes de la existencia humana;
> b. El amor no ocupará el lugar principal que en otras novellas: se tratará como cualquier otra pasión;
> c. Nada se resistirá a la necesidad, o a la pasión, del dinero;
> d. Las observaciones hechas desde un punto de vista materialista y se dirigen a todo aquello que es tangible o fácilmente comprobable;
> e. El interés por situaciones, sin que haya necesidad de poner en juego las emociones;
> f. Se harán analogías entre la sociedad y la naturaleza, se estudiarán todas las especies sociales;
> g. Los personajes elegidos serán los tipos (modelos) de una especie y valdrán para representar a todos los demás individuos de dicha especie;
> h. El novelista debe determinar las leyes que rigen la sociedad;
> i. El novelista deberá hacer la crítica de las instituciones, los gobiernos, y las clases dirigentes;
> j. Al final de la novela deben deducirse importantes conclusiones. (via Arango 141–142)

This citation is followed by Arango L.'s attempt to fuse realism with naturalism by suggesting that naturalism, as a literary movement, is really more or less realism, after the death of Balzac and under the new leadership of Zola. He goes on to define only two unique elements of the naturalist movement:

> k. Importancia de la documentación científica dentro de los hechos;
> l. La novela realista busca una verdad más intensa, más "eficaz" como documento: se pide que escoja casos de verdadero dramatismo. Por estos caminos, la novela realista cae en la fórmula del materialismo proclamado por Zola; estudio documentado del medio y concepción de la novela como experimento de laboratorio. (142)

And when one considers this definition closely, these two items essentially amount to really only one true differentiating characteristic—Zola's emphasis on scientific objectivity.

Again, Arango L. appears to be creating yet another level of literary *mestizaje*, combining realism and naturalism in Spanish America, basically arguing that the evolution of the realist movement continues to follow the same trajectory established by Balzac and simply finds new leadership under Zola after his death (142). If this is true, then it seems that Arango L.'s position is that naturalism, independent of realism, never really existed in Spanish America. This perspective makes more sense when one takes into account the fact that numerous literary scholars claim that naturalism has never really existed in Spanish America because of the region's fundamentally religious nature, especially in the late nineteenth and early twentieth centuries. The Spanish American novel during this period not only borrows from romantic and nativistic literary traditions, but it is also full of overt religious references as well, which means that it can't be the kind of deterministic, objectivistic and scientific novel originally proposed by Zola.

There are important detractors to this position, however. María Guadalupe García Barragán and Saúl Sosnowski have both written books citing numerous examples of Spanish-American naturalistic novels, using their own definitions. In *Naturalismo en México*, García Barragán acknowledges that though many of these naturalist writers were, in fact, Jewish, Catholic, etc., and only a tiny minority ascribed to Zola's determinism or Comte's positivism, introduced to Mexico through the work of Dr. Gabino Barreda, being religious, like Gamboa—a practicing Catholic—should not, in and of itself, necessarily exclude one from the roles of naturalistic writers in Spanish America (30–32).

There seems to be an important distinction being made between one who writes with a religious or moralizing narrative perspective and one who writes "objectively" about "the poor, the uneducated, the unsophisticated" in Spanish America, where the great majority of people just happen to be Catholic. *El sol de Texas* is a perfect example of this kind of distinction: though the characters in the novel are often found in prayer, making religious references and seen in various forms of spiritual practice, all of these activities are reported on with a narrative voice which appears to be *trying* to remain as "objective" as possible (Espinosa 18–21). No reward is ever given to a character in the novel as a result of his or her faithful devotion. No manna ever falls from the heavens as an answer to some dutiful supplication. Nor does any deus ex machina climax appear at the end of the text to deliver obedient disciples from their misery. Quite to the contrary, the principal characters all flee a war-torn Mexico to come to the United States in search of the American Dream and instead find nothing but poverty, exploitation and even death. In the end, the moral of Espinosa's novel is political, not religious, in nature: don't go to the United States, because nothing can save you from the pain and suffering you will find there—not even your little alabaster saints.

## Realism/Naturalism: A Literary *Mestizaje* in Spanish America

Now that we have a couple of definitions to work with, we can begin the work of determining whether or not Conrado Espinosa's *El sol de Texas* is an example of Mexican/American realism/naturalism, neither or both.

To begin, we'll simply focus on the three elements of the definition of realism that both Becker (via Pizer) and Navarro (via Arango L.) seem to hold in common and see exactly how, or even if, they apply to *El sol de Texas*.

The first criterion of the realist novel that everyone seems to agree upon is what Becker calls "verisimilitude," or Navarro's representation of the material world, that which is tangible or verifiable. In *El sol de Texas,* all of the names of cities, streets, etc., are taken from real life. Most of the novel's action takes place in or around San Antonio and Houston. The area around the Alamo and the neighboring Mexican-American district in San Antonio is all well described using the names of real streets and historical landmarks. This is an extremely important point for a translator to consider, because the signifiers used by the English and Spanish speaking communities in San Antonio for some of these places can be quite different. For example, a literal translation of "La Plaza del Zacate" (*El Sol de Texas* 18) rendered as something like "The Grassy Plaza," "The Plaza of Grass," "The Field of Grass in the Middle of the City Square" or even simply following the generally accepted translation rule that proper nouns should be left untranslated (i.e. "La Plaza del Zacate"), would undermine the realist technique employed by Conrado Espinosa when the reader in English realizes that what the writer has been referring to all along—and what the translator missed—is "Haymarket Square" (*Under the Texas Sun* 155).

Likewise, the translator needs to realize that when Espinosa employs Spanish phonetic spellings like "Poraza" (*El sol de Texas* 106), he is intentionally using the same kind of realist linguistic techniques found in the work of his contemporary American writers like Stephen Crane (1871–1900), creating intentional misspellings to reproduce the mestizo working-class vernacular for places like Port Arthur (*Under the Texas Sun* 237), a real Gulf Coast petroleum boomtown. It is also helpful to know that, unlike some other early works of Mexican-American immigrant fiction, where the pueblos of origin are purely literary inventions, Quico's Los Guajes truly is in Jalisco and Serapio's Cuitzeo, likewise, is really located in the Mexican state of Michoacán.

The second criterion for the realist novel in both the United States and Spanish America is what Becker calls the "norm of experience" or what Navarro refers to as "los sucesos communes" or "everyday events." In terms of the representation of common, normal or run-of-the-mill life experiences, instead of being driven by intricate plot structures, featuring spectacular settings, peopled by colorful and heroic characters, *El sol de Texas* follows two families from rural Mexico to areas of Texas which are primarily experiencing industrialization and urbanization. We watch them eat in a restaurant for the first time (Espinosa *El sol de Texas* 20–21); we follow them as they search for a hotel (21–22); we accompany them as they look for work numerous times throughout the novel (22–23 and 25–33); and we are with them as they pick cotton in the fields (84), work on the railroads (34–37) and work in petroleum production (120). These are hardly spectacular settings. Nor are our protagonists larger-than-life, heroic figures. The plot is simple and straightforward: Federico, also known as Quico, and his family, along with Serapio and his two sons, go to the United States to escape the chaos in Mexico at time of the Revolution only to find that times are actually harder for them in their new country, precisely because they are "the poor, the uneducated, the unsophisticated" people that Pizer claims—when defining his first "tension"—populate the American naturalistic novel.

Finally, the last criterion that both the Becker and Navarro definitions of realism have in common is the use of an "objective" narrative voice, the sort which Navarro refers to as demonstrating "el interés por situaciones, sin que haya necesidad de poner en juego las emociones" (via Arango L. 141). The fact that these terms might also recall, for some, the urging of Zola to the use a laboratory-like "scientific" voice noted, *El sol de Texas* is an interesting text when looking at this aspect of realism/naturalism because, unlike writers like Dreiser, Norris and even British "blue book" writer Benjamin Disraeli (1804–1881), Espinosa often uses section breaks, indicated by three asterisks, to clearly differentiate between his objective and scientific ethnographical reporting and a slightly more subjective voice which is employed to establish the narrative depicting the struggles of the two Mexican migrant families while living in Texas.

This is a feature of the author's writing which is extremely important to consider when approaching the translation of the novel, because it seems to suggest that two different narrative voices are present in the text; and, therefore, two different models, one for the rendering of each voice, must be found in order to properly render a translation. The more objective and journalistic the tone of someone like a Dreiser, Norris or even Jacob Riis (1849–1914) might seem like a more appropriate model to use when attempting to translate the ethnographic portions of the text; but, the livelier and somewhat more engaging writing of someone like Crane might be a better fit for rendering Espinosa's more colloquial narrative voice which, as was previously noted, recalls Crane in its use of misspellings, contractions, etc., to represent the vernacular diction of the novel's fictional characters.

If the second criterion for the realist novel reminds one of Pizer's first naturalistic "tension," and this third criterion also seems to reflect the content of Arango L.'s two naturalistic "scientific" qualities in the Spanish-American novel, then it seems that all that is left to do to establish that Espinosa's work likewise fits both the American and Spanish-American definitions of naturalism is to address Pizer's second tension: the naturalist's characters act as though they are conditioned and controlled by environment, heredity, instinct or chance.

The characters in *El sol de Texas* leave Mexico unwillingly, due to forces beyond their control. It may not exactly be like Zola's theories of determinism based on heredity, but there is a strong sense in the novel that the actions of the character are the direct result of their political and social environment. Before the war broke out, Serapio was actually a lower-middle-class farm owner who was subsequently squeezed from his land by revolutionary forces (Espinosa *El Sol de Texas* 13–14). Likewise, when looking for work in the United States, Quico really has no recourse when established discriminatory social practices preclude him from receiving various work contracts because he was traveling with his wife and small children (24). And, finally, the "discomforting truths" of these characters' world are shown most clearly in the end of the novel, when the reader discovers that not only does Serapio lose his son José to a railroad accident (38), but Quico has also lost his son Doroteo to alcoholism and womanizing, in addition to losing his daughter Juanita to "disgrace" and possible prostitution (120–121).

If we accept the argument put forth by critics like García Barragán and Sosnowski, making room under the naturalist tent for Spanish–American works that include some religious references, as long as those references are treated with the same kind of objective and scientific voice that we would expect from an ethnographic work, then I would definitely argue that Conrado Espinosa's *El sol de Texas* is both a Mexican *and* American naturalist novel because it follows the definitions proposed by both Pizer and Arango L. But, even if one maintains that the Catholic religiosity expressed in the text precludes its inclusion among the naturalist tradition, we can certainly conclude that, at very least, Espinosa's novel is a work of realism.

Having already fulfilled all three of Becker's criteria for the American realist novel, we can quickly elucidate examples which would round out the remaining categories in Navarro's definition:

b. El amor no ocupará el lugar principal que en otras novellas:

Quico is already married when the novel opens and his wife and children are always in tow as he tries to make a life for his family in the United States (Espinosa *El Sol de Texas* 11–12). Serapio is also married, but he has left his wife and a few younger children at home, having always planned to return to Mexico as soon as he and his two sons could earn enough money to buy back the farm that they lost to the Revolution (13–14). The only romance or courtship seen in the novel at all is found in chapter eight, "La serenata," when Matías, Serapio's son, is drawn out of his dwelling by the moonlight and the music he hears emanating from a nearby house; he meets up with Juanita who has come out to admire the same music and moonlit night. By the end of the brief encounter, they have agreed to go to a dance with each other (66). But their romance fades as abruptly as it had appeared, when the two families are forced by economic realities to travel different paths once again, showing that everything, even love and romance, must take a back seat to economic necessity, García Barragán's next realist criterion.

c. Nada se resistirá a la necesidad, o a la pasión, del dinero:

As in the example above, all of Quico and Serapio's decisions are based on their economic realities. They originally leave Mexico because the Revolution has made both so poor that they can't feed their families, and there are no jobs in Mexico for them to seek. The first time the two families are forced to split up is because Serapio and his son are offered work which wasn't extended to Quico due to the fact that he was traveling with his wife and young children (24). In the end, after finding each other once again, their final separation is the result of a difference of opinion with regard to another question of economics: whether or not to take work in the petroleum industry. With his son now dead, and after having just escaped from slave-like work camp conditions, Serapio can only think about how to get back to Mexico and how to arrange to take his son's remains with him (96–97). But Quico, still hopeful that he will strike it rich in the United States, is the one who eventually loses everything, arguably, due to his passionate search for "black gold."

f. Se harán analogías entre la sociedad y la naturaleza, se estudiarán todas las especies sociales:

This criterion seems to run contrary to the "objective" narrative voice which only reports on perceivable objects and events in the "real world." But, of course, using the "romantic" technique of placing action in natural settings that underscore the tone which is being established within the scene is precisely the kind of theoretical contradiction that is often cited in the works of Balzac, Zola, Crane, etc. If the Spanish-American realist is permitted, following García Barragán's definition, to treat natural surroundings in this metaphorical manner, then Espinosa should certainly be included among the ranks of Spanish-American realists because he makes frequent use of this technique in *El sol de Texas*.

The prologue is full of metaphorical natural imagery: the sun turns the fields into an "inferno" for the migrant workers, as its bitter rays reflect and echo the foreman's mocking gaze, and the earth becomes a "silent torturer" at the campesinos' feet (Espinosa *Under the Texas Sun* 140). Even the scene in which Serapio loses his son to a railroad accident is cloaked in this metaphorical use of natural imagery: ash falls languidly from the "worm with vertigo," until José is enveloped in a halo of light cast out from the train's "powerful eye"; then night falls, leaving a "shroud" over the countryside; and, when Serapio and Matías finally reach the site of the accident, the first clue that they find when attempting to locate José's body is a strip of white cloth fluttering listlessly from the thicket (171–172).

g. Los personajes elegidos serán los tipos (modelos) de una especie y valdrán para representar a todos los demás individuos de dicha especie:

It is clear that Quico, like Serapio and those in their respective families, should be read as a typical Mexican immigrant. Quico is the poor farm laborer who brings his family to the United States in hopes of finding a better life. He sometimes dreams of going back to Mexico after he has become wealthy, to buy land and become an established member of the community (13). But his actions are typical of those who come to the United States to stay for good. Serapio, on the other hand, represents a different kind of Mexican migrant worker: he was once landed, but lost his modest holdings to political unrest. Throughout the novel, Serapio maintains that he *will* go back to Mexico, and this idea is reinforced by the fact that he has left his wife and younger children back in his homeland. The fact that both families are dealt crushing blows as a result of their respective decisions to leave their fatherland to find a new life in "El Norte" could arguably be read as a kind of "romantic" punishment for their transgression against their country of origin; but, it could also be seen as simply the objective representation of the reality experienced by many real Mexican immigrants who seldom, if ever, achieve anything which even approaches the Horacio Alger–style myth of the American Dream.

h. El novelista debe determinar las leyes que rigen la sociedad;
i. El novelista deberá hacer la crítica de las instituciones, los gobiernos, y las clases dirigentes:

These two criteria seem to be closely related, and could be merged, especially as they pertain to the novel *El sol de Tejas.* The rules of society are rules which are determined by power structures beyond the protagonists' control. Quico has no legal recourse when discriminated against by the work contractors because he has a family. Serapio can only appeal to the essentially powerless Mexican consul when he discovers that racist Texans have desecrated his son's grave (128–129). Of course, Quico and Serapio both blame their government for more or less forcing them to leave their country in order to feed their families. But perhaps the most comical and satirical critique of Mexican social and political institutions can be seen in chapter twelve, "Red, White and Green": while giving flowery speeches and public address at a public festival to commemorate Mexican independence, politicians and civic leaders are heckled by raucous men in the crowd (Espinosa *Under the Texas Sun* 220). In the end, the reader walks away from the novel understanding Espinosa's overarching social critique that the suffering of Mexican migrant families in the United States, as demonstrated through Quico, Serapio and their families, is the result of the difficult political situation in Mexico, and the exploitation and inhumane treatment of these poor, displaced individuals at that the hands of U.S. farmers and work contractors is actually systematically supported by the U.S. government and its legal system.

j. Al final de la novela deben deducirse importantes conclusiones.

This last criterion for the Spanish-American realist novel seems the easiest to prove. In the last chapter of the book, Quico and Serapio are once again united on the banks of the Rio Grande. After recounting the horrific stories about their lives since they had last seen each other, Serapio tries to convince Quico to come back to Mexico with him. Quico says that he would like to, and may at some point in the future, but for now he must decline. However, he does have a message for Serapio to take back with him to Mexico: "Go on! Tell our comrades to take it like men, to stay in their homeland . . . Here, it's easier to find death and dishonor than money and riches" (257). And as his silhouette slowly (and metaphorically) fades into the "darkness of night," few more resounding and obvious conclusions could be made at the end of this or any novel.

## An Ice Cube is Born

Knowing that the themes of rural-to-urban migration, the metaphorical use of the train to show a man's demise at the hands of industrialization, and a woman's decline into debauchery and often prostitution are all common literary tropes which also help to define realism and naturalism, and the fact that they are all present in Conrado Espinosa's *El sol de Texas* just seems to further the argument that this work should be regarded as an example of Mexican *and* American realism *and* naturalism; but, if the repeated Catholic religious references create some hesitation to recognize it as a naturalistic work, one can safely claim that, at very least, it is a work of realism. The novel's location within a particular theoretical framework and literary tradition is significant, because it is important to first establish genre and form as well as historical period before one can attempt to faithfully render the translation of any work of literature.

In this essay, we have seen how this kind of literary analysis can be useful when making decisions about how best to construct the two very different narrative voices present in the novel and where to turn to in order to find models for the rendering of these two distinct voices in the English target language: Riis as a model for early American ethnographic reportage and Crane for the vernacular of the early twentieth-century American street, for example.

Finally we discovered that the genre, form and literary conventions of a particular literary period are important for the translator to note as well, because something as simple as mistranslating a term like "La Plaza del Zacate" to anything other than "Haymarket Square" can actually undermine the entire aesthetic and historical frameworks at work within the source text, thereby taking the original ice cube and converting it into something akin to crushed ice.

Of course, once a translator has clearly established an aesthetic and historical framework for a text, this will inform all of the decisions he or she will have to make when rendering the source into the target language. After facets of the original author's voice fall away like water evaporating into thin air, replaced by the condensation of equivalent, contemporary literary models in the target language, thorough preliminary research establishing literary period and convention may be the best structure to hold the whole translation together, like an ice-cube tray, providing shape and volume in order to create ice cubes of more or less the same height, width and depth as the original.

## Works Cited

Arango L., Manuel Antonio. *Origen y evolución de la novela hispano-americana.* Bogota: Tercer Mundo Editores, 1991.

Cipolla, Gaetano. Lecture. American Literary Translators Association Conference, Montreal, Quebec. 5 Nov. 2005.

Espinosa, Conrado. *El sol de Texas*. San Antonio: Viola Novelty, 1926.

______. *Under the Texas Sun/El sol de Texas.* Trans. Ethriam Cash Brammer de Gonzales. Houston: Arte Público P, 2007.

García Barragán, María Guadalupe. *El naturalismo en México*. Mexico City: UNAM P, 1979.

Pizer, Donald. *Realism and Naturalism in the Nineteenth-Century American Literature*. Carbondale, Il.: Southern Illinois UP, 1966.

Sayers Peden, Margaret. "Building a Translation, the Reconstruction Business: Poem 145 of Sor Juana Inés de la Cruz." In *The Craft of Translation.* Ed. John Biguenet and Rainer Schulte. Chicago: U of Chicago P, 1989.

Steiner, T. R. *English Translation Theory, 1650–1800.* Amsterdam: Koninkklijke Van Gorcum & Co., 1975.

Sosnowski, Saúl. *Realismo y naturalismo.* Madrid: Editorial La Muralla, 1983.

# Contributors

**Kevin Anzzolin** is a Ph.D. student in the Department of Romance Languages and Literatures at the University of Chicago. His current research focuses on the intersection of journalism and narrative in 19th century U.S. and Mexico.

**Alejandra Balestra** is currently an independent scholar in Albuquerque, New Mexico. She received her Ph.D. from the University of Houston, where she also served as a visiting assistant professor and the coordinator of the Recovering the U.S. Hispanic Literary Heritage Project. Most recently, she served as an assistant professor at the University of New Mexico. The author of numerous published articles, she coordinated the anthologies *Herencia: The Anthology of Hispanic Literature in the United States* (Oxford University Press, 2002) and *En otra voz: antología de literatura hispana de los Estados Unidos* (Arte Público Press, 2002).

**Nancy Bird-Soto** is an Assistant Professor of Spanish at the University of Wisconsin-Milwaukee, where she teaches Latin American and U.S. Latino literature. She received her doctoral degree from the University of Wisconsin-Madison in 2006. Her main interests are gender representations and identities in the Hispanic, Latin American and Latino worlds. She has published articles on Luisa Capetillo and Josefina López in *Identidades* (UPR-Cayey, vols. 5 and 6, respectively). Currently, Bird-Soto is working on a critical edition of *Sara la obrera [y otros cuentos]* by Puerto Rican author, Ana Roque.

**Ethriam Cash Brammer de Gonzales** is a Chicano writer and scholar. He has translated a number of significant works of early Latino literature, including *The Adventures of Don Chipote: When Parrots Breast Feed* by Daniel Venegas (Arte Público Press, 2000); *Lucas Guevara* by Alirio Díaz Guerra (Arte Público Press, 2003); and *The Texas Sun* by Conrado Espinoza (Arte Público Press, 2007). His journal articles addressing issues of translation appeared in *ABC Journal* and the *Denver Quarterly*. Currently, he is Assistant Director of the Center for Chicano-Boricua Studies at Wayne State University in Detroit, Michigan, where he is a doctoral candidate in English.

**Tomás Ybarra-Frausto**, an independent scholar of Latin American and U.S. Latino arts and cultures, is the former associate director of Creativity and Culture at the Rockefeller Foundation. Previously he was a tenured professor at Stanford University. Dr. Ybarra-Frausto has written and published extensively, and has served as board chair of the Mexican Museum in San Francisco and the Smithsonian National Council. He is the recipient of the Smithsonian's Henry Medal and the Mexican government's Order of the Aztec Eagle. He lives and works in New York City.

**Timothy P. Gaster** is an ABD student at the University of Chicago in the Romance Languages Department. His dissertation deals with the representation of Japan in late nineteenth- and early twentieth-century Hispanic and Luso-Brazilian literature. His secondary interests include nineteenth-century Hispanic writers in the United States and José Martí's translations.

**Carmen Gómez Galisteo** is a Ph.D. candidate in American Studies at the Universidad de Alcalá (Madrid, Spain). She was assistant editor of *Interpreting the New Milenio* (Cambridge Scholars Publishing, 2008). Her work has appeared in international journals such as *Clepsydra* or *AdAmerican*. She is a contributor to *The Literary Encyclopedia*.

**Pilar Melero** teaches Spanish and Chicano/a literature at the University of Wisconsin-Whitewater. Her research focuses on the discursive strategies of subaltern subjects. She has presented her research and creative work in the United States, Mexico, Cuba and Peru.

**María Irene Moyna** is an assistant professor at Texas A&M, where she teaches a variety of linguistics and advanced language courses. She was the associate editor for the 5th edition of the University of Chicago Spanish Dictionary (University of Chicago Press, 2002), and her scholarly work has appeared in journals such as the Southwest Journal of Linguistics, Spanish in Context, Studies in Hispanic and Lusophone Linguistics and in several edited collections.

**Gerald E. Poyo** is professor and chair of the history department at St. Mary's University, San Antonio, Texas. In 1983 he received his Ph.D. in Latin American history from the University of Florida. His research has focused on the intersection of Latin American and U.S. Latino history, especially on the history of Cuban exile communities in the United States during the nineteenth and twentieth centuries. He has also written on the origins of Tejano identity in eighteenth century San Antonio and Latino Catholics in the United States. He is the author and editor of five books, including *'With All, and For the Good of All': The Emergence of Popular Nationalism in the Cuban Communities of the United States, 1848-1898* (Duke University Press, 1989) and *Cuban Catholics in the United States, 1960-1988: Exile and Integration* (University of Notre Dame Press, 2007).

**Alberto Varon** completed his M.A. at the University of Chicago and is a doctoral candidate in English at the University of Texas at Austin. His current project, entitled "A Literary Genealogy of Mexican American Masculinity," explores literary representations of Mexican American-masculinity from 1848-1939, and the connections between gender, nation and culture.

**Gabriela Baeza Ventura** is Associate Professor of Hispanic Literature in the Hispanic Studies at the University of Houston. She is also Executive Editor for Arte Público Press. Her publications include *La imagen de la mujer en la crónica del México de afuera* (UACJ, 2006), *Con otra mirada: Cuentos hispanos de los Estados Unidos* (Editorial Popular, 2005) and *U. S. Latino Literature Today* (Longman, 2005).